DEBATING TARGETED KILLING

DEBATING ETHICS

General Editor
Christopher Heath Wellman
Washington University of St. Louis

Debating Ethics is a series of volumes in which leading scholars defend opposing views on timely ethical questions and core theoretical issues in contemporary moral, political, and legal philosophy.

Debating Targeted Killing

Counter-Terrorism or Extrajudicial Execution?

TAMAR MEISELS AND JEREMY WALDRON

OXFORD
UNIVERSITY PRESS

OXFORD
UNIVERSITY PRESS

Oxford University Press is a department of the University of Oxford. It furthers
the University's objective of excellence in research, scholarship, and education
by publishing worldwide. Oxford is a registered trade mark of Oxford University
Press in the UK and certain other countries.

Published in the United States of America by Oxford University Press
198 Madison Avenue, New York, NY 10016, United States of America.

Library of Congress Cataloging-in-Publication Data
Names: Meisels, Tamar, author. | Waldron, Jeremy, author.
Title: Debating targeted killing : counter-terrorism or extrajudicial execution? /
Tamar Meisels and Jeremy Waldron.
Description: New York : Oxford university press, 2020. |
Series: Debating ethics | Includes bibliographical references and index.
Identifiers: LCCN 2019055842 (print) | LCCN 2019055843 (ebook) |
ISBN 9780190906917 (hardback) | ISBN 9780190906924 (paperback) |
ISBN 9780190906948 (epub)
Subjects: LCSH: Targeted killing. | Targeted killing—Case studies. |
Targeted killing—Moral and ethical aspects. | Terrorism—Prevention.
Classification: LCC HV6431.M4345 2020 (print) |
LCC HV6431 (ebook) | DDC 172/.4—dc23
LC record available at https://lccn.loc.gov/2019055842
LC ebook record available at https://lccn.loc.gov/2019055843

1 3 5 7 9 8 6 4 2

Paperback printed by Marquis, Canada
Hardback printed by Bridgeport National Bindery, Inc., United States of America

CONTENTS

ACKNOWLEDGMENTS

Many of the arguments and ideas expressed in my portion of the book are the product of my previous academic work on terrorism, counter-terrorism, and just war theory. I begin by thanking the following publications for allowing me to draw on my earlier writing on these issues, and to reuse the following published materials, or bits and pieces thereof:

> Tamar Meisels, "Targeting Terror," *Social Theory and Practice*, 30 (3) (July 2004), 297–326.
> Tamar Meisels, *The Trouble with Terror* (Cambridge: Cambridge University Press, 2008), chapters 4 and 5.
> Tamar Meisels, *Contemporary Just War: Theory and Practice* (London: Routledge, 2017), chapter 7.
> Tamar Meisels, "Assassination: Targeting Nuclear Scientists," *Law and Philosophy*, 33 (2014), 204–234.

It would be virtually impossible to name and list all the individuals and institutions that have contributed to my work on targeted killing along the way, either in support, or in controversial discussion, and/or with helpful comments. I apologize to anyone I have left out. In Israel in particular, practically everyone I know has put in his or her two cents on the issue of targeted killing. Nonetheless, several colleagues have been particularly helpful: Ariel Colonomos, David Enoch, Michael Gross, and Danny Statman. Kit Wellman initiated this debate, and his patient support and encouragement are largely responsible for its completion. Hannah Doyle and Lucy Randall at OUP have also been wonderfully helpful. Special debts of gratitude are due to my co-author Jeremy Waldron for a good fight, as ever; and last, but certainly not least, to Michael Walzer, for the influence of his momentous work, and his never-ending help and advice.

Thanks always to my family: Chaim Gans, and our daughters Abigail and Martha.

—Tamar Meisels

I am grateful to Professor Meisels for the commitment and civility with which she approached this debate; it is good indeed to argue with a friend. Kit Wellman, the series editor, was wonderful in the encouragement he offered, and Lucy Randall and Hannah Doyle have been patient editors at Oxford University Press.

I have been thinking about targeted killing for many years in many different settings. Claire Finkelstein, Jens David Ohlin, and Andrew Altman organized a terrific conference in Philadelphia in 2011. I participated in a debate on targeted killing at the Oxford Union in 2013, and I made a presentation at an Interfaith Conference on Drone

Warfare at the Princeton Theological Seminary in 2015. There was a debate at New York University Law School in 2012, and over the years I have accumulated a great debt to my NYU colleagues (including my antagonists), not least to Philip Alston, Ned Block, Cynthia Estlund, John Ferejohn, Jeanne Fromer, Ryan Goodman, Moshe Halbertal, Samuel Issacharoff, Liam Murphy, Richard Pildes, and Samuel Scheffler. I have presented bits and pieces of argumentation on targeted killing over the years at Christ Church and All Souls Colleges at Oxford, in the Knowlton Program at the University of South Carolina, at La Sapienza University in Rome, at Union College in Schenectady, at the United States Military Academy at West Point, at the University of California, San Diego, at the University of Illinois Law School, and at the University of Otago in New Zealand. In all of this, thanks to David Aaronovitch, Guido Alpa, Kenneth Anderson, Richard Arneson, Nigel Biggar, Jean Cohen, Chris Cole, Anthony Dworkin, David Dyzenhaus, Jill Frank, Amos Guiora, Adil Haque, Mark Henaghan, Heidi Hurd, Jameel Jaffer, Harold Koh, Michael Moore, Mary Ellen O'Connell, Marcela Prieto Rudolfy, Naureen Shah, Henry Shue, Daniel Statman, Benjamin Wittes, and Leo Zaibert. Finally—and as always—my very special thanks to Carol Sanger.

—Jeremy Waldron

DEBATING TARGETED KILLING

1

Introduction

TAMAR MEISELS AND JEREMY WALDRON

■□■

OUR TOPIC IN THIS BOOK is *targeted* killing—the officially authorized and premeditated killing by military or intelligence officials of named and identified individuals without the benefit of any judicial process.[1]

There is nothing new about targeted killing. Understood as "assassination," targeted killing dates back to antiquity, through the classical world and medieval Europe, up to the present-day political practices of venerable democracies such as Israel, the United States, and the United Kingdom, as well as more authoritarian states such as Turkey, China, Iran, and Russia.

In a further sense, however, the history of targeted killing is far more recent. As a routine and now well-known measure of counter-terrorism, targeted killing is a relatively novel policy, and its practice has proliferated unprecedentedly over the past decade. It bears serious consideration and scrutiny.

---

1. Here is another useful definition: Targeted killing is "[t]he use of lethal force attributable to a subject of international law with the intent, premeditation and deliberation to kill individually selected persons who are not in the physical custody of those targeting them" (Melzer, *Targeted Killing in International Law*, 5).

Debating Targeted Killing. Tamar Meisels and Jeremy Waldron, Oxford University Press (2020)
© Oxford University Press.
DOI: 10.1093/oso/9780190906917.001.0001

We will not retell this story here. Our book is not a history of targeted killing, though we frequently refer to historical cases as illustrations of our respective arguments. Ours is a normative debate between political theorists about legal and political principles, policies, and practices. As such, it engages with current events in the behavior of states and their political institutions. Our topic is the officially authorized and premeditated killing by military or intelligence officials of named and identified individuals without benefit of any judicial process. Such a policy introduces a significantly new dimension into the state's repertoire of the use of lethal force. We need to reflect on the significance of this tool in the armory of statecraft and national security.

Several authors have recounted the recent history of targeted killings. We acknowledge these works throughout without attempting to compete with them. Ronen Bergman's *Rise and Kill First* supplies its readers with a full and detailed account of Israel's history of targeted killings.[2] Uri Friedman offers a very short and concise description of America's assassination policy.[3] Many other works in Israel and the United States cover similar territory.[4] Most of our examples draw on the past activity of these two countries, for they are the ones most closely identified with targeted killings.

---

2. See Bergman, *Rise and Kill First*.

3. Friedman, "Targeted Killing: A Short History," https://foreignpolicy.com/2012/08/13/targeted-killings-a-short-history/.

4. See, e.g., Bar Zohar and Mishal, *Mossad: The Greatest Missions of the Israeli Secret Service*, and Jacobsen, *Surprise, Kill, Vanish*.

Modern Israel has been involved in assassinations even before attaining statehood in the 20th century. Famous pre-state cases include the *Lehi* (the Stern Gang) targeting of Lord Moyne and Count Bernadotte in the mid-1940s, followed by the covert actions allegedly undertaken by the State of Israel's secret services in the decades to come. Since the beginning of the 21st century, Israel has publicly acknowledged its targeted killing policy in the West Bank and the Gaza Strip. Israel does not officially accept responsibility for any targeting operations that it may or may not have conducted overseas.

Much of the modern debate centers on the use of targeted killing as a tactic in counter-terrorism, with "terrorism" being understood as the indiscriminate use of force against civilian targets, intended to advance political ends by sowing terror and insecurity in a population. But we both acknowledge that targeted killing is not defined by this one use it is put to. Targeted killing is also used as a tactic against insurgencies; and by Israel it has allegedly been used as a way of preventing the acquisition of dangerous weapons by states that are Israel's enemies, such as Syria, Iraq, and Iran. Over the years, several civilian scientists, particular nuclear scientists, have also been the victims of suspected assassinations, attributed (by foreign sources) to Israel's Mossad agency. Most recently, in August 2018, Aziz Asbar, one of Syria's leading rocket scientists, was killed by a car bomb. Asbar—a research director at a military agency linked to Syria's chemical weapons program—had apparently been working closely with the Assad regime, in collaboration with top Iranian military personnel, on developing long-range precision missiles. Mr. Asbar was allegedly also involved in coordinating Iranian and Hezbollah activities in Syria.[5] So, alongside victims labeled "terrorists" or "unlawful combatants," top enemy scientists, such as Asbar, appear to form a second major category of targets selected for assassination. Numerically, however, these instances constitute only a tiny fraction of targeted killings, falling far below assassinations associated with counter-terrorism.

Since 9/11, the United States has gradually adopted an official policy of targeted killing in Afghanistan, Yemen, Iraq, and Pakistan. American killings of this kind take place as part of what we call the war on terror or the global war against terrorism.[6] There have been thousands of such killings.[7] Far from America's first engagement with political assassination,[8] the scale, labeling, and weaponry used for these killings are nonetheless new, as is the debate launched by public knowledge of this enhanced policy of "named killing."

These American targeted killings refer to two distinct types of military strategy, often carried out by drones: "personality strikes" and "signature strikes."[9] Strictly speaking, only personality strikes are targeted killings. They involve the listing and subsequent assassination of previously identified named individuals.[10] Israel, as well as the United

5. David M. Halbfinger and Ronen Bergman, "A Top Syrian Scientist Is Killed, and Fingers Point at Israel," *New York Times*, August 6, 2018.

6. For the former president's acknowledgment of the practice, see "Obama's Speech on Drone Policy," *New York Times*, May 23, 2013.

7. See Alston, "Report of the Special Rapporteur."

8. See also discussions of the American program of assassination of thousands of local communist officials in South Vietnam in Andrade, *Ashes to Ashes* and Valentine, *The Phoenix Program*.

9. Heller, "One Hell of a Killing Machine," 90.

10. Waldron, "Death Squads and Death Lists," 292–307, 292.

States, openly engages in personality strikes when it targets leading figures in Hamas.

Signature strikes, by contrast, are mostly US drone attacks that target groups of men who have certain behavioral characteristics associated with terrorist activities or membership in al-Qaeda or its affiliates, but whose identities are unknown. As Andrew Altman explains, "Their 'signature' behavior functions as if it were the uniform of an enemy force, opening them to lethal attack, in the eyes of the U.S. government."[11] Signature strikes raise all sorts of issues, but they are not our subject of debate in this volume. Whether or not signature strikes (particularly as carried out by the United States) are justifiable in the course of combating terror, they are much more like "untargeted killing," as most wartime killings are. "Personality strikes," or named killing, can be carried out by ground forces or by conventional airplanes, and may involve the use of bullets, bombs, or poison.[12] Mostly though, at least in the American case, targeted killings are performed by "drones," unmanned aerial vehicles operated at a distance. These are also the well-publicized cases of targeted killing, attracting the greatest public attention, not least because of the collateral damage they incur, and perhaps due to the science fiction type images they invoke in popular imagination. But the focus of this volume is not drones as such,[13] but rather the principled issue of targeting

11. Altman, "Targeted Killing as an Alternative to War," 3–4.

12. As in Israel's failed targeting of Hamas leader Khaled Mashal in Jordan in 1997, when Mossad agents administered poison into Mashal's left ear, Israel was subsequently compelled to handover the antidote.

13. Cf. Waldron, "Death Squads and Death Lists," 292.

identified victims as opposed to conventional killing in war. We emphasize from the outset that our topic includes but is not limited to killings by remotely piloted aerial vehicles. We regard killings by remotely piloted aerial vehicles as only part of the broader category of targeted killings, which includes the use of special forces on the ground in various countries (like the killing of Osama bin Laden in Pakistan).

Many aspects of killing with drones are touched on in the course of this volume, such as our concerns about collateral damage and violation of sovereignty, as well as new and emerging military technologies. In all sorts of ways, drone warfare is interesting and unique, posing new and distinctive questions for any ethics of war. Drones are a new form of warfare, which seems finally to abandon any element of chivalry or reciprocity in combat. The vulnerability of targeted individuals to drone strikes from the air, alongside the vulnerability of surrounding civilians, is now coupled with the complete *in*vulnerability of those who are operating the unmanned armed aerial vehicles, often from thousands of miles away. The concern is that this presages utterly new forms of armed conflict, for which new rules, ethics, and customs will be necessary. Beyond targeted killing, some worry about drone technology itself and the way it introduces a new era of *surveillance*—yet another new era of surveillance—from the skies.

Notwithstanding, our main issue remains the killings themselves: the practice of individualized killings by our governments. While we address surrounding aspects, such as incidental harm to civilians, violations of sovereignty, the cultural significance of drone technology, and so forth, we urge the reader to maintain a steadfast focus on the essence of targeted killing, namely, the targeting for death of named and identified individuals by our states and leaders.

***

The book proceeds as follows. The debate opens with a defense of targeted killing, presenting it as a legitimate, desirable, and uniquely effective anti-terrorism strategy, which can be conducted in keeping with both just war theory and the strictures of international law. For the most part, the defense of targeted killing undertaken in the first part of this volume addresses its use in warlike contexts, against irregular, or "unlawful," combatants, usually within low-intensity armed struggles. More hesitantly, the argument for targeted killing also looks at the rarer usages of assassination against particular categories of peacetime civilians, notably the aforementioned cases of nuclear scientists. Less conclusively than the argument for targeting terrorists, this discussion suggests that some assassinations may be morally justifiable, though they are clearly illegal and ought to remain as such.

Then we move on to the case against targeted killing. Although this practice is often analogized to legitimate killings in the course of law enforcement or to combat killings under the laws of war, neither analogy really applies. The law-enforcement model does not permit extrajudicial killings on the basis of the past or future danger posed by an individual when this is unmoored from any imminent danger. And the military model does not really permit the hunting down and killing of individual combatants outside the context of immediate hostilities. Mostly the case against targeted killing turns on the question of *man-hunting*: Do we really want to allow our governments to authorize the activity of death squads to eliminate individuals named on "kill lists" as enemies of the state? The case against targeted killing also turns on the question of its abuse and its extension into areas of public policy unlike the immediate context of counter-terrorism. Any new power by the state may be abused, but the likely abuse of this power of life and death is particularly worrying.

We conclude the volume with a final exchange of ideas, briefly responding and replying to each other's arguments. Our hope is that the back-and-forth in this debate, as well as our two main contributions, will enrich and deepen readers' understanding of this vexed and difficult issue.

For

TAMAR MEISELS

■□■

Debating Targeted Killing. Tamar Meisels and Jeremy Waldron, Oxford University Press (2020)
© Oxford University Press.
DOI: 10.1093/oso/9780190906917.001.0001

PART I: INTRODUCTION

1. Outlining the Basic Argument

As the United States and Israel wage war on terror, they curiously find themselves under attack for targeting individual terrorists and their leaders. It has been argued that "targeted killing" violates international standards of legitimate warfare and that it is on a par with political assassination, or "extra-judicial execution," unequivocally banned by international law. In the extreme, it has been compared with the terrorist activity it purports to combat. Nevertheless, former US President Obama repeatedly stated and demonstrated that targeted killing was his favored counter-terrorism measure. Israel, which has long resorted to this tactic, escalated its use after the outbreak of the second Intifada.

In the following, I argue that targeting terrorists in the course of armed conflict as a preventive, rather than a punitive, measure is a legitimate act of self-defense, or defense of others, subject to necessity, proportionality, and reasonable chance of success. I follow the American and Israeli Supreme Courts in maintaining that the relevant normative framework for considering counter-terrorism measures is that of an (international/non-international) armed conflict, bringing the full privileges of belligerency into play. More generally, I suggest that where international law is unclear and indeterminate—that is, where alternative interpretations are possible—we ought to adopt an understanding of "armed conflict" that does not exclude the new wars we are fighting.

Once at war, or engaged in armed conflict, any combatant may be killed under circumstances that far outstrip those that constrain ordinary self-defense.[1] The next step in my argument for targeted killing is, then, to establish that the targeted victims are in fact combatants, albeit irregular combatants. At the very least, they belong to a type of unprotected civilians who are not unengaged in hostilities. The target's paramilitary status separates targeted killing from political assassination. Military objective—preventing terrorism rather than punishment—distinguishes targeted killing from "extrajudicial execution." Moreover, I argue that "unlawful combatants," as opposed to soldiers, may also be targeted in non-military locations.

The following arguments defend the named killings of individually identified combatants, primarily terrorist operatives, compared with the common practice of killing anonymous soldiers in war. Judged under a wartime regime, there is nothing wrong, and in fact much that is right, about targeting individual terrorists—whether by name or simply because of their part in hostilities. Killing terrorists, I argue, is a legitimate and desirable military

1. Gross, "Assassination," at 104.

objective. In terms of proportionality, it is a good to be weighed against any regrettable harm to civilians.

Regarding civilians and their surroundings, much critical attention has been focused on the collateral damage incurred in the course of targeting operations, as well as on the specifically American use of drones and their effect on the surrounding population. In war, however, armies are authorized to attack and kill enemy combatants in ways that predictably cause a considerable degree of harm to civilians. In fact, when targeted killings are carried out with due care, they actually cause less collateral damage than many conventional wartime tactics. This is the very essence of the case for pinpointed attacks.

Care and caution regarding choice of target and enemy civilians are crucial to the justification of targeted killings. Both the Israeli Supreme Court and former US President Obama publicly affirmed various conditions.[2] Whether high standards are actually met in practice is a further issue of contention. Opposition to targeted killing often points to the lack of clarity surrounding the decision-making procedure and the manner in which attacks are carried out. Such worries include suspicion of government power, fear of its abuse, lack of transparency, mistakes, misjudgments, use of unmanned aircraft, and killing by "remote control." All these are secondary arguments against targeted killing.

2. Former President Barak Obama, speech at the National Defense University, https://www.whitehouse.gov/the-press-office/2013/05/23/remarks-president-national-defense-university. *Public Committee against Torture in Israel v. Government of Israel* HCJ 769/02, Dec. 11, 2005, Para. 34.

They do not principally oppose the killings themselves but rather express concern about their execution in practice, as well as about the feasibility of carrying out such operations legitimately. At the very least, they call for institutional guarantees against abuse of government power and related dangers.

Ultimately, I deny that these objections present conclusive arguments against the permissibility of targeting terrorists. I argue that such concerns can, and should, be resolved in keeping with the general wartime framework in which these attacks are carried out. That is, we should require the standards of concern for enemy combatants and civilians, as well as the extent of oversight of administrative power, that we would normally require during wartime (e.g., review by a legal advisor) and in accordance with the standards applied to any other act of war.

One such requirement is reasonable chance of success. Disagreements over the utility of assassinating terrorists cannot be resolved in theory, but it cannot be avoided either. Considering arguments against and (mainly) for the expediency of this tactic, I suggest that targeted killing is our best shot at combating terrorism at the lowest cost to innocent human life.

Finally, not all cases of state-instigated named killings are in fact "targeted killings" defensible in this way. My argument applies only to targeting direct participants in hostilities. Where states target bona fide civilians, they engage in political murder or assassination, clearly and absolutely prohibited by law. One recent well-publicized series of assassinations concerns the mysterious deaths of several Iranian nuclear scientists over the past few years. Scientists are unquestionably noncombatants.

Nevertheless, contemporary just war theory, in all its varieties, contains resources for sanctioning attacks on key civilians under highly constrained circumstances of necessity, such as contending with an existential threat. The final sections of my portion of this book look at this type of state-sanctioned assassination, commonly described as instances of targeted killing. Ultimately, I argue that if any such cases—either historical or contemporary—appear morally justified, their defense relies on something like a supreme emergency argument.

2. The Status of the Conflict

The key to the argument that targeted killing is legitimate under international law is the contentious proposition that a state of war, or armed conflict, exists between states and various terrorist or guerrilla organizations and their affiliates. The rules about deliberate killing are starkly different in armed conflict than they are in peacetime. In war, members of the military are authorized to kill, maim, and capture. They enjoy a privileged status that renders them immune from prosecution for acts that would normally count as murder, criminal assault, kidnapping, and so on. No proportionality restriction applies to killing enemy combatants during wartime, so long as there is any military advantage to doing so;[3] and "[t]here is no 'last resort' requirement on operations aimed at killing the enemy in

---

3. Walzer, *Just and Unjust Wars*, at 138–147; Hurka, "Proportionality in the Morality of War," at 58. That this is the unanimous view within traditional just war theory is conceded even by its critics, most notably McMahan, *Killing in War*, at 18, 22–23, 29–30.

war: a legitimate target can be permissibly killed, even if capture would be costless."[4] Armies are also entitled to cause levels of collateral damage that would be intolerable in a domestic peacetime setting.

These privileges of belligerency, however, apply only in wartime. Outside of an armed conflict, combatants, just like the rest of us (including armed police), are prohibited from killing anyone at all except in self-defense against imminent danger. And here lies the trouble with targeted killing, emphasized strongly by a variety of scholars: It may be defensible as a wartime tactic, but not as a peacetime measure. Killing belligerents in the course of war is common practice, but drawing up kill lists in a domestic peacetime setting is not.

Which set of rules apply when states fight terrorists? This question has been hotly debated by lawyers and philosophers.[5] Does a state of war exist between Israel or the United States and various terrorist organizations as the political and military leaders of these states assert?

Prior to the 9/11 attacks, the United States had responded to terrorism primarily from a law-enforcement perspective. The law-enforcement model treated terrorists

4. Altman, Introduction to *Targeted Killing—Law and Morality in an Asymmetrical World*. 6. Gross, *Moral Dilemmas of Modern War*, at 106.

5. Blum and Heymann, "Law and Policy of Targeted Killing," at 155–165. Determining the appropriate framework for discussion— laws of war versus domestic peacetime rules—is raised and discussed by nearly all of the contributors to Finkelstein et al., *Targeted Killing— Law and Morality in an Asymmetrical World*, e.g., Altman, "Introduction," at 5–8; Maxwell, "Rebutting the Civilian Presumption," esp. at 36–38; Ohlin, "Targeting Co-Belligerents," esp. at 60–61; McMahan, "Targeted Killing: Murder, Combat or Law Enforcement," 135–155, throughout; and Finkelstein, "Targeted Killing as Preemptive Action," at 156–183.

as criminals, to be arrested, tried, and afforded certain rights. After the attacks, the United States changed its posture toward terrorism from one of law enforcement to an armed conflict paradigm. Shortly after 9/11, Congress authorized the president to use military force against terrorist organizations and their members, as well as against individuals and states who aid and harbor terrorists, effectively recognizing the existence of an armed conflict between the United States and terrorist organizations.[6] Congress approved the Authorization for the Use of Military Force (AUMF) against "those nations, organizations, or persons that . . . planned, authorized, committed, or aided the terrorist attacks that occurred on September 11, 2001, or harbored such organizations or persons in order to prevent any future act of international terrorism against the United States"—essentially allowing the United States to go to war.[7]

Since that time, the United States has increasingly adopted a strategy of targeted killing, mirroring Israel's policy of targeting Hamas leaders in Gaza, and using drone technology pioneered by Israel. The official American position is that its *personality strikes* always take place as part of this approved armed conflict with al-Qaeda, the Taliban, and other associated forces.[8] Despite difference in style and

6. Maxwell, "Rebutting the Civilian Presumption," at 37–38.

7. Daskal and Vladeck, "After the AUMF," at 120; Friedman, "Targeted Killing: A Short History," https://foreignpolicy.com/2012/08/13/targeted-killings-a-short-history/.

8. Heller, "One Hell of a Killing Machine," at 92. The situation of signature strikes is different. The United States maintains that although they may take place within the armed conflict and justified under the AUMF, signature strikes may also be launched outside this mandate for reasons of self-defense.

rhetoric regarding the war on terror, a succession of US administrations continues to contend that targeted killing is justified under the Law of Armed Conflict because we are in a full armed conflict with al-Qaeda and its affiliates.[9]

In Israel, a series of Supreme Court rulings, most notably on targeted killing, maintain that the relevant normative framework for considering counter-terrorism measures is that of an international armed conflict. Led by its former president, Aharon Barak, the Court stated:

> The general principled starting point is that between Israel and various terrorist organizations active in Judea, Samaria and the Gaza Strip a continuous situation of armed conflict has existed since the first Intifada. The Supreme court has discussed the existence of that conflict in a series of judgments. (HCJ 769/02, Para. 16)[10]

In one of these previous judgments, Justice Barak wrote of the situation at the start of the second Intifada: "Since late September 2000, severe combat has been taking place in the areas of Judea and Samaria. It is not police activity. It is an armed struggle" (HCJ 7015/02).[11] Moreover, the Court maintains, time and time again "this approach is in line with the definition of armed conflict within the international literature" (HCJ 769/02, Para. 16), and the judges cite a long list of sources by legal scholars to support

9. Former President Barack Obama, speech at the National Defense University.
10. HCJ 769/02.
11. HCJ 7015/02 Ajuri v. IDF Commander, http://www.hamoked.org/files/2010/110_eng.pdf.

their view. This, armed conflict, they maintain, accurately reflects what is taking place.

And what was true in the fall of 2000 and later in 2005, when the Court ruled on targeted killing, has certainly remained true in Israel vis-à-vis the Gaza Strip post disengagement. As the Court noted back in 2005:

> the state of Israel is under a constant, continual, and murderous wave of terrorist attacks directed at Israelis because they are Israelis—without any discrimination between combatants and civilians or between men, women and children. . . . (HCJ 769/02, Para. 16).
> . . . [T]he fact that the terrorist organizations and their members do not act in the name of a state does not turn the struggle against them into a purely internal state conflict. . . . Confronting the dangers of terrorism [the Court concluded] constitutes a part of the international law dealing with armed conflicts of international character. (HCJ 769/02, Para. 21).

Under the relevant laws applicable to armed conflicts of an international character, Andrew Altman notes:

> Not only is a qualified combatant authorized to kill enemy combatants, even when he could disarm and capture them at a slightly increased cost to his side in the war effort; he is licensed to attack the enemy in a way that foreseeably causes death and injury to civilians, as long as the anticipated harm to civilians is not disproportionate, i.e., not "excessive in relation to the direct and concrete military advantage." (AP I, 57 2b)[12]

12. Altman, "Targeted Killing as an Alternative to War," at 19. Protocol I, Art. 57 2b, http://www.icrc.org/ihl.nsf/7c4d08d9b287a42141256739003e636b/f6c8b9fee14a77fdc125641e0052b079.

Of course, one need not accept the interpretation of the Israeli Court regarding the applicability of the laws of international armed conflict to counter-terrorism or the relevance of this ruling outside the Israeli case. The Court notes a number of alternative interpretations raised in the legal literature, including some that involve a mixture of different legal regimes. Nonetheless, the Israeli Court is a world leader in legal discussions of these timely issues, and its judges are unusually familiar with the real-world experience of terrorist threats.[13] Justice Barak's ruling on targeted killing has been described as "probably the most comprehensive judicial decision ever rendered addressing the legal framework of the 'war on terrorism.'"[14] Other scholars simply assume various aspects of the Israeli Supreme Court decision as the current legal standard.[15]

As opposed to the Israeli ruling, though not essentially in contrast to it, the US Supreme Court has favored classifying the conflict with al-Qaeda and associate forces as a *noninternational* armed conflict.[16] Considering targeted killing, Gabi Blum and Philip Heymann suggest that the preference of the American Court is actually less restrictive than that

13. As Justice Barak described himself and his colleagues in the *Beit Sourik* judgment (on the security fence): "We are members of Israeli society. Although we are sometimes in an ivory tower, that tower is in the heart of Jerusalem, which is not infrequently hit by ruthless terrorism." HCJ 2056/04, Beit Sourik Village Council v. The Government of Israel, Para. 86 (cited in HCJ 769/02, Para. 63).

14. Blum and Heymann, "Law and Policy of Targeted Killing," at 156.

15. E.g. Maxwell, "Rebutting the Civilian Presumption," at 44.

16. Maxwell, "Rebutting the Civilian Presumption," at 49; Blum and Heymann, "Law and Policy of Targeted Killing," at 157.

of the Israeli Court: "This choice was possibly motivated by the fact that international armed conflicts are subject to more regulation under international law than their non-international counterparts, thereby further constraining the government."[17]

Rejecting both versions of the "armed conflict" model, some scholars have pointed out that the laws of war, traditionally applicable to old-fashioned wars between states, are not a perfect fit for dealing with asymmetrical struggles with terrorists, and accordingly inappropriate for assessing our governments' response to terrorism.[18] Terrorism has been described as a "super-crime"—a grave and deadly criminal activity incorporating some characteristics of warfare but crime nonetheless.[19] Consequently, it ought to be perhaps, by and large, handled in keeping with law-enforcement procedures, albeit subject to adjustments required by the specifics of the situation.[20] From this criminal law perspective, targeted killing is often criticized as grossly violating the basic rights of the accused, deviating inexcusably from the most minimal standards of "due process" required of any well-functioning liberal state.[21] In response, advocates

17. Blum and Heymann, "Law and Policy of Targeted Killing," at 157. For further discussion of the *non-international* armed conflict model and the applicability of Protocol 2, see Maxwell, "Rebutting the Civilian Presumption," at 40–41, 49–50.

18. E.g. Finkelstein, "Targeted Killing as Preemptive Action." Meyer, "The Privilege of Belligerency and Formal Declarations of War, 183–219. Fletcher, *Romantics at War—Glory and Guilt in the Age of Terrorism*, at 3–9.

19. The term "super-crime" comes from Fletcher, "The Indefinable Concept of Terrorism," at 894, 900.

20. Altman, Introduction to *Targeted Killing*, at 5–6.

21. Altman, Introduction to *Targeted Killing*, at 5–6.

of the Laws of Armed Conflict framework retort by stressing the inadequacy of domestic law-enforcement measures to combat terrorists operating overseas and emphasizing states' unquestionable responsibility to protect their own citizens.[22]

In fact, the most powerful objection to the law-enforcement framework is not legal or philosophical, nor even practical. It is the commonsense observation that terrorists clearly operate within the military, rather than the civilian-criminal, sphere. Terrorists, like other irregular forces, confront a state, or states, against which they conduct their attacks. Their goals are political, and they strive to attain them by killing members of the states and regimes they oppose.[23] "Thus, Al Qaeda attacks the United States for its support of Israel and the Saudi regime, seeking to drive America out of the Middle East."[24]

Moreover, there may be far less distinction between interstate wars and wars against terrorist organizations than first meets the eye. As Altman points out, "terrorist organizations are often supported by friendly governments that provide resources such as money, forged documents, weaponry, training camps, and safe haven."[25] Israel's prime minister, Benjamin Netanyahu, made this point in his 2001 address to Congress, little more than a week after 9/11.

22. Altman, Introduction to *Targeted Killing*, at 6.
23. Netanyahu, *Fighting Terrorism*, at 7–8. Altman, Introduction to *Targeted Killing*, at 7.
24. Altman, Introduction to *Targeted Killing*, at 7–8.
25. Altman, Introduction to *Targeted Killing*, at 8.

There is *no* international terrorism without the support of sovereign states. International terrorism simply cannot be sustained for long without the regimes that aid and abet it. Terrorists are not suspended in midair. They train, arm, and indoctrinate their killers from within safe havens on territory provided by terrorist states. Often these regimes provide the terrorists with intelligence, money, and operational assistance, dispatching them to serve as deadly proxies to wage a hidden war against more powerful regimes.[26]

Consequently, Netanyahu argued, "Victory over terrorism is not, at its most fundamental level, a matter of law enforcement or intelligence."[27] It is a war against terrorists and their supporting states.

In the forthcoming arguments, I follow the Israel and US Supreme Courts, as well as their political leaders, assuming that the appropriate legal and moral framework for considering the targeted killing of "terrorists" is the existence of an "armed-conflict."

To win this war, we must fight on many fronts. The most obvious one is direct military action against the terrorists themselves. Israel's policy of preemptively striking at those who seek to murder its people is, I believe, better understood today and requires no further elaboration.[28]

26. Benjamin Netanyahu's address to the US Congress, September 20, 2001, in Netanyahu, Foreword to *Fighting Terrorism*, at xiii.

27. Netanyahu, *Fighting Terrorism*, at xxiv.

28. Netanyahu, *Fighting Terrorism*, at xxiii.

Notwithstanding, the following elaborates on this policy, arguing for its relative merits as a wartime tactic. Judged as an act of war, targeted killing is a particularly limited and fastidious form of combat and as such, often morally preferable to alternative modes of belligerency commonly employed in war.

3. Terrorism

Strictly defined, terrorism is the worst type of political violence imaginable. As Michael Walzer describes it in *Just and Unjust Wars*, terrorism is the intentional, random, and indiscriminate murder of defenseless noncombatants, many of whom are innocent even by the assailants' own standards (e.g., infants, children, the elderly and infirm, and foreign nationals), with the intent of spreading mortal peril amidst a civilian population as a strategy designed to advance political ends.[29]

Walzer's understanding of terrorism as distinct from milder forms of political violence—guerrilla warfare directed at armies and political assassination directed at state officials—has become the term of reference for practically every discussion of terrorism. Nevertheless, this definition is admittedly controversial, and I argue for it elsewhere.[30] There is to date no canonical, universally agreed upon definition of terrorism, either legally, philosophically, or in ordinary usage. For the purposes of

29. Walzer, *Just and Unjust Wars*, at 197, 203.
30. Meisels, *The Trouble with Terror*, Chapter 1.

defending targeted killing, however, it is not necessary to get bogged down in terminological controversy. Those who contest Walzer's understanding argue for a wider, more inclusive, definition of terrorism that would necessarily include the one offered here. They might also include attacks on military forces or more limited attacks on specific civilians.

The argument advanced in the following sections suggests that irregular belligerents, whether "terrorists" or otherwise, are targetable as combatants, albeit unprivileged or "unlawful combatants." Like soldiers, they may be killed during armed conflict, whether they are members of a genuinely terroristic organization like al-Qaeda or simply insurgents fighting the army. As irregulars, they are ineligible either for the legal immunities guaranteed to lawful combatants or for the protections of the criminal justice system. This argument about unprivileged combat and the legitimacy of targeting its perpetrators does not entail any theoretical controversy over the precise definition of "terrorism" as distinct from other forms of irregular warfare. Paramilitary forces and their members are subject to wartime attack.

Nonetheless, Walzer's classic distinctions are important because they highlight the difference between targeted killing and non-targeted warfare; they also serve to favorably distinguish targeted killing from the related practice of political assassination, to which it has been derogatively compared. Part II deals exclusively with the targeted killing of irregular combatants, rather than with any other type of state-sanctioned assassination. Part III considers some civilian targets of assassination, particularly nuclear scientists.

PART II: TARGETING TERROR

1. What's Wrong with Targeted Killing?

In the normal course of events, all individuals—the good guys and the bad guys—are legally and morally immune from attack. As Walzer observed long ago: "[T]he theoretical problem is not to explain how immunity is gained, but how it is lost. We are all immune to start with; our right not to be attacked is a feature of normal human relationships."[31] Professor Waldron makes a similar point with regard to civilian immunity: The default position is the moral prohibition on murder—"Thou shalt not kill"—and the challenge is to explain what justifies the privileging of certain killings in wartime that would otherwise be murder.[32]

For most of us, this challenge is met; we are not pacifists. For the pacifist, fighting and killing are always unconditionally wrong; specific opposition to targeted killing would never arise in such circles. The controversy over targeted killing begins with the non-pacifist viewpoint whereby it is sometimes morally justified to fight and kill other people.[33]

There is also little disagreement among citizens of liberal democracies concerning the immorality of terrorists and their abhorrent deeds.[34] Like pacifism, support for

---

31. Walzer, *Just and Unjust Wars*, at 144–145.
32. Waldron, *Torture, Terror and Tradeoffs*, at 109–110.
33. Cf. Statman, "Jus in Bello and the Intifada," at 133.
34. An exception to this putative anti-terrorism consensus in the West is, e.g., Honderich, *After the Terror*, at 46–51, and throughout

terrorism is rarely, if ever, the source of liberal opposition to targeted killing. Instead, the arguments most characteristic of the opposition to named killings suggest that targeting terrorists is not the morally appropriate response to their murderous actions.

Such claims typically run along the following lines. First, it is argued, assassination, is illegal, that is, it violates international law, as well as immoral, constituting extrajudicial execution. On this view, either terrorists ought to be captured and tried or, at the very least (when this is impractical), decisions concerning their assassination ought to be placed under judicial scrutiny and supervision. Additionally, it is sometimes suggested that targeted killing is an ineffective means of combating terrorism as it only strengthens the commitment of the victims' co-nationals to engage in belligerent activity against the assassins and their compatriots and erodes the prospects of peace. Furthermore, it is argued, assassination is both inexpedient and immoral in a further respect: While its professed aim is to target a specific culprit, it often causes grave harm—whether negligently or inevitably—to innocent bystanders.

Advocating the morality of targeted killing requires answering all these challenges. Controversies over the expediency of this tactic, far from being distinctly pragmatic are, to a large extent, part and parcel of the normative issue. As for the law, international law remains inexplicit on the specific issue of targeting terrorists. The laws of armed conflict are, however, clear on other, related wartime issues, such as who may and may not be killed in

the book. This is at least partly due to Honderich's rejection of liberal morality. Another dissenter is Noam Chomsky.

combat. Clear-cut conventions often reflect shared moral values and intuitions, which can shed light on the controversial issue at hand. I begin with these.

2. Civilians and Combatants

The routine way of determining who may, and who may not, be killed in war distinguishes between combatants (i.e., uniformed soldiers as well as irregular belligerents) on the one side and unarmed civilians on the other. Most opponents of targeted killings accept that, within certain constraints, soldiers may legitimately kill (and be killed) in war in the name of "self-defense." Within the just war tradition, soldiers have been assumed (by Walzer and others) to have lost their immunity from attack by virtue of the threat they pose to their adversaries.[35] Legally, soldiers are granted mutual immunity from prosecution for attacking their opponents in the course of armed conflict. As Israel's Supreme Court justices put it in their decision on targeted killing: "In general, combatants and military objectives are legitimate targets for attack. Their lives and bodies are endangered by the combat. They can be killed and wounded."[36] The condemnation of targeted killing then necessarily hinges in the first instance on a normative distinction between killing enemy soldiers on the one hand and targeting terrorists on the other.

Clearly, the combatant/noncombatant distinction, which renders immunity to the latter, cannot facilitate

35. Walzer, *Just and Unjust Wars*, at 144–145.
36. HCJ 769/02, Para. 23.

arguments against targeting terrorists. As Walzer pointed out recently:

> Military leaders are obviously legitimate targets in wartime. A sniper sent to a forward position to try to kill a visiting colonel or general is engaged in targeted killing, but no one will accuse him of acting extra-judicially and therefore wrongly. . . . Individuals who plan, or organize, or recruit for, or participate in a terrorist attack are all of them legitimate targets.[37]

In the Israeli case, typical Palestinian targets have included Ibrahim Bani Odeh, a well-known bombmaker; Fatah leader Hussein Abayyat; Yahya Ayyash, the famous explosives "engineer," assassinated in Gaza in 1996; Tanzim leader Raed Karmi; Mahmoud Abu Hanoud, a high-ranking Hamas commander assassinated in November 2001; Hamas military leader Salah Shehade, assassinated by Israel in July 2002.[38]

More controversially, in 2004, an Israeli helicopter targeted Sheik Ahmed Yassin, the founder of Hamas, perceived as the organization's "spiritual leader." Yassin—a sight-impaired and wheelchair-bound quadriplegic imam—was targeted while being wheeled out of morning prayers, raising criticism over his liability as a legitimate wartime target. The following month, the Israeli air force killed pediatrician

---

37. Walzer, "Targeted Killing and Drone Warfare."
38. Cf. Gross, *Moral Dilemmas of Modern War*, at 112. For details on Ayyash's life and death (as well as his successor—"engineer number 2"—Mohi al-Dinh Sharif), see Bergman, *Rise and Kill First*, at 420–422, 436–442, 444, 472–473. On Abayyat, see Bergman, at 494–495, on Karmy, at 507–508, on Shehade, at 516–525.

Dr. Abdel Aziz al-Rantisi, Yassin's newly appointed successor as the political leader and spokesman of Hamas.

Some of the misgivings raised over Israel's choice of targets were later echoed in the US debate about targeted killing. In particular, the killing of Anwar al-Awlaki in Yemen
in 2011, raised similar concerns about the assignment of
combatant status. Professor Waldron writes:

> A case can be made that Anwar Al-Awlaki was a bad person,
> whose activities were certainly not in the interests of the
> United States: he was an able propagandist and recruiter and
> he incited terroristic actions. He was not, as far as I know,
> a combatant. Targeting him would be like targeting a high
> enemy civilian official in a regular war.[39]

High enemy officials are immune from wartime attack,
even though they declare and conduct wars, recruit soldiers and encourage participation, spread propaganda and
incite violence. These regular wartime immunities rely on
the delicate separation maintained by states between the
military and civilian-political spheres and are justified primarily on pragmatic utilitarian grounds: We do not want
an international setting in which it is legal and legitimate
to go around eliminating political opponents, however bad
they may be.

A norm permitting the killing of civilian-political officials would erode the workings of politics and peaceful
diplomacy. (I return to this point about the rationale for
the prohibition on political assassination and its distinction from targeted killing, in Section 2.8). Maintaining the

---

39. Waldron, "Death Squads and Death Lists," at 13.

immunity of high-ranking state officials, often clearly complicit in acts of war, promotes civilian immunity by protecting the enemy community's leaders during wartime, and looks forward to the prospect of a negotiated resolution in its aftermath.

Viewed purely in terms of moral liability, however, the wartime protections accorded to enemy officials and political leaders (ministers of defense, commander-in-chief) are largely artificial. Arguably, such niceties ought not to be extended to informal paramilitary organizations, much less to unscrupulous indiscriminating terrorists, who do not respect the civilian-military dichotomy. This diplomatic distinction between political functionaries and military leaders or between political and military wings or echelons, rendering the former immune from attack is not only dubious but also untenable in connection with terrorist organizations that maintain no such divisions.

Leaders and active members of paramilitary organizations engaged in armed conflict are direct participants in hostilities, legally and morally liable to military attack. For various pragmatic reasons, Israel has at times attempted to distinguish between the political and military arms of organizations such as the Palestine Liberation Organization (PLO) and Hamas, but it is not clear that they are required to do so. No one, I assume—to take the extreme example—would argue for Osama bin Laden's immunity as a political leader of al-Qaeda. That is part of the occupational hazard of participating in an organized militia, particularly by choosing terrorism as a career. One cannot conceivably claim civilian immunity as a political or media figure while being deeply involved in the activities of a terrorist organization, whether laying out policy, recruiting or inciting, planning operations, issuing orders, overseeing, or carrying out murderous attacks.

In the Israeli case, Yassin and Rantisi were cofounders and active leaders of Hamas that proudly claimed responsibility for numerous suicide attacks against Israeli civilians. As part of his vision of establishing a Muslim theocracy from the Jordan River to the Mediterranean sea, Yassin developed and disseminated his doctrine of martyrdom. Advocating and instigating the use of suicide bombings, Yassin differentiated the acts of the *Shahid* from ordinary suicide prohibited by Islam and promised "the martyr" (and his family) a place in paradise. Toward the end of his life, Yassin also encouraged the use of female suicide bombers in the "holy war" against Israel. Both leaders—Yassin and Rantisi—were actively involved in directing and planning Hamas terror against Israelis, openly inciting and recruiting for, as well as organizing, countless deadly attacks.[40]

Anwar al-Awlaki, an imam like Yassin, was a senior terrorist recruiter and motivator, an active operational affiliate of al-Qaeda—described by former US President Obama as "the leader of external operations for Al-Qaeda in the Arabian Peninsula"—and was (allegedly) involved in plotting and planning specific attacks against American civilians.[41] His public preaching, openly calling for jihad and the killing of non-Muslim Americans, appear to back

40. For details of Yassin's terrorist activity and assassination, see Bergman, *Rise and Kill First,* at 410–417, 549–555; on Rantisi, at 555–556.

41. https://www.youtube.com/watch?v=x43omN1yhxw, President Obama's speech, praising the killing of al-Awlaki, September 30, 2011, AP.

up the Obama administration's allegations. In his numerous YouTube videos and other widespread Internet propaganda, al-Awlaki (dubbed by the Saudi's as "bin Laden of the Internet") made no bones about his enthusiastic affiliation with al-Qaeda and his active involvement with their belligerent (murderous and terroristic) operations. What more must one do to count as a direct participant?

By their own admission, terrorists are not civilians: They are the instigators, organizers, recruiters, commanders, and operatives of an armed struggle. Terrorists controversially regard themselves as "freedom fighters" or guerrilla warriors but never claim to be unengaged in hostilities. On the contrary, terrorist leaders and the organizations they represent are always proud to publicly accept responsibility (as opposed to guilt) for the atrocities they plan and execute—bin Laden or "card-carrying" members of Hamas, to cite extreme examples.

It is also instructive to note in comparison who counts as a combatant in regular wars. Targetable members of the military include numerous soldiers who contribute only marginally to the execution of war; for the most part, they do so less freely and willingly than enthusiastic volunteers for terrorist organizations. Once enlisted, many of the men and women who don a military uniform will never see the battlefield, and of those who do see it, a great number of them will never even fire their gun, let alone kill anyone at all.[42] Nevertheless, all count as legitimate wartime targets by virtue of affiliation with a belligerent organization,

---

42. Many, if not most, soldiers are "non-firers." See Walzer, *Just and Unjust Wars*, at 139.

though most will participate far less actively and directly in armed conflict than either al-Awlaki or Yassin did.

Like all soldiers, terrorists are legitimate wartime targets. Aside from the obviously warlike character of the activity they are engaged in, and for which they are pursued, they themselves do not deny the military nature of their deeds; indeed, they take pride in it. More often than not, they bear militaristic titles of command, as do various "military commanders" of Hamas. Al-Awlaki apparently held the rank of "regional commander" within al-Qaeda. At times, terrorists wear military-style uniforms or identifying dress (as Yasser Arafat often did), though they remain irregulars, unprotected by the rules of war. On no account are they protected civilians, even civilian criminals, nor do they sincerely profess to this status.

3. Location

Assuming now that terrorists are liable targets, it might still be pointed out in objection that their targeting is often carried out in civilian settings (e.g., at their desks, in their cars, or even in their beds), and that this fact distinguishes their killing from legitimate combat on the battlefield. While this is slightly more plausible than classifying terrorists as protected civilians, it is ultimately destined to the same fate.

Killing combatants in irregular settings does not breach any international laws or moral conventions, though under normal circumstances it may fall short of an officer and a gentleman's ideal. "Soldiers may be killed in self-defense under circumstances that far outstrip those that constrain ordinary self-defense. Any soldier may be killed during armed conflict at any time whether armed or unarmed, whether posing a grievous threat or idly standing by, and whether innocent or non-innocent."[43] Walzer explains in *Just and Unjust Wars*: "It is not against the rules of war as we currently understand them to kill soldiers who look funny, who are taking a bath, holding up their pants, reveling in the sun, smoking a cigarette."[44] No doubt we feel uneasy about killing soldiers in such circumstances, as Walzer clearly does, but there is no rule against doing so.

In the case of terrorists, it is unclear that we should even experience a lack of ease about targeting them in unexpected, unordinary, contexts, for example, in their office or on their way to it. Killing combatants in their military headquarters, on their way to or from a military activity (in their cars) or accompanied by their bodyguards is entirely legitimate even in conventional wars.

Admittedly, soldiers may not be killed in civilian locations, when on leave out of uniform, back home, or vacationing with their families. Why is it legitimate to kill an enemy officer in his office or on the way to it but illegitimate to kill him in a hotel? How does the change in location serve to provide immunity to an otherwise legitimate wartime target? Should such immunizing rules apply to irregular combatants who do not abide by them?

The limitation on targeting combatants in civilians settings is the product of convention, though one with a morally significant rationale, that of confining wartime

43. Gross, "Assassination," at 104; See also Fletcher, *Romantics at War*; at 107–108; Statman, "Targeted Killing," at 195.
44. Walzer, *Just and Unjust Wars*, at 142.

violence to the battlefield and its immediate vicinity.[45] Elsewhere, Professor Waldron has pointed out that many seemingly arbitrary, technical or artificial, wartime protections are in fact "Deadly Serious Conventions," mitigating the horrors of warfare and preventing it from degenerating into an entirely morally horrific situation.[46] Assassinating terrorists in non-military settings admittedly defies such conventions. Terrorists are often targeted in their homes or hideaways. Sheik Ahmed Yassin was killed exiting a mosque.

Defending Israel's policy of targeting terrorists in civilian locations, Daniel Statman distinguishes between rules based purely on convention and those based on strict moral ground, such as the prohibition against targeting civilians, killing children, genocide, or torture. Unlike rules founded on strict moral grounds that hold regardless of the enemy's transgressions, some conventional prohibitions (even ones with a moral rationale) depend on mutuality.[47] The irregular organizations confronted by Israel and the United States do not refrain from attacking soldiers in civilian settings or even from targeting civilians directly.

> Since groups like Al-Qaeda, the Tanzim and the Hamas, have no regard whatsoever for the conventions of war, the party fighting against them is released from these conventions too, though not from the strict moral rules of conduct.[48]

45. Statman, "Targeted Killing," at 196.
46. Waldron, *Torture, Terror and Tradeoffs*, at 109. Statman, "Targeted Killing," at 196.
47. Statman, "Targeted Killing," at 196.
48. Statman, "Targeted Killing," at 196.

In fact, both types of rules that Statman refers to are enshrined within international conventions. However, his point is that those norms that derive primarily from convention require mutuality in order to retain their moral force while the latter do not. "[K]illing officers in their homes (during war) is not, in itself, morally worse than killing them in their headquarters; therefore, if one of the sides violates this convention, it loses its moral force."[49]

Jeff McMahan makes a similar point about the limited binding force of conventions:

> [I]t is widely accepted that the violation of a convention by one side tends to release the other side from its commitment to respect the convention. . . . It is not obvious, for example, that poison gas is inherently more objectionable morally than artillery, provided that its use is confined to the battlefield; yet the convention that prohibits its use is widely obeyed, mainly because we all sense that it would be worse for everyone, ourselves included, were the taboo to be breached.[50]

49. Statman, "Targeted Killing," at 196. Fletcher suggests a slightly different explanation of the significance of changing location. A soldier in uniform, Fletcher explains, assumes a collective identity as an enemy agent, which renders him threatening to the other side and thus vulnerable to attack (Fletcher, *Romantics at War*, at 107–108). This suggests that when he is off-duty, while vacationing for example, the same individual resumes his civilian identity and as such cannot be targeted personally. Here, too, it is clear that the relevant distinctions are conventional in the sense of requiring some form of artificial construction (such as the notion of "collective identity") rather than appealing directly to a moral prohibition. It is equally apparent, however, that the laws and customs of war aspire to minimize suffering by confining the fighting to a distinct class of individuals—namely, soldiers—and protecting civilian populations from direct attack.

50. McMahan, "The Ethics of Killing in War," at 732.

It is admittedly difficult to discern and starkly distinguish the more inherently moral type of conventions from those that essentially require reciprocity. Clearly, not all conventions require mutuality. The conventions that constitute the rules of armed conflict need not be of this type. They may require only that sufficient others follow them in order to make them morally significant, and that moral significance does not go away merely because one's opponent then violates them in some particular conflict.[51] On the other hand, as Statman's and McMahan's comments suggest, some conventional rules of war make sense only if they are mutually, or multilaterally, adhered to.

The rule about location is based on the morally worthy aspiration to separate the battlefield from the home front, protecting civilians and their surroundings, limiting the harm and the destruction of war.[52] The case is similar to the wartime immunity of state leaders, discussed in the previous section. These legal protections are largely artificial, though they have some very good utilitarian justifications. Protected locations safeguard civilians, while the artificial protection of political leaders upholds diplomacy and political alternatives to war. Moreover, off-duty soldiers lay down their arms (and uniforms), relinquishing their threatening nature and thus any justification for killing them. Terrorists who do not maintain conventional rules— specifically those rules that confine fighting to the battlefield and uphold civilian immunity—are not entitled to the

---

51. On the conventions that constitute the rules of armed conflict and their importance, see Waldron, *Torture, Terror and Tradeoffs*, Chapter 4: "Civilians, Terrorism and Deadly Serious Conventions."

52. Statman, "Targeted Killing, at" 196.

same protection. On-/off-duty immunities cannot extend to combatants who do not express this distinction by way of external insignia or by limiting their military activities to specific locations. How is one to know whether they are on or off their "battlefield"?

In the case of terrorism, it is doubtful whether there even is a front line or conventional battlefield to consider. When a soldier relinquishes an opportunity to shoot his opponent while the latter is relaxing behind enemy lines, he retains the realistic prospect of confronting him or his indistinguishable comrades in a more conventional context when the battle resumes. Terrorists "on the run," however, do not ordinarily expose themselves to such risks. Unlike the soldier who may honorably spare his enemy when engaged in non-belligerent activity only to confront him again on tomorrow's battlefield, the opportunity to combat terrorism on the conventional front line will never, by definition, arise at all. By fighting among civilians, terrorists create intolerable battle situations intentionally rendering the separation between civilians and military settings impossible to maintain.

There seems, therefore, to be little, if any, reason to uphold unwritten codes concerning optimal battle settings (which do not apply officially even to conventional soldiers) or even those limiting combat to non-civilian settings, in the case of terrorists. Any active member of a terrorist organization is a legitimate target "even when he is asleep in his bed—unlike a soldier on leave who has taken off his uniform."[53] The very existence of a battlefield setting as

---

53. Cf. Bergman, *Rise and Kill First*, at 510 (for the Israel Defense Forces interpretation of liable "illegal-combatants" and its limits).

distinct from the home front depends on both sides adhering to this distinction. Otherwise, as Statman notes, "the side adhering to them would simply be yielding to the side that refuses to follow them."[54] When combatants fight as civilians among other civilians, it is both impossible and unwarranted to grant them the war rights of soldiers who abide by the laws of war.

4. Unlawful Combatants

The traditional conventions of war explicitly accord equal rights and obligations to all uniformed soldiers as well as to those members of resistance movements who assume the risks of overt combat and abide by the laws of war. The relevant legal rules, those agreed on at The Hague and Geneva Conventions, supply little guidance about how to proceed against terrorists.[55] They do not clearly apply to members of organizations who habitually abstain from the legal requirements.

Consequently, Israel and the United States assume terrorists are never immune from attack, not even in their homes or in their beds. Like soldiers, they may be killed during armed conflict at any time, whether armed or unarmed, whether posing a grievous threat or idly standing by.[56] Unlike soldiers, however, they may also be killed in purely civilian settings, from which they continue to pose a threat.

54. Statman, "Targeted Killing," at 196.
55. Fletcher, *Romantics at War*, at 95.
56. On the license to kill enemy combatants, see Walzer, *Just and Unjust Wars*; Fletcher, *Romantics at War*, at 107; 139–142; Statman, "Targeted Killing," at 195; Alan Dershowitz, "Killing Terrorist Chieftains is Legal," *The Jerusalem Post*, April 22, 2004.

Aside from their unprotected legal status, the moral rationale for the license to kill them concerns the lack of reciprocal rule keeping. Irregulars do not expose themselves to conventional risks, nor do they uphold any conventions concerning the appropriate contexts for combat.

Traditionally, the rights and duties of war applied to state armies and their soldiers. The Hague and Geneva Conventions extended these rights to militia and volunteer corps, stipulating the conditions under which they are entitled to the war rights of soldiers, specifically prisoner of war (POW) rights when captured. In order to achieve this status, combatants must wear "a fixed distinctive sign visible at a distance" and must "carry their arms openly."[57] Two further conditions are that combatants form part of a chain of command within an organization that obeys the customs and the laws of war.[58]

After World War II, the Third Geneva Convention explicitly included members of "organized resistance movements" as potentially eligible for full-combatant status under the law, provided such militias fulfill the aforementioned conditions, notably that of overt combat and "that of conducting their operations in accordance with the laws and customs of war."[59]

57. The Hague Convention (October 18, 1907), Annex to the Convention, Section I "On Belligerents," Chapter I "The Qualifications of Belligerents," Art. 1. Geneva Convention relative to the Treatment of Prisoners of War (August 12, 1949), Part I—General Provisions, Art. 4. Fletcher, *Romantics at War*, at 106; Walzer, *Just and Unjust Wars*, at 182.

58. Ibid.

59. Convention (III), ibid, 1949, Art. 4.2.

More recently, Additional Protocol 1 (1977) partly, and controversially, waived the uniform requirement but only in exceptional cases in which "an armed combatant cannot so distinguish himself."[60] Even in these presumably rare instances when distinctive dress is utterly impossible, the Protocol nonetheless requires that such combatants clearly separate themselves from noncombatants by carrying their arms openly at all times.[61] Only combatants who fulfill these requirements—who distinguish themselves outwardly as combatants—enjoy the full privileges of lawful belligerency. Protocol I also requires membership in an armed force that enforces international law as a condition for attaining combatant status and lawful participation in armed hostilities.[62]

Why deny un-uniformed guerrillas the full war rights of soldiers? Some insurgents fight against "colonial domination, alien occupation or racist regimes,"[63] while armies do not always pursue just causes or treat their adversaries in strict accordance with the law. Nevertheless, there are broadly two moral arguments for the unprivileged status of irregulars: First, irregular combatants place civilians at risk; second, lack of reciprocity—irregulars who do not abide by the rules themselves are ineligible for their protections.[64]

As for the first: The obligation to wear uniforms and fight overtly is intrinsically tied to the protection of

60. Protocol I, Art. 44(3).
61. Protocol I, Art.44(3).
62. Protocol I, Art. 43.
63. Protocol I, Preamble.
64. Cf. Scheipers, *Prisoners in War*, at 316–317.

civilians, which forms the cornerstone of the morality and laws of war.[65] In the words of Protocol 1:

> In order to promote the protection of the civilian population from the effects of hostilities, combatants are obliged to distinguish themselves from the civilian population while they are engaged in an attack or in a military operation preparatory to an attack.[66]

Walzer stresses this point even when considering the most justified case of insurgency imaginable—that of the resistance against Nazi occupation. Fighting in civilian guise, irregulars endanger the surrounding population by blurring the distinction between combatants and civilians. Disguised irregulars effectively "invite" the opposing army to fight them among civilians with no ability to accord the latter their required protections. However noble the cause is, distinguishing soldiers from civilians by means of external insignia remains essential to protect civilians from attack. This is a central moral reason for denying irregulars the war rights of soldiers, such as "off-duty" immunity from attack.

As for lack of reciprocity: Maintaining civilian immunity by distinguishing oneself as a soldier carries a heavy price—it marks combatants as legitimate targets, optimally

65. Bugnion, "Just War, Wars of Aggression and International Humanitarian Law," at 16; the status of POWs, for example, protects both sides because it not only confers rights but also restricts the category of persons who can engage in hostilities while being entitled to claim this status if captured. Distinction protects soldiers as well as civilians by warning civilians that they cannot take up arms without losing their immunity.

66. Protocol I, Art. 44(3).

drawing the fire toward them and away from the civilians. Guerrillas in civilian clothes share no such risks of overt and identified warfare. As George Fletcher explains:

> Those who refuse to wear a uniform or a "distinctive emblem recognizable at a distance" do not expose themselves to this reciprocal risk. They claim the right to be aggressors in wartime without paying the price, and this they may not do. . . . The unlawfulness derives from the deliberate refusal to share in the risks of warfare.[67]

The category of those who do not abide by these rules remains something of a "no man's land," in that it is not clear what rules, if any, apply. Irregulars who operate within paramilitary organizations (whether terrorists or otherwise) and confront states, clearly function within a military context. Nonetheless they do not live up to the criteria specified in the war conventions—they conceal their weapons and disguise themselves as civilians—and thus fail to secure the full status and protections accorded by the laws of war.

While no distinction between lawful and unlawful combatants is explicitly laid down within international law, it is widely accepted, and its reasoning can be traced back to international agreement and practice.[68] The status of

67. Fletcher, *Romantics at War*, at 108. See also Scheipers, *Prisoners in War*, at 317, on lack of reciprocity and fairness as a core argument for the unprivileged status of irregulars.

68. Israeli Supreme Court ruling on targeted killing, HCJ 769/02, Para. 25. Justice Barak citing Ex Parte Quirin 317 U.S. 1 30 (1942); and Hamdi V. Rumsfeld, 542 U.S. 507 (2004). See also Para. 31 on "unlawful combatants." Fletcher, *Romantics at War*, 96–112, esp. at 107; Nabulsi, *Traditions of War*, at 32, describing the treatment of irregulars during the Napoleonic wars.

unlawful combatants can be deduced negatively from the positive definition of combatants eligible for POW status under The Hague and Geneva Conventions. This was the move made by The US Military Commissions Act of 2006, which defines enemy combatants as unlawful if they do not belong to a certain type of organization, do not wear identifying insignia, carry their arms openly, or abide by the rules of war.[69] Nevertheless, the term "unlawful combatant" is never explicitly employed either in The Hague or Geneva Conventions nor elsewhere in international law.

Precisely this vagueness in international law, alongside the terrorists' failing to live up to its requirements, led Israeli Supreme Court Justice Aharon Barak to shy away from directly classifying Palestinian terrorists as "combatants" as opposed to "civilians." In his judgment on targeted killing, Justice Barak preferred to reach the "unlawful combatant" conclusion via a slightly different avenue. Rather than regarding terrorists as combatants acting unlawfully, Barak explains that according to existing (rather than desirable) international law, terrorists or irregulars do not by their belligerent actions lose their civilian status. However, as civilians who illegally participate directly in the hostilities, they lose the protections accorded to civilians in wartime and are therefore effectively "civilians who are unlawful combatants." For such time as a civilian partakes directly in hostilities, he loses his civilian immunity,

69. The US Military Commissions Act of 2006, Chap. 47A, Sec. 948a&b.

though he remains a civilian who does not acquire the war rights of soldiers.[70]

> He is subject to the risks of attack like those to which a combatant is subject, without enjoying the rights of a combatant, *e.g.* those granted to a prisoner of war. True, his status is that of a civilian, and he does not lose that status while he is directly participating in hostilities. However, he is a civilian performing the function of a combatant. As long as he performs that function, he is subject to the risks which that function entails and ceases to enjoy the protection granted to a civilian from attack. . . . That is the law regarding unlawful combatants. As long as he preserves his status as a civilian— that is, as long as he does not become part of the army— but takes part in combat, he ceases to enjoy the protection granted to the civilian, and is subject to the risks of attack just like a combatant, without enjoying the rights of a combatant as a prisoner of war. Indeed, terrorists who take part in hostilities are not entitled to the protection granted to civilians. True, terrorists participating in hostilities do not cease to be civilians, but by their acts they deny themselves the aspect of their civilian status which grants them protection from military attack. Nor do they enjoy the rights of combatants, e.g. the status of prisoners of war.[71]

Determining who is a direct participant in hostilities is analogous to identifying legitimate targets, which is

70. HCJ 769/02, Para. 31; and Paras. 27–31 for Justice Barak's characterization of "civilians who are unlawful combatants."

71. HCJ 769/02, Para. 31. On "civilians who are unlawful combatants," Paras. 26–31. See also Protocol I, Chapter II: Civilians and Civilian Population: Art. 51(3): "Civilians shall enjoy the protection afforded by this section, unless and for such time as they take a direct part in hostilities."

admittedly no easy task.[72] Earlier I mentioned Sheik Ahmad Yassin as a controversial Israeli case in point and the killing of Anwar al-Awlaki by the United States as raising similar concerns about combatant versus civilian status. Both men were regarded by the relevant authorities as "direct participants," constituting legitimate targets; in both cases not everyone accepts their designated status.

Undeniably, both Israel and the United States take a wide view of what it means to be a "direct participant," but this cannot be a limitless view either.[73] Certainly, we cannot in good faith classify all men of a relevant age group as legitimate targets.[74] The class of direct participant can properly only include active members of terrorist organizations who pose a continuous threat. Consequently, the Israeli Court recognized that "there is no escaping going case by case," calling for a careful evaluation of each and every potential target.[75]

5. Named Killing

Case-by-case evaluation of individual wartime targets is very different from the normal practice of killing anonymous

72. Altman, "Targeted Killing," at 28–29.

73. The criteria for direct participation are extremely controversial. See ICRC, "Interpretive Guidance on the Notion of Direct Participation in Hostilities under International Humanitarian Law," at 997. The interpretation of "direct participation" has been a serious issue of contention with regard to Israel's and the United States' policy on targeted killing. See, e.g., Eichensehr, "On Target?," 1873–1881.

74. Cf. Walzer, "Targeted Killing and Drone Warfare." For the Israeli Court discussion of "direct part in hostilities" see HCJ 769/02, Paras. 33–40.

75. HCJ 769/02, Para. 34.

soldiers in war, personalizing the killings considerably. One further argument against targeted killing points to the anonymity of soldiers, as opposed to the personalized identity of named terrorists, as grounds for a morally relevant distinction between the two cases.[76]

Even if terrorists are like combatants, it is argued, soldiers lose their right to life, not as individuals, but only as representatives of an enemy political entity. They are vulnerable to acts of aggression due to their collective and anonymous identity that supersedes (or is at least combined with) their individual ones, rather than to any personal grievance held against them.[77] Moreover, as named private individuals, most soldiers are completely innocent of any personal crimes or responsibility for the instigation of wars in which they participate.[78] Their vulnerability stems solely from their role as military agents of their political communities.[79] It is only as such that they constitute

76. Gross, "Assassination," esp. at 103–107; Gross, "Fighting by Other Means," esp. at 362–363.

77. Zohar, "Collective War and Individualistic Ethics," 606–622. Gross, "Fighting by Other Means in the Mideast," at 362; Gross, "Assassination," at 103–107, takes anonymity to be the main feature which sets soldiers apart from named targets of assassination. See also Waldron's criticism of the US kill lists, in Waldron, "Death Squads," at 6, 17–18.

78. Walzer, *Just and Unjust Wars*, at 138; Gilbert, *New Terror, New Wars*, at 14: The requirements for *jus ad bellum*—for having the right to go to war to begin with—are constraints placed on statesmen and political leaders rather than soldiers. Soldiers are responsible only for their own conduct in wartime. Revisionist morality of war contests this view.

79. Gross, "Assassination," at 107: "The difficulty with assassination is its need to re-personalize the state of war," at 112.

morally legitimate targets.[80] As Rousseau commented, war is "something that occurs not between man and man, but between states. The individuals who become involved in it are enemies only by accident."[81] In contrast, civilians who are "unlawful combatants," or who perform the function of a combatant, are often pursued individually and targeted by name.

Lifting the "veil of ignorance" from the personal identity of the enemy-victim allegedly transforms the morality of war.[82] Accordingly, adopting an assassination policy changes the moral landscape, and re-imports into the battlefield the same moral rules that govern relationships between individuals, in particular rules governing the use of lethal means. Failing to work through conventional legal channels in order to punish terrorists, resorting instead to unregulated brute force, illegal and immoral, as would be in any criminal case.[83]

As opposed to the combatant-civilian distinction, the present argument succeeds in identifying a morally relevant difference between killing soldiers in battle and assassinating specific terrorists. This distinction, however, actually works against the terrorists, and in favor of targeted killing. It is entirely counter-intuitive to suggest that killing innocent combatants (soldiers) in battle purely

---

80. For an interesting account of the collective identity of the soldier, and its limits, see Fletcher, *Romantics at War*, at 5, 54–55, 92–96.

81. Rousseau, *The Social Contract*, Bk. I, Chap. 4.

82. Cf. Statman, "The Morality of Assassination: A Reply to Gross," 776–777.

83. This objection is commonplace among the Israeli left and is reflected in Gross, "Assassination," throughout.

because they represent the "enemy" is morally preferable to targeting particular combatants who readily admit their responsibility for the actions attributed to them. Like soldiers, particular terrorists are targeted not because of who they are, but because of the specific strategic role they play within the armed conflict.[84] What is more, while soldiers are not personally responsible for the instigation of, or for the means employed in, the armed conflicts in which they are engaged, terrorist activists and leaders share direct responsibility for both. Moreover, this special responsibility is one they acquire voluntarily. As opposed to conscripted soldiers, terrorists are motivated volunteers.

Furthermore, even where soldiers are concerned, neither the law nor the morality of war prohibits the personalized killing of key targets during wartime. Shooting down the Red Baron (Manfred von Richthofen) in April 1918 was not an anonymous, or impersonalized, killing. In 1943, the United States intentionally shot down the plane carrying Admiral Yamamoto, commander of the combined Japanese fleet and chief architect of the attack on Pearl Harbor.

This is not to deny that re-personalizing the situation by naming the targets may transpose our normative evaluation of killing. In the case of terrorists, however, this transformation strengthens the assassins' moral case rather than that of their victims. Admittedly, while ordinary soldiers may kill in war in the name of self-defense regardless of the material and moral innocence of their opponent-victims, normally once victims are named they may be killed only if

---

84. Statman, "The Morality of Assassination," at 777; Statman, "Targeted Killing," at 190.

materially and morally non-innocent.[85] Killing of the first type—regardless of personal responsibility—is legitimate self-defense only so long as anonymity is preserved and the victims are killed solely as agents of a threatening enemy power.[86] The anonymity factor (the fact that soldiers are depersonalized in war) helps explain why it is legitimate to kill soldiers regardless of their moral and material innocence whereas it is normally forbidden to kill particular innocent, nonthreatening individuals.

Moral opposition to assassination based on the distinction between named and anonymous killing, however, holds water only so long as the victims *are* morally and materially innocent, which terrorists never are.[87] The distinction between personalized individuals and amorphous soldiers can only explain why, in military circumstances, it may be legitimate to kill innocent human beings even when they do not pose any immediate threat, despite the fact that under normal circumstances it is entirely illegitimate to do so. The anonymity factor cannot in itself explain why it is legitimate to kill innocent anonymous combatants but illegitimate to kill identified *guilty* combatants, that is, specific combatants particularly responsible for intentional killings.

At most, naming the target paves the way toward arguing that in war, as in civilian life, when a culprit is identified, he or she ought to be tried and sentenced rather than extrajudicially murdered.[88] At the very least, individualized kill

85. Gross, "Assassination," at 109.
86. Gross, "Assassination," at 109.
87. Cf. Gross, "Assassination," at 111.
88. Gross takes up this argument in "Fighting by Other Means," at 352–354.

lists raise suspicions about our governments' motivations in singling out a particular set of individuals for assassination. Certainly, as Professor Waldron cautions, we should be circumspect about the names placed on these lists, safeguarding against any possible political abuse of power or ulterior motives.[89] Both challenges concern named killing specifically, calling for due process of law as well as suspicion of power.

6. Due Process

Notwithstanding the distinction between terrorists and civilian criminals, there is a strong argument against *punishing* terrorists by assassination in defiance of due process. If a particular person is suspected of a crime—whether civilian or military—and however grave, he or she ought to be brought to trial, though this is not always practicable.

The legal option is usually resisted by armed forces on the grounds that arresting terrorists can be extremely costly in terms of human life. As opposed to targeted killing, it will usually require ground forces to infiltrate hostile populations, endangering both soldiers and enemy civilians.[90] As Israel's Supreme Court noted in its ruling on targeted killing: "Arrest, investigation, and trial are not means which can always be used. At times the possibility does not exist whatsoever; at times it involves a risk so

89. Waldron, "Death Squads," at 5, 17–18.
90. Gross, "Fighting by Other Means," at 353; Walzer, "Targeted Killing and Drone Warfare."

great to the lives of the soldiers, that it is not required."[91]
Similarly, Walzer notes:

> It would be better to capture them and bring them to trial, but
> this is often not a reasonable option—the risks are too high;
> innocent bystanders would be killed in the attempt; the plan-
> ning would take time, and the terrorist attacks are imminent
> or actual. In cases like this, the phrase "war on terror" makes
> sense.[92]

More often, Walzer worries, "the 'war' is police work,
and targeted killing is not permitted for the police. *If the
terrorist campaign has ended*, only the police can deal with
the men and women who organized it—and lawyers and
judges after the police."[93]

Trying terrorists in accordance with basic criminal justice procedures may create an unusual, and at times insur-
mountable, obstacle to indicting them. Proving specific
identity, affiliation, and direct responsibility in accordance
with strict legal procedures can prove particularly problematic when dealing with underground organizations.
Gathering evidence, often available only on enemy territory,
and enlisting witnesses to testify against terrorist suspects
will often be extraordinarily difficult and raise overwhelming hardships in proving guilt beyond reasonable doubt.
These considerations, however, cannot in themselves justify discarding the rule of law. Procedural difficulties may

91. HCJ 769/02, Para. 40.
92. Walzer, "Targeted Killing and Drone Warfare,"
https://www.dissentmagazine.org/online_articles/
targeted-killing-and-drone-warfare.
93. Walzer, "Targeted Killing and Drone Warfare." My emphasis.

arise when dealing with domestic criminals as well, and that would not justify sending in hit squads to shoot them.

Punitive assassination may indeed be regarded as extrajudicial execution. "Like torture, it is unequivocally banned by UN conventions without regard for 'a state of war or threat of war, internal political instability or any other public emergency.'"[94] Unarguably, "What is certainly forbidden is targeted killing for the sake of justice or vengeance."[95] Furthermore, offenders need not be civilian criminals in order to warrant the protections of due process. As Gross points out, "the closest analogy to terrorists are war criminals. . . . War criminals are judged by other states, usually the victors. But the point is that they are judged; a suspected war criminal cannot be summarily executed but must be captured and tried."[96]

Construing "targeted killing" as executing a death sentence without trial also solicits familiar opposition to the death penalty in general. Some objections relate to the possibility of wrongful conviction and the irreversibility of capital punishment. With targeted killing in particular, there is always a danger of mistaking an innocent individual for the appropriate target and killing the wrong person by mistake. In January 1974, Israel's Mossad attempted to target Ali Hassan Salameh, the mastermind of the 1972 Olympics massacre, but instead mistakenly killed a Moroccan waiter,

94. Gross, "Assassination," at 111, citing UN High Commission on Human Rights, *United Nations Principles on the Effective Prevention and Investigation of Extra Legal, Arbitrary and Summary Executions, Economic and Social Council, 1989/65.*

95. Waldron, "Targeted Killing."

96. Gross, "Assassination," at 112. See also Gross, *Moral Dilemmas of Modern War*, at 107.

Ahmed Boushiki, in Lillehammer, Norway.[97] Moreover, even when a target is accurately identified, military agents can accidentally hit the wrong man. Trials matter, even in wartime, inter alia as a means of avoiding mistakes and preventing harm to the innocent.

On the other hand, trials are not required in order to carry out deadly military operations, despite the regrettable fact that such operations sometimes misidentify their target and often harm civilians, usually on a far larger scale than targeted killings do. In 1944 the RAF set out to bomb Gestapo headquarters in Copenhagen, Denmark, but mistakenly hit a hospital instead, killing scores of children.[98] Nonetheless, no one denies that bombing enemy headquarters is a legitimate act of war. Rare mistakes in identifying military targets do not render acts of war unjustifiable, and the same goes for targeted killings.

The appropriate rebuttal to the "due process" argument is that targeted killing should not be employed as punishment for prior misdeeds. Punishment ought indeed be pursued by due process of law. Contemporary targeted killing, by contrast, is essentially a preventive measure with prior offenses serving primarily as indication of future intentions rather than justification for punishment. Israel's Supreme Court ruling was clear on this point:

---

97. Aside from the identity issue, this case also involved the violation of a third party's sovereignty in peacetime, which I am reluctant to defend. The present argument supports a policy of targeted killing in the course of an ongoing armed struggle.

98. Netanyahu, *Fighting Terrorism*, at xxi; Netanyahu, *Terrorism— How the West Can Win*, at 9.

> [A] civilian taking a direct part in hostilities one single time,
> or sporadically, who later detaches himself from that activity,
> is a civilian who, starting from the time he detached himself
> from that activity, is entitled to protection from attack. He is
> not to be attacked for the hostilities which he committed in
> the past.[99]

Speaking at the National Defense University, former President Obama stated, "America does not take strikes to punish individuals; we act against terrorists who pose a continuous and imminent threat to the American people, and when there are no other governments capable of effectively addressing the threat."[100]

Purely punitive or vengeful killings cannot be defended along these lines. If the terrorist campaign has in fact ended, or if the terrorist has ended his involvement in it, only the police, and subsequently lawyers and judges, can deal with him/her.[101] Targeted killing, by contrast, is a military tactic employed within the context of an armed struggle as part of a wider attempt to avoid future attacks, to ferret out active terrorists, to repulse rather than punish terrorists and harboring states.

Undeniably, further, secondary motivations may accompany a defensive act of targeted killing, such as personal or national revenge, pacifying collective outrage, even punishment or a sense of just desert. Following the assassination of Osama bin Laden, President Obama told the

99. HCJ 769/02, Para 39.
100. Former President Barak Obama, Speech at the National Defense University. https://www.whitehouse.gov/the-press-office/2013/05/23/remarks-president-national-defense-university
101. Cf. Walzer, "Targeted Killing and Drone Warfare."

nation that justice had been done.[102] As Professor Waldron commented quite rightly at that time, however, "the only possible justification for the shooting of bin Laden was as a legitimate act of war,"[103] that is, as an act of national self-defense in wartime "under the auspices of Article 51 of the United Nations Charter. That is where the justificatory debate should be focused."[104]

Back in 1943, the assassination of Admiral Yamamoto was dubbed "operation vengeance," boosting morale among allied soldiers and demoralizing the Japanese, but it was also intended to hamper Japan's future ability to wage war.[105] Mixed motives may be present in the most routine acts of war. Defensive tactics are often accompanied by feelings of rage or vengeance or penal intent, none of which delegitimizes them or casts a shadow over their justification as acts of self-defense.

Pursuing and assassinating active terrorists with the intent of impeding further incursions is a preventive measure of national self-defense, whatever the emotions or politics that accompany this goal happen to be. In the context of armed struggle, it is puzzling even to consider capture and trial as a first and preferable (albeit often impractical) option. There is no wartime requirement to attempt capture and trial of either soldiers or other direct

102. Macon Phillips, Osama Bin Laden Dead, The White House, May 2, 2011. https://obamawhitehouse.archives.gov/blog/2011/05/02/osama-bin-laden-dead

103. Waldron, "Targeted Killing," https://www.lrb.co.uk/blog/2011/may/targeted-killing

104. Waldron, "Targeted Killing."

105. Gross, "Fighting by Other Means," at 361; Gross describes Yamamoto as a target of immense strategic importance.

participants in combat, rather than killing them as a first resort. Distinguishing targeted killings from unlawful assassinations, State Department legal advisor Harold Koh pointed out in a 2010 speech: "A state that is engaged in an armed conflict or in legitimate self-defense is not required to provide targets with legal process before the state may use lethal force." Adding that though the technology may be new, the concept is not, and he cited the World War II targeting of Admiral Yamamoto as a case in point.[106]

Notwithstanding the liability of combatants to be killed in self-defense without due process, the decision-making procedures under which targeted killings are carried out raise additional concerns. Not all critics of targeted killing are opposed to this strategy in principle. Much opposition concerns the process leading up to targeting operations in practice, questioning whether we ought to entrust unsupervised military and political personnel with making such crucial decisions.

7. Judicial Review

In Israel, the power to authorize targeted killings lies ultimately in the hands of the prime minister and his defense minister. A certain lack of clarity surrounds the procedures that lead up to the final order, certainly not specified in law, but some general details are familiar to the Israeli public. In each instance, the prime minister is expected to secure his defense minister's formal consent to any particular operation. In practice, while the balance of power between the

---

106. Quoted in Friedman, "Targeted Killing: A Short History."

prime minister and the defense minister leans toward the former, the significant role played by the military in this decision-making process must not be under estimated. In most, if not all, cases, the defense minister is personally involved in the decision, as are the chief of staff, the commander of the air force, and other military commanders in charge of planning, as well as high-ranking military intelligence officers.

Often, the prime minister will consult other members of the cabinet, though not necessarily the government as a whole. At times, a proposed targeting operation will be brought to a vote, though this too will usually be within a restricted forum of select cabinet ministers. Such decisions rely heavily on military intelligence and expertise and give considerable, even decisive, weight to the advice and opinions of high-ranking officers. In some cases, the executive decision authorizes the killing of a specific target, leaving the military in charge of the specific time and place. More sensitive cases (such as the assassination of Sheik Ahmed Yassin) appear to require an additional last-minute, on-the-spot authorization from the prime minister.

As for the American targeted killings, Professor Waldron critically describes the process as follows:

> The President and a committee of his high national security advisors maintain one or more lists of persons whose continued existence is deemed to be not in the best interests of the United States. (The variety of lists may be theater-specific.) The lists contain names, photographs, and dossiers, drawn up on the basis of intelligence. These are the death lists. Names on these lists are ranked according to the prioritization of their destruction. From time to time, as the opportunity presents itself, names are taken up from this list or lists and

assigned to officials who arrange for the killing of the named individuals, usually by drone strikes from the air or by the use of death squads on the ground.[107]

In view of this questionable decision-making procedure, one further source of criticism calls for the judicial supervision of the administrative power over targeted killings. Objections along these lines need not necessarily assert that terrorists must be under all circumstances brought to trial. Instead, they warn against placing the authority to assassinate in the hands of a small cabal of unsupervised members of the executive branch. The requirement of accountability applies to both punitive and preventive actions undertaken by governments and is perhaps best stated by analogy, not with punishment or with killing soldiers, but with the proper attitude and course of action that ought to be adopted toward serial criminals. Why, for instance, don't we want to have police death squads? The answer has nothing to do with violating the rights of serial "bad guys." Possibly, like terrorists, they are morally liable to defensive harm and haven't any entitlement not to be killed as a preventive measure (given plausible background assumptions concerning their unquestionable guilt and certain qualifications). The point is rather that we do not trust the police to make the necessary decisions in all cases. This is a kind of secondary argument against targeted killing (which does not make it any weaker) because it does not question the legitimacy of named killing in principle.

107. Waldron, "Death Squads and Death Lists," at 292. See also in this volume, at 196. On lack of judicial review or due process, see "Death Squads," at 294, 302.

This is a different sort of argument: Even if there is nothing wrong with the killing itself, we want institutional guarantees against abuse.

Similar considerations to those that prevent us from supporting police death squads may apply in the case of targeting terrorists as well. The problem is not their right to life, but rather that we might not have enough confidence in military and political personnel to entrust them with making such crucial decisions. This line of thought is not only a good general argument against absolute power and its effects but also represents a particularly plausible suspicion in the relevant cases.[108]

Suspicion of power is possibly the most serious worry concerning government-instigated targeted killing and probably the most difficult to contend with in practice. Nevertheless, concerns about potential abuse and calls for government accountability do not present conclusive arguments against the moral permissibility of targeted killing of terrorists. At most, such concerns suggest that targeting operations ought to be placed under some type of judicial (i.e., nonmilitary and nonpolitical) scrutiny and supervision. Legal constraints would prevent placing decision-making on life and death issues solely in the hands of an exclusive group that might abuse its power or make fatal mistakes. Generals may be too dominated by purely militaristic conceptions. Politicians may be insincere or misuse their power to advance partisan political ends rather than purely security-oriented goals under the guise of preventing terror attacks on civilian populations. Again, political

108. I am grateful to David Enoch for raising this objection and for the accompanying analogy.

leaders might misuse, or overuse, targeted killing to pacify an outraged terrorized public or be adopted out of sheer vindictiveness.

Naturally, any *national* judicial body would never be entirely clear of such suspicions either. Judges are not infallible, and they are potentially biased in favor of their nation's cause; not unlike politicians and military personnel, judges may be influenced by public opinion. In the United States, the Supreme Court is a politicized institution. Nevertheless, placing decisions concerning targeted killings under judicial supervision would presumably mitigate the dangers of misuse and introduce some level of accountability and transparency.

Imminent terrorist threats requiring immediate action might supersede our concerns about government abuse, lack of transparency, and accountability. However, even when an executive decision to target a particular terrorist is carried out in the face of immediate danger, the government could still be held retroactively accountable and required to show good cause for its belief that the threat was indeed imminent, and that targeting the terrorist immediately was the only feasible remedy. Similarly, other operational considerations, such as an isolated opportunity to strike down a life-threatening terrorist in a particular place and time, might also justify an unauthorized assassination. Such urgent decisions could still be judicially scrutinized retrospectively.

Moreover, most targeted killings are not carried out in the face of literally imminent danger nor entail immediate action. In most cases, targeted killing rests on the broad understanding of "self-defense" in wartime against a wide range of enemy targets poised to command or engage in an attack in the near future. In these more common cases, where the confronted threat falls short of immediacy, proposed killings could reasonably be required to undergo (swift) judicial scrutiny designed to establish whether their objectives were truly defensive rather than purely punitive, vengeful, or otherwise politically motivated.

Israel is particularly alert to the dangers of unsupervised attacks especially in cases involving potential harm to civilians. In its confrontation with Hamas in Gaza, as well as with Hezbollah in Lebanon, Israel uses legally trained IDF officers to supervise attacks in civilian areas.[109] This places at least some legal, though not judicial, supervision and restriction on the carrying out of administrative power in wartime.

For all the merits of legal supervision, however, it is noteworthy that imposing specifically *judicial* review and restrictions on anti-terrorist operations—however feasible and justified in the abstract—would place targeted killing totally out of step with all other types of military action. Military and political personnel are normally authorized to make a wide range of on-the-spot decisions, including, for instance, waging war, embarking on particular battles, and a vast array of tactical and strategic decisions made and carried out in belligerent situations. These decisions are also

109. On Lebanon (2006), see Alston, "Report of the Special Rapporteur," Para. 35: "Both for principled and pragmatic reasons, Israel set certain limits on the conduct of its hostilities with Hezbollah. The mission was informed by IDF representatives that Israel followed its practice of drawing up lists of potential targets, with each individual target, as well as the type of weapon to be used, being reviewed by an IDF expert in humanitarian law."

rarely carried out under circumstances of immediate and dire peril. Any such decision, which is totally free of judicial review, will usually affect the lives of numerous individuals, most of whom are totally innocent.

The largely unsupervised wartime authority vested in generals and politicians in all such belligerent situations is subject to potential abuse and misuse in a variety of ways not dissimilar to those which raise concerns vis-à-vis targeting terrorists—and on a far larger scale. Nevertheless, in the name of "national security" or personal safety, we resign ourselves to these negative side effects and remain satisfied with retaining only the power to punish gross moral digressions in military decision-making and action (such as massacres or other extreme violations of human rights) if they are uncovered. It is puzzling that the lives of terrorists warrant calls for extraordinary judicial protection that are not imposed on other types of military action in which the lives of innumerable innocent individuals are at stake. Unless there is something about terrorists in particular that warrants preferential treatment, there seems little justification for placing decisions concerning their targeting under judicial review that is not imposed on any other type of military decisions.

Why single out targeted killing for extraordinary supervision, distinguishing it from other forms of deadly military force? One reason might be its apparent affinity with political assassination. Admittedly, the two practices share certain basic features, in name as well as deed, when compared with either conventional warfare or terrorist activity. Both are types of named and extrajudicial killings, and their comparison is a further source of opposition to targeted killing.

Undeniably, targeted killing of individuals named on "kill lists" shares key normative features with acts of political assassination, but there are also significant differences between the two practices. A brief comparison suggests that targeted killing exhibits additional moral qualities that serve to distinguish these two types of named killings in favor of its anti-terrorist form.

8. Political Assassination

Walzer's *Just and Unjust Wars* supplies a detailed analysis of revolutionary political assassination, distinguishing it from both guerrilla warfare and from terrorism. Assassination, Walzer explains, necessarily involves the drawing of a fine line "between people who can and people who cannot be killed."[110] The former consist exclusively "of officials, the political agents of regimes, thought to be oppressive."[111] Not unlike the laws of war, the assassin's "political code" *aims* narrowly at its victim and refrains from targeting large categories of people whom the assassin regards as immune from attack.[112]

Whether in the hands of revolutionaries or states, assassination, as opposed to terrorism, does not kill randomly or indiscriminately. At times, avoiding all-out war and/or large-scale collateral damage is the very purpose of resorting to this limited tactic. The assassin aims narrowly

110. Walzer, *Just and Unjust Wars*, at 199. As Paul Gilbert comments, "Assassination is, however, far from the worst offence against the prohibition on attacking civilians that we witness in new wars," *New Terror, New Wars*, at 94.
111. Walzer, *Just and Unjust Wars*, at 199.
112. Walzer, *Just and Unjust Wars*, at 198–199.

at a civilian representative, or operative, of a regime regarded as oppressive or dangerous. Ultimately, Walzer tells us, "we judge the assassin by his victim, and when the victim is Hitler-like in character, we are likely to praise the assassin's work, though we still do not call him a soldier."[113] Such praise, however, will depend entirely on our political assessment of the target in question. Where the assassin's political views differ from our own, we rightly regard him as nothing but a murderer.[114]

How does targeted killing compare with political assassination? Comparison suggests that targeted killing shares certain morally favorable aspects with political assassination without partaking of its normative shortcomings. Conventional laws of war, "political codes" of assassins and state-initiated targeted killings all *aim* at their target and attempt to avoid harm to wider categories of people.[115] None of these tactics kills indiscriminately, and, for all three, private citizens retain their immunity from attack. Political assassination and targeted killing are both "named killings," setting them apart from conventional warfare: They aim specifically at identified individuals regarded as culpable aggressors rather than targeting anonymous groups of soldiers functioning as representatives of the enemy power.

As we saw in Section II.5, this distinguishing feature—naming the victim—serves as a source of opposition to targeted killing. I argued to the contrary that assigning

---

113. Walzer, *Just and Unjust Wars*, at 199–200.
114. Walzer, *Just and Unjust Wars*, at 200.
115. Cf. Walzer, *Just and Unjust Wars*, at 200 and Walzer, "Targeted Killing and Drone Warfare," at 1.

personal responsibility and killing named combatants is morally preferable to the wholesale anonymous killing of innocent soldiers in wartime. Regarding political assassination, Walzer comments paradoxically that we "might even feel easier about killing officials than about killing soldiers, since the state rarely conscripts its political, as it does its military agents; they have chosen officialdom as a career."[116] This applies with greater force to terrorist or guerrilla chieftains and operatives.

Nevertheless, political assassination remains illegal, as well as morally problematic, for the following two reasons: First, regardless of moral liability, targets of political assassination are civilians, political leaders, and officials, rightly protected by war conventions and international law. "In wartime, international law bars the killing of political leaders on the grounds that they are the ones who will in the end negotiate the peace treaty."[117]

Second, while the lawful killing of soldiers in war is judged independently of the justice of their cause, judging political assassination requires taking a substantive stand on the political struggle engaged in by the assassins: "[W]e judge the assassin by his victim."[118] While justifiable at times, assassination is not a practice that lends itself to politically neutral, internationally acceptable rules or guidelines regarding its legitimacy.[119] As Walzer

---

116. Walzer, *Just and Unjust Wars*, at 200.
117. Walzer, "Targeted Killing and Drone Warfare."
118. Walzer, *Just and Unjust Wars*, at 199.
119. Waldron, "Can Targeted Killing Work as a Neutral Principle?," at 1–9; "Justifying Targeted Killing with a Neutral Principle," at 112–120, esp. 112–113, 116–120.

restates more recently, it all depends on our moral and political evaluation of the assassin's cause and that of his opponent and target: "Justice in assassination depends on the character of the targeted official, the character of the regime he or she serves, and the immediate political circumstances."[120] In the case of state instigated political assassinations, we would have to trust state leaders to get all this morally right, rather than murdering their political opponents or any individuals branded "enemies of the state."[121]

None of this, however, applies to targeting irregulars: terrorists and insurgents are armed belligerents rather than protected persons. Just like officials but unlike many soldiers, most terrorists are willing volunteers rather than conscripted recruits.[122] Unlike officials, however, the role they have chosen to take on is a militant, rather than civilian, one.

When the targets of assassination policies are insurgents rather than civil officials, the situation regains the threatening nature that characterizes and legitimizes killing soldiers in war. While targeted terrorists may not always pose an immediate threat to life or limb (though they often do), they always present a clear and present danger, at least to the degree posed by soldiers when they are caught off-guard. It is implausible to regard the threat posed

120. Walzer, "Just and Unjust Targeted Killing and Drone Warfare," at 12; see also "Targeted Killing and Drone Warfare."
121. Waldron, "Death Squads," at 301, 302, 304. See also Waldron, "Targeted Killing."
122. Statman, "Targeted Killing," at 185–186.

by terrorist instigators, organizers, and commanders—charged with recruitment, planning, ordering, and carrying out armed attacks—as less obvious and imminent than the threat posed by a soldier who may be shot in his barracks while showering, relaxing, sunbathing on camp grounds, or lighting a cigarette. [123]

Possibly, some insurgents currently denounce as terrorists will later emerge as state leaders and play a role in peaceful negotiations and politics.[124] This, however, is equally true of conventional high ranking military officers, generals in conventional armies, who often go on to hold high political office. Nonetheless, military leaders are obviously legitimate targets in wartime, for such time as they participate in hostilities, regardless of the future peacetime role that may or may not lay in store for them. No one, I think, doubts that General Eisenhower was a legitimate target throughout World War II; or that General Moshe Dayan was a legitimate target as IDF chief of staff during the Sinai campaign, though he later played a pivotal role in negotiating the historic peace treaty between Israel and Egypt. Countless other examples present themselves, notably the liability of irregular (terroristic) leaders in Palestine prior to the establishment of the State of Israel. Targeting military personnel, leaders, and active members of paramilitary organizations is not political murder or assassination,

123. Cf. Walzer, *Just and Unjust War*, at 142.
124. Walzer, "Just and Unjust Targeted Killing and Drone Warfare," at 13; Waldron, "Targeted Killing"; and Waldron in this volume, at 243–244.

no matter which side of the political struggle one finds oneself on.

To recap: We might respect assassins for drawing limits to their actions, but we outlaw and deplore political assassination because (a) politicians and statesmen are noncombatants and killing them endangers peaceful diplomacy, (b) judging political assassination depends on political views—who is right and who is wrong in the conflict. Neither of these problematic features obtain when killing direct participants in armed struggles rather than protected civilians. As for the moral evaluation of their actions, targeted killing requires no case-by-case political judgment of the victim and his cause (though great vigilance is required in identifying and selecting targets and carrying out the mission with due care).

Terrorists function as combatants and are targeted for the role they play and the tactics they employ within an armed conflict, rather than for the ends they serve. At most, judging their assassination requires taking a stand against terrorism, while all other specific political debates over substantive issues are left open by this basic moral stance. One can condemn terrorism and still support Palestinians in their struggle to pry concessions from Israel. One can feel sympathy for Third World nations and attribute a large part of their plight to Western economic exploitation and other global policies, without condemning the Americans for pursuing al-Qaeda operatives. Whether terroristic in the strictest sense or otherwise engaged in guerrilla warfare or insurgency, irregular enemy forces and their militants are legitimate wartime targets because of the paramilitary function they perform rather than for the political cause they serve.

9. Reasonable Chance of Success

The ethical controversy over targeted killing is inseparable from the debate over its estimated expediency. In the public political arena, both sides to this debate enlist "military expertise" and empirical assessments of utility, which coincide with, and reinforce, their respective normative positions.

Moral condemnation of targeted killing often goes hand in hand with the objection that such strikes are ineffective. Such killings, Michael Gross suggests, may solicit acts of retaliation and consequently escalate rather than diminish the level of conflict. Targeted killing deepens hostility and mistrust, which jeopardizes the chances of attaining peace between the warring parties, thus not only enhancing but also prolonging the conflict.[125] Aside from the antagonism caused by the assassination itself, collateral damage to the surrounding community may increase hatred and radicalization. Consequently, its critics argue that targeted killing is overall inexpedient, ineffective (even counterproductive) in reducing hostility, as well as plainly immoral because it often exceeds its target and kills innocent bystanders.

Some instances of targeted killing are immediately followed by further terrorist attacks (which may or may not have been carried out otherwise) and are often described by their instigators as retaliation for the assassination of their brethren. Whether these terror attacks are in fact reactions to targeted strikes is always an issue of contention. While policymakers often deny this, opponents of targeted killing

125. Gross, "Fighting by Other Means," at 352, 356–358; "Assassination," at 100–103, 113; Gross, *Moral Dilemmas*, at 111.

view subsequent terrorism as proof of the policy's failure and of the role they attribute to assassination in the continued cycle of violence.[126] In the long run, critics argue, assassination (alongside the collateral damage that often accompanies it) contributes to feelings of mistrust, humiliation, and festering resentment within the victim's community, which in turn damage prospects for attaining an eventual peaceful resolution to the hostilities.[127]

These various objections represent two general types of utilitarian considerations for fighting limited wars and excluding certain forms of combat. These are, Walzer tells us, concerned "not only with reducing the total amount of suffering, but also with holding open the possibility of peace and the resumption of pre-war activities. . . . And if that is to be possible, the war must be fought, as Sidgwick says, so as to avoid 'the danger of provoking reprisals and of causing bitterness that will long outlast' the fighting."[128]

Sedgwick's and Walzer's utilitarian concerns assume initially that there is a war that must be fought. This is less obvious in debating the utility of targeted killing. In this case, the first round of practical argument addresses alternatives: Targeted killing as opposed to what? Targeted killing (any killing) remains indefensible as against realistic

126. For example, Gross, "Fighting by Other Means," at 356–357; Gross, "Assassination," at 102, 109–110. Gross also argues that the use of local collaborators and informers, often employed by the assassin-state (most notably Israel), enhances feelings of resentment on the part of the targets' compatriots.

127. Gross, "Fighting by Other Means," at 359; *Moral Dilemmas*, at 111–113.

128. Walzer, *Just and Unjust Wars*, at 132, with reference to Sidgwick, *The Elements of Politics*, at 264.

prospects of negotiating international disagreements. From any just war perspective, utilitarian and otherwise, targeting one's opponents does not fare well as "an alternative to negotiating with them or respecting their human rights or allowing them to take part in national politics."[129] Where civilized diplomacy and a peaceful resolution of hostilities are feasible, targeted killing is a nonstarter.

If the terrorism of al-Qaeda, the Taliban, ISIS, or Hamas can be overcome peacefully—by "compromise, negotiation, the addressing of grievances, and so on"[130]—this is a *jus ad bellum* argument against resorting to war as a last resort. It is not an argument against targeted killing (or drone warfare) specifically, any more than it is an argument against bullets or bayonets. The debate over targeted killing—for or against—is primarily a *jus in bello* issue (or else it is a *jus ad vim* issue),[131] which begins after the decision to resort to force has already been made. Once the fighting begins, targeted killing is an option to be compared with other available measures within the military's toolkit.

How does targeted killing fare in comparison with alternative forms of combat in terms of achieving legitimate military goals, as well as complying with the requirements of distinction and proportionality? In a recent contribution to the *Oxford Handbook of the Ethics of War*, Daniel Statman puts the answer better than I can:

---

129. Waldron, "Death Squads," at 294.
130. Waldron, "Death Squads," at 303.
131. For *jus ad vim,* the just use of force short of war, see Walzer, *Just and Unjust Wars*, Preface, esp. at xv–xvi.

If war, rather than law-enforcement, is the appropriate model for dealing with such situations, then targeted killing becomes the most logical way of conducting it. The alternative would be to engage in a ground attack causing many more deaths and much more harm—to both sides—with no guarantee of better results in neutralizing the relevant threats. In practice, denying the legitimacy of targeted killing in asymmetric warfare would amount to a rejection of the war model as a means of dealing with such conflicts. But this denial is not very convincing.[132]

Judging the expediency of targeted killing is admittedly fraught with difficulties. "Thwarted attacks remain unobserved, and counterfactuals—attacks that would have been launched had there never been a firm assassination policy—are difficult to gauge."[133] Certainly, the expediency of assassinating terrorists cannot be resolved by political theorists (though it cannot be entirely avoided either). It is difficult for anyone, even military experts, to establish absolutely the utility of targeting individual terrorists. This severely complicates the moral issue, as it requires tackling it without resolving the practical questions to everyone's satisfaction.

As Statman points out, however, "Morally speaking, wars are a risky business. Still, according to just war theory one is allowed to use lethal measures if there are good reasons to believe they will be efficient in self-defense."[134]

132. Statman, "Drones and Robots," Sec. 6, at 9, available at http://lecturers.haifa.ac.il/en/hcc/dstatman/Documents/Drones_and_Robots.pdf.

133. Gross, "Fighting by Other Means," at 357; Gross, "Assassination," at 101. See also Gross, *Moral Dilemmas*, at 114–117.

134. Statman, "The Morality of Assassination," at 778.

Jus ad bellum, governing the initial resort to war, requires among other things that a war have a reasonable chance of success. In keeping with *jus in bello*, we also need not be absolutely sure (nor can we be) that a particular strategy is conducive to our defense; we need only employ it in good faith on the general assumption that it has a reasonable hope of success and show good cause for this belief.[135]

> . . . [H]ow effective is targeted killing in deciding asymmetric conflicts? . . . The level of evidence required to establish the effectiveness of attacks in conventional warfare is pretty low. Soldiers are permitted to kill enemy soldiers with no need to establish that the killing of some specific individual or group of individuals is necessary for victory. If asymmetric warfare is perceived under the war model, it is unclear why the burden of establishing the effectiveness of the measures used, especially of targeted killing, should be any higher.[136]

Proponents of targeted killing readily admit that assassinations do not annihilate terrorism in one fell swoop. No one argues that targeted killing presents an overall solution to terrorism or that it brings peace. Targeted killing is a military means of "conflict management"—limiting negative aspects of a prolonged conflict—not an overall political solution. Those of us who support it believe that a sustained policy of targeting terrorists, particularly leaders, can dramatically reduce terrorist hostility and save many lives. Israel's success in overcoming Palestinian suicide terrorism in the early 2000s is a strong case in point, whatever one's

135. Statman, "Targeted Killing," at 193.
136. Statman, "Drones and Robots," Sec. 6, at 9.

view on the surrounding political issues may be.[137] Ronen Bergman's recent book concludes his detailed discussion of this period of time in Israel as follows:

> Israel deployed a number of measures in its war against Palestinian terror in the second Intifada, including IDF ground forays to conduct extensive arrests and the construction of a barrier between the West Bank and Israel that made it more difficult for suicide terrorists to enter into Israel. But while these measures somewhat hampered the terror organizations, *statistics clearly show* that they continues their attempts to execute murderous attacks after those measures were initiated, and *that the terror attacks ceased only after a massive number of targeted killings of terrorist operatives and—* in Operation Picking Anemones—*the assassination of terrorist leaders*.[138]

Within continuous low-intensity armed conflicts, targeted killing serves both as a deterrent (rather than punishment) and as an impediment in the face of terrorist organizations and their leaders. Arguably, such killings weaken terrorist organizations, cause demoralization among their members, force them into hiding, and restrict their movements and activity. Underground terrorist groups with little internal structure often rely on the personal charisma or professional skills of the leaders and key figures of certain organizations. It is reasonable to believe that killing such individuals will gradually make it harder for the terror machinery to function.[139]

137. See Bergman, *Rise and Kill First*, at 539–565, esp. 539, 563.
138. Bergman, *Rise and Kill First*, at 563 (emphasis added).
139. Statman, "Targeted Killing," at 192; "The Morality of Assassination," at 778.

Moreover, assessing the efficacy of assassination policies involves evaluating not only their long-term (rather than merely immediate) effects but also their psychological impact. It is a reasonable observation that terrorist leaders do not always wish to die for their cause. They often conceal themselves in the midst of civilian populations and disguise and reposition themselves constantly when faced with personal danger. The consistent and vivid threat posed by the "long arm" of their enemy, which is out there waiting to pluck them out of any place perhaps when they least expect it, presents a considerable emotional and practical obstacle. Wanted arch-terrorists do not go about their business as usual. Instead, they move around incessantly hoping to confound their enemy, presumably at considerable cost to their missions and public image.[140]

As the Israeli Court noted, apprehending terrorists as an alternative to assassination is operationally difficult and costly in human life;[141] it is also unlikely to meet with the cooperation of local authorities. Gross points out that "governments headed by the Palestinian authority or Taliban do not readily extradite suspected terrorists."[142] Left to their own devices however, there is every probability that terrorists will resume their activities. Exhausting the difficult and costly option of arrests is not legally required.[143] In war, the law authorizes the use of lethal force as first resort against

---

140. Cf. Bergman, *Rise and Kill First*, at 503, who describes such precautions taken by Israel's targets during the second Intifada in the hope of escaping assassination, e.g., moving around rapidly, changing vehacles, wearing disguises, etc.

141. HCJ 769/02, Para. 40.

142. Gross, "Assassination," at 111.

143. HCJ 769/02, Para. 40.

enemy persons and objects within the parameters of the armed conflict.[144]

Furthermore, even in the absence of wholly conclusive factual evidence as to its efficiency, targeted killing has at least one definite consequential benefit, namely it carries with it a far lower risk of *bad* moral results than any other available military strategy. Assuming we must take some forceful action against terrorists, their assassination is, at the very least, "our best shot."[145] As Gross notes, nations fighting terrorists who intentionally target noncombatants "are faced with very difficult questions of appropriate response. The stronger power cannot, in good conscience, target non-combatants on the other side. . . . In this context, assassination has much to offer. It avoids the pitfalls of disproportionality, nondiscrimination (by targeting only the terror suspect) and the fear of violating noncombatant immunity."[146]

> Assassination has the singular virtue of substantially reducing collateral damage and harm to noncombatants while eliminating grave, military threats. In an age when low intensity war is increasingly replacing conventional armed conflict, and pinpoint attacks against combatants are preferred to indiscriminate assaults on mixed populations of civilians and soldiers, assassination should be particularly attractive.[147]

144. Corn, "Back to the Future," at 1347–1348.
145. Statman, "The Morality of Assassination," at 778; Statman, "Targeted Killing," at 193.
146. Gross, "Assassination," at 113.
147. Gross, *Moral Dilemmas of Modern War*, at 101; See also, Gross, "Assassination," at 99.

Assuming it achieves at least some of its goals, targeted killing is preferable to other forms of combat because it succeeds to a large extent (though admittedly not entirely) in sparing civilian lives. It never deliberately targets the innocent.

10. Collateral Damage

Admittedly, as in any other assault on military targets in war, a certain degree of unintentional collateral damage to civilians is to be expected. These foreseeable harms are increased by the fact that terrorists almost invariably fight among civilians (whether inevitably or by choice). The collateral ills of targeted killing, most notably resulting from air strikes, have been the source of condemnation by human rights groups worldwide.

Justification appeals to the doctrine of double effect, which permits the performance of certain acts of war even though they are likely to have evil consequences, specifically the killing of noncombatants. The stringency of the prohibition on killing noncombatants in wartime does not apply to unintended effects. Civilian casualties are justifiable insofar as they are sincerely unintended byproducts of attacking a legitimate target, aimed at narrowly in a genuine attempt to avoid peripheral harm.[148] Additionally, even unintended harm to civilians must be proportionate in relation to the anticipated military advantage.[149] Moreover, the

---

148. On the doctrine of double effect see Walzer, *Just and Unjust Wars*, at 151–159, 257, 277, 280, 283, 317, 321.

149. Protocol I, Art. 57 (2), (iii). Walzer, *Just and Unjust Wars*, at 153–155.

military must take care to minimize civilian casualties,[150] possibly even at some risk to their mission and their own soldiers.[151] That said, Walzer tells us, "There are, after all, unintended deaths and legitimate military operations, and the absolute rule against attacking civilians does not apply. War necessarily places civilians in danger; that is another aspect of its hellishness."[152]

Avowed, "card-carrying" terrorists are legitimate wartime targets if ever there were ones. Furthermore, there are, at the very least, reasonable grounds for the belief that targeting terrorists is conducive to self-defense. Certainly, incurring civilian casualties does not set these operations apart from other acts of war such as bombing military targets or destroying military supplies or ammunition reserves. On the contrary, targeted killing fulfills the requirement of aiming narrowly at an acceptable target to the very highest degree. Achieving the direct effect, hitting the target (and no one else), is clearly the agent's single intent. Targeted killing is not unique, nor is it delegitimized, by the fact that it results in civilian casualties.

Moreover, targeted killing cannot be accused of inflicting a degree of harm to civilians that is disproportionate in relation to the operation's military objective or to the overall objective of preventing terror attacks. The danger posed by a targeted strike (or a succession of targeted killings) to members of the surrounding community is necessarily smaller than the risk faced by noncombatants caught up in the midst of any conventional type of military operation.

150. Protocol I, Art. 57 (2), (i) and (ii).
151. Walzer, *Just and Unjust Wars*, at 155.
152. Walzer, *Just and Unjust Wars*, at 156.

Civilians are at far lower risk when an enemy air force aims at a pinpointed target within a very definite and confined area than they are by conventional acts of aviation warfare, such as the classic case of bombing of an ammunition factory in an enemy town. Statman makes a similar point: "Bear in mind still that the alternative to targeted killing is not no-killing (some form of pacifism), but *non-targeted* killing; namely, ordinary military operations which are far less sensitive to differences in moral liability."[153]

This is not a point of logic or merely an estimate or observation. When contemplating the standard of proportionality alongside the requirement to minimize harm to civilians, consider the figures put forward by B'tselem—The Israeli Information Center for Human Rights in the "Occupied Territories" (an organization not noted for underestimating the number of civilian fatalities caused by Israel) at the absolute height of Israel's assassination policy:

> In the course of the Al-Aqsa Intifada (between Sept 29 2000 and December 2003), at least 126 Palestinians were "extra judicially executed" by Israel. Of these, 67 assassinations were carried out by the Israel Air Force and 59 of them, were carried out by ground forces. In the course of these assassinations 85 additional Palestinians were killed, 75 of them in assassinations carried out by the Israel Air Force and 10 of them in assassinations carried out by ground forces.[154]

153. Statman, "Drones and Robots," Sec. 6, at. 9.
154. http://www.btselem.org. This website no longer displays the statistics from the early 2000s, but their recent figures equally indicate relatively low collateral damage in targeted killing.

By August 2008, Israel had targeted 232 named combatants, while killing 154 civilians.[155] Gross reports, "When
asked, B'tselem had no doubt that the intended objects of
targeted killings were all members of one military organization or another."[156] All subsequent figures by B'tselem
consistently indicate that Israel continues to maintain
an overall average ratio of less than 1:1 between genuine militants who are the object of attack and additional
casualties.[157]

B'tselem's website never mentioned whether any "additional Palestinians" caught in the close vicinity of the target
victim—often in his car or office—were themselves involved
in terrorist activity. In some cases, additional victims have
included the target's bodyguards or driver, and other members of his organization. Undeniably, some of the casualties
have been innocent bystanders, even children. In the worst
of such cases to date, the aforementioned July 2002 attack
on Salah Shehade far exceeded its goal by killing not only
the arch-terrorist but also over a dozen civilians, including
Shehade's wife and teenage daughter. A hundred and fifty
people were reported injured.[158]

Once again, however, civilian casualties do not set targeted killing apart from conventional warfare. To the extent

155. Gross, *Moral Dilemmas*, at 114, citing B'tselem.
156. Gross, *Moral Dilemmas*, at 119.
157. http://www.btselem.org/statistics/
fatalities/after-cast-lead/by-date-of-event/gaza/
palestinians-killed-during-the-course-of-a-targeted-killing.
158. For details of the attack, see Bergman, *Rise and Kill First*, at
525. The singularity of the attack, the fact that it always appears as the
example of collateral damage, attests in itself to the infrequency of its
occurrence.

that concern for civilians draws a distinction between various military tactics, it does so in favor of pinpointed attacks on combatants. Moreover, in those cases in which terrorists are targeted by ground forces, the danger posed to civilians is reduced even further while soldiers assume a greater degree of risk. The use of "assassins" or "death squads on the ground"[159] as an alternative to airstrikes—however dishonorable this may appear in the abstract[160]—actually minimizes civilian casualties as special forces assume the lion's share of risk involved in fighting terrorists, rather than offloading it onto surrounding civilians.

In the more common case in which the targeting is carried out from the air, due care for civilians is often exhibited by the choice of weapon (e.g., the weight of a bomb, its precision, the flight altitude, etc.) as well as the timing of the attack and the precise location of the operation. Above all, targeting specific terrorists, as opposed to any other available military course of action, exhibits the distinct moral advantage of singling out and aiming at combatants. Moreover, it does so within a type of war in which such distinctions are increasingly blurred by the terrorists themselves. Certainly, assassinating terrorists cannot be accused of disproportionality in relation to the terror strikes it is designed to combat.[161]

159. Waldron, "Death Squads," at 292.
160. Waldron, "Can Targeted Killing Work as a Neutral Principle?," at 10.
Waldron, "Justifying Targeted Killing with a Neutral Principle," at 125, with reference to Kant, "Toward Perpetual Peace," at 70 (8:346).
161. For the Israeli Supreme Court discussion of the proportionality requirement and its application to targeted assassination of Palestinian terrorists, see HCJ 769/02, Paras. 41–46. See also Gross, "Fighting by Other Means," at 357.

Admittedly, there is always the fear that the anger provoked by such operations and the collateral damage they incur will impede future peaceful negotiation and political cooperating with the communities involved. Aside from its part in calculations of expediency considered in the previous section, increased bitterness and hostility amongst enemy civilians due to collateral damage might also weigh heavily on the negative side of the proportionality calculus. The object of just war is ultimately attaining a just peace. Hence Walzer's and Sedgwick's reminder to fight with an eye on "holding open the possibility of peace," refraining, as far as possible, from actions "'provoking reprisals and of causing bitterness that will long outlast' the fighting."[162]

Traditional post-bellum considerations notwithstanding, conflicts involving terrorism typically include deep animosity, long-standing feelings of bitterness and injustice, as well as unsettled scores. Within this context, particular resentments brought on specifically by targeted killing are likely to be negligible, aside from being indistinguishable and immeasurable within the sea of existing hostilities. It is, for instance, improbable that conflicts with groups such as al-Qaeda, and the deeply felt hatred they foster toward the West and its ways, are affected by any specific strategy adopted by the United States in response to 9/11. Even in the Israeli case, it is doubtful that targeting terrorists in particular contributes significantly to the existing list of Palestinian grievances against Israel. On a more optimistic note, it is also unlikely that targeted killing will destroy the necessary basis for establishing future peace. As Gross

162. Walzer, *Just and Unjust Wars*, at 132, with reference to Sidgwick, *The Elements of Politics*, at 264.

points out: "Nations commit unspeakable horrors and still cease fighting and restore relations when it is in their interest to do so."[163]

11. Drones

What about collateral harm and resentment caused by drone warfare, as well as further objections directed at the use of unmanned aerial vehicles (UAVS) "killing by remote control"?[164] As Statman notes, although there is no essential connection between the use of drones and targeted killing, the two issues are at least contingently connected and the moral debate about drones is very much entangled with the debate about the morality and the legality of targeted killing.[165] Some disentangling is in order.

First and most obviously: Regardless of academic debate, drones are here to stay. To quote the American film *Good Kill*: "Drones aren't going anywhere. In fact they're going everywhere."[166] Perhaps quite soon everyone will have them,[167] though the feasibility of non-state actors successfully operating formidable drone programs in American or Israeli skies appears most unlikely.[168]

163. Gross, "Fighting by Other Means," at 356.

164. Strawser, *Killing by Remote Control*.

165. Statman, "Drones and Robots," Sec. 1, at 2; see also Sec. 6, at 8.

166. *Good Kill* (2014), http://www.imdb.com/title/tt3297330/.

167. Walzer, "Targeted Killing and Drone Warfare"; Walzer, "Just and Unjust Targeted Killing and Drone Warfare," at 18.

168. The popular notion that anyone can buy a drone is comically reflected in the BBC series *Episodes*, where Matt Leblanc tells Sean he's thinking of buying a drone, to do drone stuff. https://www.youtube.com/watch?v=VT3wRBueTJY (*Episodes*, Season 4, Episode 7). I doubt this potential is a source for concern. It seems a far cry from watching

So this is the second point about drones, they are asymmetrical weapons both morally and strategically. Arguably, this is actually one of their advantages. Running an effective drone program requires, among other things, sophisticated satellite systems, large infrastructure, and trained manpower, where state-level air superiority is already established and working in cooperation with the drone operations. Drones offer a built-in advantage to powerful states that are capable of operating such large-scale schemes. Despite the remote-control imagery, Walzer explains, "drones are actually flown from bases fairly near their targets and it requires some 170 people to maintain the drones and get them into the air."[169]

Given the expense and complexity of running an effectively lethal drone system, as well as the anti-aircraft defenses operated in Israel and the United States, drones are going to be far less effective in the hands of individuals or terrorist organizations flying over countries with anti-aircraft capability.[170]

the tops of birds to launching successful drone warfare against mighty nations such as Israel and the United States.

169. Walzer, "Just and Unjust Targeted Killing and Drone Warfare," at 15.

170. Strawser explains:

> Many speak of drones not as individual weapons, but more as "drone systems." Each drone flight involves the drone itself (or drones, usually many drones working in tandem), but also involves the integrated satellite systems that navigate them and communicate with them anywhere on the planet, the ground uplink stations themselves that send and receive this communication, as well as sophisticated secondary satellite systems the piloting teams draw upon for navigation. It is this—the large infrastructure that is required for even minimally successful drone operations—that is only plausible for states to possess; and far out of the reach of

Notwithstanding, there is a growing concern among
military experts, as well as scholars, that smaller, less
sophisticated off-the-shelf drones that are rapidly becoming readily available, may be used by terrorist organizations
to carry out indiscriminate attacks. Walzer cautions us to
"imagine a world, in which we will soon be living, where
everybody has drones."[171] A recent article in *The New York
Times* quotes J. D. Johnson, a retired general who previously commanded the threat-defeat agency, warning that
terrorist drones constitute a very real danger: pointing out
"these things are really small and hard to detect, and if they
swarm in groups, they can overload our ability to knock
them all down."[172] There have been numerous articles to
this effect in the Israeli and American press.[173]

even the most well-funded non-state actor groups. Additionally, without
state-level air superiority, drones are incredibly ineffective. They are slow,
lumbering planes that can *easily* be shot down by even the most basic
anti-aircraft defenses. They would be like shooting down a slow moving,
low flying Cessna, or even easier. The only reason they are effective where
we use them is because we use them in places where complete air superiority is already established and working in cooperation with the drone
operations. Non-state actors almost never have this. As such, even if they
somehow COULD co-opt the massive infrastructure needed for an effective drone program (which I don't think they could), their drones would
be pathetically and easily shot down out of the sky almost instantly. (personal communication)

171. Walzer, "Just and Unjust Targeted Killing and Drone
Warfare," at 18.
172. Eric Schmitt, "Pentagon Tests Lasers and Nets to Combat a
Vexing Foe: ISIS Drones," *New York Times*, September 23, 2017.
173. Yossi Melman, "Hamas Increases Its Efforts to Develop
Unmanned Aerial Vehicles," [Hebrew] *Maariv*, January 20, 2018, http://
www.maariv.co.il/journalists/Article-618572; Hudson, "Drone Attacks
Are Essentially Terrorism by Joystick."

At the start of 2018, a *Washington Post* headline warned: "Drones Keep Entering No-Fly Zones over Washington, Raising Security Concerns."[174] The low-cost, low-operational skill requirement, off-the-shelves availability may make airborne IEDs (improvised explosive devices) an ideal weapon for terrorists. This seems to be the opinion of the Pentagon, which sent technical specialists to Iraq, Syria, and Afghanistan to protect US and local troops from ISIS drones.[175]

Nevertheless, the basic point about asymmetry holds: While terroristic drone attacks pose a potential threat, the asymmetry in capabilities will probably remain. A distinction needs to be drawn here between highly advanced US and Israeli military drones, and satellite-operated drone systems, versus airborne IEDs. Moreover, drones are particularly effective where complete air superiority is established, as is the case with the US drone program in Afghanistan, Pakistan, and Yemen. Non-state actors do not have this. While a cause for concern, terrorist drones are likely to be far less efficient than a massive drone program run by a superpower like the United States or a regional superpower such as Israel. However effective they ultimately become, terrorists with drones will be least effective over American

174. Michael Laris, "Drones Keep Entering No-Fly Zones over Washington, Raising Security Concerns," *Washington Post*, January 13, 2018, https://www.washingtonpost.com/local/trafficandcommuting/drones-keep-entering-no-fly-zones-over-washington-raising-security-concerns-and-illustrating-larger-problems/2018/01/13/1030159a-db7d-11e7-b1a8-62589434a581_story.html?undefined=&utm_term=.4b7f42cc03fc&wpisrc=nl_headlines&wpmm=1.

175. Schmitt, "Pentagon Tests Lasers and Nets to Combat a Vexing Foe."

and Israeli skies, well protected by anti-aircraft defenses. Moreover, as terrorist capabilities improve (if they do improve), so most likely will our technology of detecting them and shooting them down.

I do not wish to belabor this point about strategic asymmetry because I am no expert on emerging technologies, and I may have already strayed irresponsibly into the realm of predictions. More importantly, I cannot figure out how imagining what may come to pass when everyone has drones affects the ethical debate over targeted killing with drones in the present. Terrorists will do what they can, with whatever means at their disposal, totally irrespective of what we do or do not do with drones. (Neither are we, for that matter, likely to affect the practices of states such as China, Iran, Russia, or Turkey, among others, all of whom already manufacture, as well as possess, operational drone technology.)

As for moral asymmetry within our war on terror: Drones are not only currently weapons of state but also particularly useful to law-abiding states aspiring to distinguish combatants from civilians. Asymmetry may seem unfair, but it is actually a moral point in favor of killing with UAVs. Drones are precision weapons, offering the possibility of careful compliance with the laws of war, to those who wish to comply. In terms of upholding traditional *jus in bello*, drones are useful to the "good guys," though we know that good states will not always act well. Drones offer a built-in advantage to states that try to distinguish between combatants and civilians over murderous terrorist organizations that kill indiscriminately.

To recap: At present, drones favor powerful states that wish to minimize collateral damage and should be used to that effect. It is quite possible that in the foreseeable future, less sophisticated drones, requiring lower construction and operational costs, could inflict terroristic destruction, but I deny this has any normative bearing on what we ought to do in our struggle with terrorism today. Terrorists may soon be able to harness drone technology effectively to their fiendish purposes of carrying out indiscriminate murderous attacks. I cannot predict the extent to which we might be capable of refining our anti-aircraft defenses to contend with this threat. I fail to see the connection between these warnings and our ethical questions about if and how to use drones right now. ISIS is not likely to refrain from drone technology if only we would do the same.

Given these previous points (drones are not going away, and they currently favor relatively law-abiding states), the relevant question is how—not if—to use them. The laws and customs of war supply the answer: Aim narrowly at identified combatants, sparing civilians whenever possible. Drones have this capacity to refine, rather than dull our moral sensibilities, and enhance compliance with the laws about distinction and proportionality, minimizing collateral damage. If they are not used to this end, then humans are at fault, not the machines they employ.

Many of the earlier arguments about targeted killing pertain to the use of drones as well. Assuming the war model and last resort, Statman poses and answers the appropriate question: "Are civilians put at higher risk of harm by the use of drones than by the use of alternative measures?"[176] Here again:

> The crucial point to remember here is that the alternative to the use of drones is not the avoidance of violence altogether, which would entail zero-risk to civilians but the use of other, more conventional, lower-tech measures, such as tanks, helicopters, and so on. (Of course, if the use of force were not necessary, there would be no justification for using force even when no harm to civilians was to be expected). But such imprecise measures would almost certainly lead to more civilian casualties rather than to fewer.[177]

More critical of drone warfare generally, Jeff McMahan nonetheless concedes that the advantage of remotely controlled weapons is their ability to be highly discriminating in the targets they destroy:

> What differentiates the newer models of remotely controlled weapons from traditional long-range precision-guided munitions is that they allow their operators to monitor the target area for lengthy periods before deciding whether, when, and where to strike. These are capacities that better enable the weapons operators to make morally informed decisions about the use of their weapons.[178]

Similarly, Walzer notes, drones "combine the capacity for surveillance with the capacity for precise attack."[179] (Note

176. Statman, "Drones and Robots," Sec. 2, at 2; Statman, "Drones, Robots and the Ethics of War," at 41–45, 41.
177. Statman, "Drones and Robots," Sec. 2, at 2; Statman, "Drones, Robots and the Ethics of War," at 41–45, 42.
178. McMahan, Forward to *Killing by Remote Control*, at ix–xiv, ix.
179. Walzer, "Targeted Killing and Drone Warfare."

the variety of scholars from conflicting just war traditions making this moral point in favor of drones and their precision capabilities. A rare moment of agreement between Michael Walzer and Jeff McMahan, and between just war theory and the revisionist morality of war.)

Solving one moral problem, however, may in this case entail another. Drones that hover above for lengthy periods of time enable better informed moral decisions, but what about the psychological collateral harms they inflict, as the costs of increased precision is offloaded onto surrounding civilians "living under drones."[180]

The undoubtedly terrifying experience of daily life under the continuous buzzing of circling predator drones overhead, monitoring their target area for lengthy periods of time, is by now well documented, as well as quite easily imaginable.[181] Israelis, in particular, cannot be impervious to this argument that counts psychological harm to civilians in wartime proportionality calculations. This type of damage to civilians has been repeatedly appealed to by Israel in justifying massive military incursions into the Gaza strip, in response to relatively few casualties on the Israeli side. Both in 2008–2009 and more recently, Israel has effectively suggested that its proportionality calculus

180. *Living under Drones: Death, Injury, and Trauma to Civilians from US Drone Practices in Pakistan*, International Human Rights and Conflict Resolution Clinic, Stanford Law School; Global Justice Clinic, NYU School of Law (September 2012).

181. *Living under Drones*, esp. Chapter 3, 59–101, the core section of the report, including firsthand accounts describing the emotional trauma, as well as the total disruption of every aspect of private and social life, caused by drone attacks in Pakistan. See also testimony in Appendix A.

accounts not only for the physical costs inflicted by Hamas but also the psychological implications to its southern population living under the continuous threat of Hamas rocket attacks. Advocating for Israel in these matters commonly involves reference to the devastating, life-disrupting, emotionally traumatic and economic costs to terrorized civilians, rather than merely to the number of actual fatalities on the ground.[182] And what is true when making "the case for Israel" must apply with even greater force in the case of civilians under drones in Pakistan and elsewhere.

I have no experience of living under drones and only short-term experience of living under ineffective Hamas rocket attacks (as well as Scud missiles from Saddam Hussein's Iraq in 1991). Despite the statistically low risk, shrieking rockets (not to mention buzzing drones) imminently threatening sudden death or injury from the skies is admittedly quite an unsettling and unnerving experience, most notably for children. All the more so, I can only imagine, in the case of effective lethal aerial vehicles circling in the sky for extended stretches of time, threatening to strike at any moment.[183] Professor Waldron is quite right to point out that the relevant perspective for assessing the terrorizing effects of drones is that of the people who actually endure them rather than professional risk assessments.[184]

Terror on the ground (far more so in Pakistan than in Tel-Aviv) must be accounted for in any proportionality

182. Dershowitz, "Israel's Policy Is Perfectly Proportionate."
183. *Living under Drones*, at 81, where one man recounts this harrowing experience, describing the reaction to the sound of the drones as "a wave of terror" coming over the community: "Children, grown-up people, women, they are terrified. . . . They scream in terror."
184. Waldron, "Death Squads," at 296.

calculation, whether *ad bellum* (as in the Israeli case) or *in bello*, when the United States chooses its weapons for combating terror. Nevertheless, psychological harm to civilians, just like any other collateral damage in war, has to be balanced alongside, and against, other considerations such as military objectives and the costs of alternative weapons.

One significant factor in comparing terrorized populations with the terrifying effects of drones is the question of intent. Is the harm to civilians intentional, or is it a side effect of a legitimate objective? In the case of terror bombings, civilian casualties are directly intended, providing a just cause for war, as are the additionally terrorizing effects of these indiscriminate attacks. Similarly (though not entirely equivalently), drones ought not to be deployed deliberately to "hover visibly and audibly precisely in order to terrify the villagers, so that they expel Taliban militants hiding among them."[185] In the case of drones, psychological harm is justifiable to the extent that it is incurred sincerely as an undesirable side effect of the war on terror. Moreover, unlike physical collateral damage, justifiable solely with reference to military objectives, the frightening effects of drones are primarily the byproduct of their surveillance capacity, focusing their aim and minimizing concrete harm to civilians.

Consider the following important point by Michael Walzer in response to Stanford/NYU Clinics' reports. Notwithstanding clear evidence of constant fear and buzzing drones, Walzer notes that

185. Walzer, "Just and Unjust Targeted Killing and Drone Warfare," at 16.

the very effectiveness of drone attacks raises questions about these accounts of the fear they provoke. Attacking drones must hover at such high altitudes that they can't be seen or heard. If they didn't do that, the intended targets, who presumably know they are targets, would simply stay out of sight.[186]

Walzer adds:

> Even the most nuanced accounts are contradictory: Gusterson quotes reporters who liken the sound of drones to "lawnmowers in the sky," but then describes a successful killing that happened "without warning."[187]

Undeniably, reconnaissance drones hover (and hum) at lower (visible and audible) altitudes. But they do so precisely in order to allow for accurate targeting of a particular individual. While, "[t]he buzz of a distant propeller is a constant reminder of immanent death,"[188] it should also serve as a reminder of our attempt to spare civilians.

Is there nonetheless something about killing at a distance that makes drones particularly objectionable or prone to misuse? Historically, hurling flying cannon balls, tearing people apart across the battlefield, must also have seemed like terrifying remotely controlled weapons in their time. "The crossbow, when it was introduced, was considered a

186. Walzer, "Just and Unjust Targeted Killing and Drone Warfare," at 16.
187. Walzer, "Just and Unjust Targeted Killing and Drone Warfare," at 16, note 10, with reference to Hugh Gusterson, *Drone—Remote Control Warfare*.
188. Waldron, "Death Squads," at 296, 305, note 43, citing firsthand report by David Rohde, "The Drone Wars," Reuters Magazine.

terrible and indiscriminate weapon, "hateful to God and unfit for Christians," because it could penetrate the armor of knights."[189] Pierre Terrail, seignior de Bayard (1473–1527), *"le Chevalier sans peur et sans reproche"* is said never to have given quarter to a musketeer. (Ultimately, *"le bon Chevalier"* was mortally wounded on an Italian battlefield by an arquebus ball.)[190]

Defending the usefulness of artillery in the 16th century, Machiavelli contested, "the universal opinion of many" in his time "that by means of artillery, men cannot show their virtue as they could in antiquity."[191] He also addressed the concern "that war will in time be reduced to artillery," a 16th-century version of Walzer's futuristic warning about drones: Imagine a world in which hand-to-hand combat will be obsolete, and "war will be conducted altogether by artillery."[192]

UAVs are, admittedly, altogether and entirely distanced from the battlefield and offer their operators (though not necessarily everyone involved in maintaining the drones

189. Davidson, *The Nuremberg Fallacy*, at 284.

190. Also in Davidson, *The Nuremberg Fallacy*, at 284. I am grateful to Azar Gat for this, and other, historical examples, as well as for the forthcoming references to Machiavelli.

191. Machiavelli, *Discourses on Livy*: "How Much Artillery Should Be Esteemed by Armies in the Present Time; and Whether the Opinion Universally Held of It Is True," at 163–168. In the *Discourses*, Bk. II, Chap.17, Machiavelli also notes the asymmetry of artillery warfare, favoring those who take the offensive over the defending army, at 163–165.

192. Machiavelli, *Discourses*, at 166–167, 166. For further debate on the use of artillery, see also Machiavelli, *The Art of War*, Bks. 2 and 3 (esp. the battle scene described in Bk. 3), at 33–83.

and getting them airborne)[193] the advantage of risk-free combat. Various writers have suggested that riskless warfare is a bad in itself, either because it renders one's opponent nonthreatening and therefore non-liable to attack in self-defense,[194] or because it is dishonorable, unfair, and (again) lacking in military valor.[195] Some of these arguments are close relatives, or modern descendants, of the objections raised by Machiavelli's 16th-century contemporaries to the use of artillery.

Some objections to drone strikes—those concerning asymmetrical warfare, distant engagement, the loss of old-fashioned military virtues, and defenseless targets facing a faceless death—apply equally to long-range missiles[196] and, though perhaps to some lesser degree, also to aerial bombardment by manned aircrafts.

Several answers have been put forward to these objections, most notably by B. J Strawser and Danny Statman. Drones are economical: Morally, they have the capacity to minimize casualties among civilians and combatants; financially, they are relatively cost-effective for states to produce and deploy in relation to inhabited planes carrying out similar missions, freeing shared resources for welfare

193. Walzer, "Just and Unjust Targeted Killing and Drone Warfare," at 15.

194. Kahn, "The Paradox of Riskless Warfare," at 2–8, 3. For discussion of this argument, see McMahan, Forward to *Killing by Remote Control*, at xi–xii; and in Statman, "Drones and Robots," Sec. 3.3., at 4; Statman, "Drones, Robots and the Ethics of War," at 44.

195. Statman, "Drones and Robots," Sec. 3.4: "Wars without Virtue," at 5; Statman, "Drones, Robots and the Ethics of War," at 43–44.

196. Statman, "Drones and Robots," Sec. 3.2, at 4; Sec. 5, at 8. Statman, "Drones, Robots and the Ethics of War," at 44.

expenditures.[197] Consequently, Strawser argues for a moral
duty to employ UAV's as opposed to exposing soldiers to
unnecessary risk, contending "that in certain contexts UAV
employment is not only ethically permissible, but is, in fact,
ethically obligatory."[198] Statman points to the motivational
benefits of safe warfare in enlisting risk-averse nations to
take part in humanitarian military interventions.[199]

In "Targeted Killing and Drone Warfare," however,
Walzer worries that this capacity for riskless warfare makes
drones dangerously tempting. The ability to kill the enemy
without risking our soldiers makes killing too easy, leading
to a relaxation of the targeting rules and actually increasing
general unfocused warfare.[200] Moreover, unlike soldiers in
conventional wars, drones and their remote operators cannot demonstrate "due care" for civilians by assuming risks
on their behalf.[201] Walzer invites "us to imagine a war in
which there won't be any casualties (on our side), no veter-
ans who spend years in VA hospitals, no funerals. The easi-
ness of fighting with drones should make us uneasy. This
is a dangerously tempting technology."[202] This diagnosis

197. Strawser, "Moral Predators," at 344.
Statman, "Drones and Robots," sec. 2, at 2–3; Statman, "Drones,
Robots and the Ethics of War," at 42–43.
198. Strawser, "Moral Predators," at 344. Also, Strawser, *Killing by
Remote Control*, at 17–20.
199. Statman, "Drones and Robots," Sec. 2, at 3; "Drones, Robots
and the Ethics of War," at 42–43.
200. Walzer, "Targeted Killing and Drone Warfare."
201. On "due care" for civilians and Walzer's requirement that
soldiers take demonstrative risks in order to prevent excessive harm
to civilians, see Walzer *Just and Unjust Wars*, at 155–156; Walzer and
Margalit, "Israel: Civilians and Combatants," at 6.
202. Walzer, "Just and Unjust Targeted Killing and Drone
Warfare," at 15.

appears painfully plausible—zero-risk warfare encourages trigger happiness.

The appropriate remedy is less clear, bearing in mind the images of war paraplegics and body bags invoked by Walzer's comment. It seems entirely preposterous, even slightly grotesque and obscene, to place our young soldiers, and probably also enemy civilians, in greater physical danger by reverting to lower tech weapons. Walzer does not suggest this.

Perhaps this comparison between drones versus costly conventional weapons is mistaken. The idea may be, as Professor Waldron suggests in this volume, that the ability for precision strikes at a distance enables us to carry out too many military operations that endanger enemy civilians "where, in the past, we would not otherwise have undertaken *any* killing operations. In which case, the number of real-world civilian casualties overall goes up rather than down."[203]

If targeted killing with drone technology enables more anti-terrorism operations—moreover more successful and less costly counter-terrorism missions—surely that is a good thing. Less opposition to terrorism—fewer military incursions that bomb training camps and weaponry, kill terrorists and disrupt their fiendish plans—does not seem like a good solution, nor is it required by the laws of war. Armies are not required to surrender their military objectives, or forgo their targets, because the fighting will cause harm to civilians. On the contrary, proportionality of civilian casualties stands in relation to the mission's anticipated

203. Waldron in this volume, "Collateral Damage." at 157.

success and its military significance, or overall objectives. Better precision weapons in the hands of nations fighting terrorism, achieving greater military advantage at the lowest cost to civilians is precisely what the rules of war suggest. They do not require surrender or retreat—carrying out fewer counter-terrorism missions—unless attaining the military objective will incur excessive civilian casualties.

In fact, the only appropriate response in keeping with *jus in bello* is more targeted warfare: Using drone capacity to focus the aim as narrowly as humanly and technologically possible, attempting to hit the enemy-target and preferably no one else. Any other use of drones is clearly unacceptable, as is any other use of a slingshot or a bow and arrow. Complaints about the misuse and overuse of drones,[204] intentionally or negligently terrorizing populations,[205] ought rightly be aimed at particular policies and policymakers, rather than at the technology.

12. Targeted Killing in the War on Terror

To take stock: Assassinating avowed terrorists in the course of an armed conflict as a preventive, rather than punitive, measure is a legitimate act of self-defense, no less, and perhaps more so, than killing soldiers in combat. Certainly, it is more defensible than related acts of political assassination, which we tend to condone when we share the assassin's judgment of his victim. In the case of terrorists, there is little possibility of disagreement among liberals concerning the moral evaluation of the targets in light of the horrific

204. Walzer, "Drone Warfare."
205. Waldron, "Death Squads," at 295.

nature of their deeds. While the debate over the expediency of targeted killing remains inconclusive and contested, there are at least good reasons to believe that targeting terrorists is conducive to defense, which is all that can be reasonably required of any military strike. Moreover, since military operations—specifically those aimed at terrorists—are often something of a gamble, targeted killing (with drones or otherwise) bears the distinct moral advantage of aiming narrowly at combatants and minimizing civilian casualties.

PART III: TARGETING ENEMY SCIENTISTS

Thus far, my argument has focused exclusively on the wartime killing of irregular belligerents. The justification I offered rests entirely on assigning combatant status to the intended targets, within the framework of an "armed conflict."[206] This justification clearly does not apply to extra-judicial killings of civilians. Many of the important arguments against "targeted killing," however, actually refer to the related practice of state-instigated assassination. In the United States, there remains considerable controversy over the assignment of combatant status to individuals who are labeled as "terrorists" and "shortlisted" for assassination. Anwar al-Awlaki remains a controversial case in point.

Factual discrepancies over the affiliation of particular targets—combatant or civilian—may be difficult to settle in the absence of full intelligence information. The

206. Cf. Guiora, "Targeted Killing as Active Self-Defense," at 327–330.

remaining issue concerns the principled liability of civilians. Regardless of the policies of an administration, states have certainly been known to target civilians alongside combatants, both in the course of armed struggles and sometimes as part of their peacetime foreign policy.

When states target bona fide civilians, rather than wartime members of irregular belligerent organizations, opposition to targeted killing really comes into its own. One notable set of cases concerns the targeting of Iranian nuclear scientists over the past decade, as well as a variety of enemy scientists going back as far as World War II. To the best of my knowledge, this is the only contemporary case study of targeted killing in which a democracy (perhaps Israel or the United States) supposedly assassinated a succession of unarmed, indisputably civilian (non-terrorist) targets in a series of perfidious, undercover operations overseas.

Scientists are unquestionably genuine civilians whose targeting remains unequivocally prohibited by law. Nevertheless, I suggest, illegality may not always exhaust our moral thinking on assassination or settle all controversy over the status of its potential targets.

1. Background

In the early 1950s, Israeli Mossad agents allegedly carried out a series of assassination operations against prominent Arab scientists. Most notably, Israel was assumed responsible for the death of Egyptian theoretical physicist Dr. Ali Mustafa Mosharafa. According to Ronen Bergman, the Mossad's targeted killing unit also attempted the assassination of various German scientists developing Egypt's missile program during the 1960s.[207] Israel's attack on Iraq's Osirak nuclear facility was apparently preceded, earlier in 1980, by the targeting of several nuclear physicists and engineers involved in the Iraqi program.[208] On March 22, 1990, Gerald Bull, a Canadian rocket scientist producing missiles and cannons for Saddam Hussein, was shot dead outside his Brussels apartment.[209] More recently, since 2007, at least five Iranian nuclear scientists have died under mysterious circumstances, most with motorcycle-borne assailants attaching small magnetic bombs to the exterior of the victims' cars.

Various issues of principle arise in these cases. Some concern the preemptive nature of attacks on citizens of states that are not in an official state of war with each other and the violation of state sovereignty. Recent assassinations in Iran were carried out outside the framework of any internationally recognized official state of hostility. At best, they were preemptive hostile acts perpetrated on foreign soil (though Iran and Israel are continuously engaged in a proxy conflict). There also remain considerable disagreements about the authenticity, gravity, and immediacy of any Iranian threat to which these assassinations are allegedly responding, as well as about the feasible and appropriate means of contending with it. I set aside these surrounding *jus ad bellum* issues of preemptive action, such as whether any military action against Iran (and/or in Syria), can be

207. Bergman, *Rise and Kill First*, at 61–85.
208. Bergman, *Rise and Kill First*, at 350–353.
209. Bergman, *Rise and Kill First*, at 357–358.

justified at the present time.[210] Moreover, as Professor Waldron rightly points out regarding targeted killings carried out by CIA agents, the perpetrators of these covert attacks are at best "unlawful combatants" who lack the war rights of soldiers.[211] The following, however, focuses exclusively on the civilian status of the victim, questioning the legitimacy of selecting scientists as direct targets of attack. Are scientists whose work forms part of their nations' armament program ever liable to attack, even in wartime or in the course of legitimate preemptive self-defense?

The traditional answer given by just war theory, as well as by international law, has always been that they are not. Men and women of science, even nuclear science, are clearly civilians. *Jus in bello* rules—both legal and moral—prohibit the targeting of civilians in wartime, while peacetime rules prohibit murder. Even where combatants are concerned, assassination may fall under the Geneva Conventions' prohibition on killing by perfidious means if it involves "acts inviting the confidence of an adversary to lead him to believe that he is entitled to, or is obliged to accord, protection under the rules of international law applicable in armed conflict, with intent to betray that confidence."[212] Such acts include the assailant's feigning of civilian status, as assassins commonly do.[213]

While there are good moral reasons for upholding all these rules, as I shall in-dicate throughout, an absolute

210. For a discussion of these issues, see Meisels, "Preemptive Strikes—Israel and Iran"; Meisels, *Contemporary Just War—Theory and Practice*, Chap. 6.

211. Waldron, in this volume, at 161–162.

212. Protocol I, Art. 37; Gross, "Assassination," at 100.

213. Protocol I, Art. 37(c).

moral ban on assassination is difficult to justify. For example, few, if any, would argue that the assassination of Nazi leaders, officials or key weapons manufacturers would have been morally undesirable during WWII, or in the years leading up to it. I doubt there is anyone who does not support some (non-hypothetical) instance of assassination or political murder throughout human history. (How many of us oppose the assassination of Heydrich?).

Section 3.2 distinguishes assassination from the cases of targeted killing discussed in the previous sections, as well as from terrorism, and considers the compelling moral arguments against assassination specifically. While these forceful arguments support the legal ban on perfidious killing, I argue that they are ultimately inconclusive in determining the right course of action in every case and cannot prescribe an absolute moral prohibition on assassination.

Sections 3.3 and 3.4 discuss perfidious killing and the violation of civilian immunity involved in targeting scientists, as well as the suggestion that targeted killing involves an unraveling of the norm against homicide.[214] Civilian immunity notwithstanding, the reigning theories of just war suggest that some civilians may lose their natural immunity from attack when they contribute directly to the business of fighting and not only when actively participating in combat. From a consequential perspective, this part of the book points once again to the advantage of pinpointed attacks in attaining military goals with a minimum of casualties.

---

214. Waldron, "Can Targeted Killing Work as a Neutral Principle?";
Waldron, "Justifying Targeted Killing with a Neutral Principle."

Section 3.5 pursues the analogy between weapons scientists and munitions workers. Arms manufacturers, their factories, and employees are accorded less than absolute protection within just war theory, and even by international law. Both the traditional account of just war theory and its contemporary revisionist versions allow for the partial extension of combatant status to civilians who are either threatening or responsible for an unjust threat. Considering these arguments helps to illuminate our thinking on contemporary cases, suggesting that scientists involved in weapons manufacturing may in some cases be morally liable to targeted attack.

Preemptive strikes, nuclear deterrence, weapons manufacturers, and assassinations on foreign soil fall within the remit of just war theory.[215] Recent dramatic events compel us to think through this issue of targeting civilian arms producers in a principled manner, whatever our views on the Iranian case may be. Political judgments concerning the specific targets recently selected for assassination will remain an open question.[216] In the Iranian case, the assassination of scientists may well form part of a combined, and unfolding, strategy. If an Israeli attack on Iran's nuclear facilities is forthcoming, these preceding assassinations will have deprived Iran of some of the individuals who could have contributed to the rehabilitation of its nuclear capacity, rendering a military strike more effective

215. Walzer, *Just and Unjust Wars*, Chap. 5: "Anticipations," at 74–85; Chap. 12: "Terrorism," on assassinations see esp. at 197–204; Chap. 17: "Nuclear Deterrence," at 83.
216. For analysis of concrete cases of assassination—past and present—and of the practical pros and cons of covert assassination policies, see Tobey, "Nuclear Scientists as Assassination Targets."

and its results more durable. All this remains unknown and arguable. Surrounding issues concerning preemption, state sovereignty, the Iran-Israel proxy war, necessity, and the practical utility of particular attacks all exceed the scope of this chapter.

Several further caveats: The succeeding discussion does not take place at any "deep moral level" of the type notably suggested by Jeff McMahan for reflecting on the rules of war.[217] All the following moral arguments are intended to guide action, not merely appraise it, and hence apply at every level of morality, if there is in fact more than one. I will not argue for any incongruence between the laws of war—prohibiting the direct targeting of noncombatants—and a deep morality of war that may recognize civilian liability to attack. Morality rightly prohibits the targeting of civilians, as is well reflected in the Laws of Armed Conflict, and this prohibition ought to be sustained for reasons of deep morality and not merely out of practical considerations. The discussion considers the possibility of rare exceptions to the existing, and morally justified, legal rules. I will not propose a change in the contemporary laws of armed conflict or adjustment of our morality of war in view of modern realities such as the emergence of nuclear power or the prevalence of asymmetric warfare.[218] Instead, I apply existing moral theories and legislation to new cases.

Finally, the discussion does not concern the paradox, suggested by Michael Walzer, whereby a political leader

---

217. E.g. McMahan, "The Ethics of Killing in War"; McMahan, *Killing in War*.

218. Gross, *Moral Dilemmas of Modern War*, considers adjusting our ethics of war to suit the realities of asymmetrical conflict.

may at times be right, even required, to "dirty his hands" in doing what it is morally wrong for him to do.[219] The issue at hand concerns possible moral justifications for particular assassinations rather than excuses. Are there exceptional cases in which we ought to be sympathetic toward assassins—morally justifying them and cheering them on—even as we recognize their breach of morally worthy legal rules?[220]

2. Assassination Revisited

The assassinations of key civilians are not typical cases of what is called "targeted killing," which usually refers to a state targeting members of irregular belligerent organizations, commonly dubbed "unlawful combatants." We saw (in Sec. 2.4) the Israeli Court defined the targets of Israel's assassination policy in the West Bank and Gaza during the Second Intifada as "civilians who are unlawful combatants."[221] This cannot be said of Iranian scientists, who are unquestionably noncombatants. Partly for this reason, no one (not even Israel) takes responsibility for their assassination.[222]

Scientists are civilians, and the assassination of civilians is illegal. As Walzer maintains regarding political

219. Walzer, "Political Action: The Problem of Dirty Hands," at 64–65; Waldron, "Death Squads," at 299: refers this line of argument in connection with target killing.
220. Cf. Walzer, *Just and Unjust Wars*, at 199–200.
221. HCJ 769/02, Para. 28.
222. Tobey, "Nuclear Scientists as Assassination Targets," at 65, lists deniability as an advantage (viewed from the perspective of the attacking nation) of targeting scientists with covert action.

assassination, "Characteristically (and not foolishly) law-yers have frowned on assassination."[223] Not foolishly, once again, because even in war, assassination targets non-military personnel who stand clearly under the protection of the war convention and positive international law.[224] The requirement of distinction between soldiers and civilians is the central principle of *jus in bello*, restricting warfare and preventing it from deteriorating into wholesale slaughter.

Whatever the arguments for war, there is obvious moral merit in narrowing the cycle of violence by limiting the scope of legitimate targets, most notably by upholding the legal protection of civilians.[225] If not always entirely inno-cent or nonthreatening, civilians are almost always entirely defenseless, supplying an additional, non-consequential, moral reason for their comprehensive immunity.[226] Nevertheless, following Walzer, the assignment of particu-lar categories of people to the class of protected noncom-batants may only partially represent our common moral judgments about their assassination.[227]

While assassinations target civilians, they are not, strictly speaking, incidents of terrorism, though they are sometimes described in these terms. As Walzer

223. Walzer, *Just and Unjust Wars*, at 199.

224. Walzer, *Just and Unjust Wars*, at 199–200.

225. This objective is clearly stated in the preamble to The Hague Convention.

226. Lazar, "Necessity, Vulnerability, and Noncombatant Immunity"; Lazar, *Sparing Civilians*, esp. Chap. 1: "Killing Civilians Is Worse than Killing Soldiers," and Chap. 5: "Vulnerability and Defenselessness," at 101–122. Meisels, "In Defense of the Defenseless," and Meisels, *Contemporary Just War*, Chap. 2.

227. Walzer, *Just and Unjust Wars*, at 199.

notes: "Randomness is the crucial feature of terrorist activity" because it is precisely the fear of arbitrary death, by pure chance, that terrorizes civilians at large and is intended to induce political surrender to the terrorists' cause.[228] In the case of enemy scientists, assassination may spread fear within a small subset of the scientific community but it is not random, though it may serve as a terrorizing deterrent to other scientists or the states that employ them. Either way, assassinations aim at particular people whose direct contribution to an aggressive threat is deemed significant, and their removal believed beneficial to impeding it. This, for example, was the case when the United States considered assassinating German physicist, Nobel laureate Werner Heisenberg, believed to be working on an atomic bomb for Adolf Hitler in the early 1940s.[229]

Most civilian targets of assassination are not "Hitler-like" cases, and judgment of the victim and his assassin are likely to be controversial.[230] Terrorists, I argued, should raise no such controversy because irregular combatants are legitimately targeted for their direct participation in armed conflict, rather than for the cause they serve. Moreover, terrorists are particularly liable to attack because their murderous tactics are unquestionably illegal and immoral. The case is not the same with civilians.

Unlike the neutral *in bello* laws of war that apply regardless of just cause on either side, our moral assessment of

228. Walzer, *Just and Unjust Wars*, at 197, and 203. This definition is admittedly controversial, and I defend it elsewhere.
229. On Heisenberg and other cases since, see Tobey, "Nuclear Scientists as Assassination Targets," at 62–64.
230. Cf. Walzer, *Just and Unjust Wars*, at 199.

any particular civilian assassination *does* require taking a substantive stand on the political struggle engaged in by the assassin, as well as of the threat to be averted.[231] Professor Waldron argues persuasively against assassination precisely on these grounds that a norm permitting such killings cannot work as a neutral principle. In the case of terrorists or guerrillas, no new norms are required to permit the killing of irregulars in wartime. There is nothing new about a norm that regards irregulars as legitimate wartime targets and licenses the killing of key combatants; both appear universally applicable. In the case of targeting civilians, however, Professor Waldron's reproach is entirely warranted.

When contemplating the incorporation of a new norm permitting targeted killing within the international laws of armed conflict, Professor Waldron cautions us to consider whether we would be comfortable with such a norm in the hands of our adversaries, as well as the potential abuse such a norm might generate in the hands of our own governments.[232] Understood as a pragmatic warning, this argument certainly has much merit. When instituting a

231. Walzer, *Just and Unjust Wars*, at 200–201: "The threatening character of the soldier's activities is a matter of fact; the unjust or oppressive character of the official's activity is a matter of political judgment. For this reason the political code has never attained the same status as the war convention. . . . In the eyes of those of us whose judgment of oppression and injustice differ from their own, political assassins are simply murderers, exactly like the killers of ordinary citizens."

232. Waldron, "Can Targeted Killing Work as a Neutral Principle?"; "Justifying Targeted Killing with a Neutral Principle," esp. at 112–113, 117–120; Waldron, "Targeted Killing"; and in this volume, Waldron, Part IV: "Getting Out of Hand."

new norm—either by legislation or even by international practice—we have to worry about the ways in which our enemies (perhaps even our own leaders) might act on it, possibly interpreting it in ways anathema to us and to our disadvantage. Several attempts to assassinate Israeli diplomats, probably in retaliation for the killing of Iranian scientists, are cases in point.[233]

This pragmatic consideration, however, cannot in itself yield an absolute prohibition on assassination or offer a decisive consideration regarding the introduction of a new, permissive, norm into the international arena.[234] It is in the nature of practical consequential considerations that they can pull in various directions. It is certainly not inconceivable that the benefits of a particular act or set of assassinations, and the drawbacks of refraining from them, will be so overwhelming to outweigh even the bad consequences of harm to the general rule. Moreover, some adversaries (such as al-Qaeda and Hamas) are unlikely to uphold restrictive norms of war, regardless of the actions of our governments.

Beyond any practical warning, however, there is obviously also the related deontological requirement of universalizability. Taken as a normative warning in this case, testing the universalizability of assassination does not require us to consider practical obstacles such as "the bad guys" taking hold of our permissive rule and abusing its

233. In February 2012 an explosion hit an Israeli diplomatic car near the Israeli embassy in New Delhi, injuring the wife of an Israeli diplomat stationed in India. In Georgia, an explosive device was found in a non-consequential employee's car and was neutralized safely.
234. Waldron, "Can Targeted Killing Work as a Neutral Principle?," at 1; Waldron, "Justifying Targeted Killing with a Neutral Principle," at 112.

license. It is an intellectual exercise, which requires us to consider the application of the norms we select, interpreted accurately and in good faith, by our adversaries. In concrete terms, it might require us to put a different face on the targets we are considering.

Applied to the issue at hand, endorsing a permissive norm allowing the assassination of civilians, such as atomic scientists (or diplomats) would commit us to regard our own scientists, professors of physics and weapons manufacturers, as liable to personal attack by foreign forces in comparable circumstances. Would Israel, for example, be comfortable with the application of such a norm to the 6,000 or so employees of Rafael (Authority for the Development of Armaments) or IAI (Israel's Aerospace Industries)? What if Palestinian militants, unable to attack a munitions facility, were to target one of the buses collecting these employees for work every morning, thus (let us suppose) setting back the latest stage of Israel's drone program that they regard as threatening?

As in the actual cases of atomic scientists, we can assume little if any collateral damage, while key targets are killed by those who regard them as significant threats and their killings as a form of self-defense. The guerrillas may have no other recourse for halting the weapons program. In that sense the hypothetical attack is necessary and proportionate (for attaining the military goal), and it is effective. In both the hypothetical and the actual cases, the targets carry with them significant replicable knowledge that they can recreate if their facility is destroyed.[235] Nevertheless,

235. I am grateful to Michael Gross for this example and the accompanying analogy. See also Bergman, at 608.

we do not usually view our own scientists as threatening and liable to assassination.

3. Perfidy

One powerful utilitarian argument against targeted killing points to post-bellum considerations, questioning the impact of assassination on the prospect of attaining future peace. In the war on terror, I suggested, emotions run high regardless, and prospects of a postwar era (e.g., with ISIS or al-Qaeda) are rather vague. The concern for postwar peace appears more pertinent in traditional conflicts, certainly in cases involving clandestine operations that assassinate civilians working for foreign governments. Here it is quite plausible to worry that the antagonism and mistrust caused by assassination, particularly where perfidy is involved, could ultimately undermine efforts at postwar peace and reconstruction, as well as about the adverse effects of assassinations on our own secret agents.[236] Professor Waldron cites *The Metaphysics of Morals* (1797), where Kant wrote:

> A state against which war is being waged is permitted to use any means of defense except those that would make its subjects unfit to be citizens. . . . Means of defense that are not permitted include using its own subjects as . . . assassins or poisoners (among whom so-called snipers, who lie in wait to ambush individuals, might well be classed).[237]

236. Gross, *Moral Dilemmas of Modern War*, at 111,119. Gross, "Fighting by Other Means," at 352, 356–358; Gross, "Assassination," at 100–103, 113. Cf. Section 2.9 and 2.10 in this volume.

237. Kant, *The Metaphysics of Morals* (6:347), cited in Waldron, "Can Targeted Killing Work as a Neutral Principle?" Sec. 7, at 10. Waldron, "Justifying Targeted Killing with a Neutral Principle," at 124–125.

Professor Waldron goes on to explain that

> [s]ome of the reasons Kant adduced for his position have
> to do with the longer term prospects for peace. In his ear-
> lier essay on "Perpetual Peace" . . . Kant said: "No nation at
> war with another shall permit such acts of war as shall make
> mutual trust impossible during some future time of peace"
> and he cites "the use of Assassins (*percussores*) [and] poison-
> ers (*venefici*)" as examples.[238]

Waldron argues that we should take what Kant says very
seriously because

> [s]uch stratagems make murderers of our citizens,
> and . . . being a murderer in this sense is not just a fact about
> killing someone (like being a soldier on active service). It is
> something vicious one becomes, a dishonorable character one
> takes on, one that cannot then be sloughed off just as soon as
> the circumstances that call for targeted killing have ended.[239]

Kant's primary example for this argument, however,
in both *The Metaphysics of Morals* and "Perpetual Peace,"
is the use of spies.[240] In "Perpetual Peace" Kant cautions
against the perfidious nature of spying (just as he argues in
The Metaphysics of Morals against the use of sharpshooters
lying in wait to ambush individuals), and he takes this to

238. Waldron, "Can Targeted Killing Work as a Neutral Principle?,"
at 10; Waldron, "Justifying Targeted Killing with a Neutral Principle," at
125 with reference to Kant, "Perpetual Peace" (8:346).

239. Waldron, "Can Targeted Killing Work as a Neutral Principle?,"
at 10–11; Waldron, "Justifying Targeted Killing with a Neutral
Principle," at 125.

240. Kant, "Toward Perpetual Peace" (8:346); Kant, *The Metaphysics
of Morals* (6:347), in *Toward Perpetual Peace and Other Writings*, at 143.

be a prime example of dishonor. Moreover, Kant cautions that, once used, any of "these malicious practices would be carried over into peacetime and thus destroy its purpose altogether."[241] Spying is also Kant's first example in the relevant section of *The Metaphysics of Morals* of methods to be wholly excluded: "using one's own subjects as spies . . ."[242]

Perhaps Kant was right, as he certainly was in "Perpetual Peace," about espionage spilling over into peacetime. Nevertheless, the international community has not suspended its use of spies on the basis of this argument, and it remains unclear how conclusive it is, in and of itself, with regard to any of the other dishonorable measures to which Kant refers. In spite of Kant's compelling argument, few nations refrain from spying, either in war or in peacetime, and there is no crime of spying under international law.[243] It is not clear that we should treat assassination any differently, at least on the basis of this argument alone.

Admittedly, spying contributes less directly to killing than assassination does, but this was not Kant's objection to assassination. In the case of both espionage and assassination alike, Kant's concern was for maintaining mutual trust with a view to future peace, as well as the honor of

241. Kant, "Toward Perpetual Peace" (8:346), at 71.
242. Kant, *The Metaphysics of Morals*, at 144.
243. Dinstein, *The Conduct of Hostilities*, at 208–211: International law and practice effectively regard spies as irregular combatants, leaving them virtually unprotected, though they are guaranteed a trial prior to punishment. Their "unlawful" identity, however, is not in itself an offense under international law. Like assassins, spies lack any war rights of soldiers and are rightly subject to prosecution and punishment, imprisonment, or execution "but only on the basis of the national criminal legislation of the belligerent state against whose interests he acted" (at 211). See also Fletcher, *Romantics at War*, at 106, 110.

combatants. These are weighty, but not exclusive, considerations, and have not tipped the balance in the case of espionage, though Kant was concerned primarily with this practice. In some cases, attaining mutual trust, reducing hostilities, and negotiating peaceful solutions may not even be feasible, regardless of any assassination or spying.[244] It remains indeterminate how conclusive we should regard this specific Kantian argument about maintaining trust and attaining peace in any particular case, attractive as it may be at some deep moral level.[245]

That said, Additional Protocol 1 does prohibit some of the wartime measures Kant considered particularly diabolical and malicious. Article 37 of Additional Protocol I (and its precursor, Article 23(b) of the Hague Regulations) prohibits perfidy that results in killing, injuring, or capturing an enemy.[246] This is the source of the specific prohibition on assassination (as opposed to the more general prohibition on murder and the *jus in bello* prohibition on targeting civilians), and it applies to the perfidious killing of soldiers

244. Tobey, "Nuclear Scientists as Assassination Targets," at 66–7, discusses the negative effects of assassination on mutual trust and the prospect of negotiating peaceful solutions in the Iranian case, while at the same time recognizing the inconclusive nature of this consideration. Killing Iranian scientists raises levels of hostility and mistrust and hardens Teheran's position. Nevertheless, "it is not clear that a negotiated solution to the nuclear crisis is or ever was possible" (p. 67).
245. Cf. Waldron, "Can Targeted Killing Work as a Neutral Principle?," at 11; Waldron, "Justifying Targeted Killing with a Neutral Principle," at 125.
246. Protocol I, Art. 37. The Hague Regulations (IV) Sec. II Chap. I, Art. 23(b). Article 23(a) prohibits the use of poison. See also Dinstein, *The Conduct of Hostilities*, at 201; and Gross, "Assassination," at 100.

as well as civilians, most notably by means of feigning non-combatant status.

Even with the crime of perfidious killing, however—in which case we may accept Kant's logic as the rule—it is difficult to view the resulting norm as an absolute moral prohibition. An example of what many might consider a moral exception to the rule against perfidious killing, albeit of combatants, can be found in Walzer's retelling of an account provided by a German officer in World War II, Captain Helmut Tausend, of an ambush on German soldiers as they marched through the French countryside in the years of the German occupation. His story is recorded in a scene from the documentary film *The Sorrow and the Pity*:

> They passed a group of young men, French peasants, or so it seemed, digging potatoes. But these were not in fact peasants; they were members of the Resistance. As the Germans marched by, the "peasants" dropped their shovels, picked up guns hidden in the field, and opened fire. Fourteen of the soldiers were hit. Years later, their Captain was still indignant. "You call that 'partisan' resistance? I don't. Partisans for me are men who can be identified, men who wear a special armband or cap, something with which to recognize them. What happened in that potato field was murder."[247]

---

247. Walzer, *Just and Unjust Wars*, at 176. Walzer recognizes the partisans' act of perfidy as clearly illegal, regarding their execution by Germans as legitimate. Nonetheless, he refrains from morally condemning the partisans' perfidious killing. He sums up his view of the situation at 178: "resistance is legitimate and the punishment of resistance is legitimate as well."

4. Murder

Kant's argument is inconclusive in determining international law and not comprehensive in determining our moral judgment in all cases of treacherous killing. Despite Kant's powerful arguments about trust and honor along with its post-bellum rationale, the Law of Armed Conflict does not prohibit spying. While perfidious killing is legally prohibited, few would argue for an absolute moral prohibition applicable in every instance.

Professor Waldron supplies a final argument against assassination, in keeping with his more general defense of civilian immunity.[248] Professor Waldron worries rightly about the unraveling of the norm against homicide, particularly when politicians face challenges, such as insurgencies, to which assassination presents a tempting response.[249] He reminds us that the point of orientation in the area of deliberate killing is the prohibition on murder—absent the Law of Armed Conflict we are prohibited from killing anyone at all—and so any argument favoring the killing of anyone, even in wartime, carries a heavy burden of proof to justify moving us away from this default position.[250] According to Professor Waldron, we accept the traditional

248. Waldron, "Can Targeted Killing Work as a Neutral Principle?," at 13. On civilian immunity, see Waldron, *Torture, Terror and Tradeoffs*, Chap. 4.

249. Waldron, "Can Targeted Killing Work as a Neutral Principle?," at 13.

250. Waldron, "Can Targeted Killing Work as a Neutral Principle?," at 11–14; Waldron, *Torture, Terror and Tradeoffs*, at 109. Walzer, *Just and Unjust Wars*, at 144–145: "the theoretical problem is not to explain how immunity is gained, but how it is lost."

principle of discrimination that permits the killing of soldiers "not because good reasons can be identified for allowing combatants to be killed, but largely because it looks as
though this offers one line of constraint that can be held in
the midst of an activity that is otherwise comprehensively
murderous."[251] Lacking any realistic prospect of prohibiting
war altogether, he argues, we adopt the principle of discrimination largely because it has "proved roughly sustain-
able and administrable. . . . We cling to it not because we
think the killing of combatants is OK but because we are
doubtful of our ability to hold any other line."[252]

But now, Professor Waldron worries, the arguments
supporting targeted killing seem to be moving in the oppo-
site direction, assuming as their point of departure the
proposition that we are entirely justified in killing certain
people in wartime (i.e., soldiers) and working their way per-
missively outward from that assumption:

> [I]t seems that the first instinct is to search for areas where
> killing is already "alright"—killing in self-defense . . . or kill-
> ing combatants in wartime . . . —and then to see if we can
> concoct analogies between whatever reasons we can associ-
> ate with such licenses and the new area of homicide we want
> to explore. In my view, *that is how a norm against murder
> unravels.*[253]

251. Waldron, "Can Targeted Killing Work as a Neutral
Principle?," at 11.
252. Waldron, "Can Targeted Killing Work as a Neutral Principle?,"
at 12. See also at 14.
253. Waldron, "Can Targeted Killing Work as a Neutral Principle?,"
at 14, emphasis is in the original.

Understanding the moral background as the prohibition on murder along with the precariousness of sustaining limitations on killing in war should make us extremely cautious, Professor Waldron argues, about attempts to introduce permissive changes into the Law of Armed Conflict.[254] Killing is never "alright," only unavoidably tolerated in wartime, and it is therefore morally erroneous, and often opportunistic and inherently abusive, to proceed to unravel the taboo against killing by reasoning that "[w]e are allowed to kill some people by principles we already have; surely, by the same reasoning, there must be other people we are also allowed to kill."[255]

Professor Waldron's argument admittedly poses a significant challenge to any defense of assassination policies, most certainly including the targeting of scientists, because any plausible argument for expanding liability beyond the category of combatants has to proceed precisely in this way. This is not to say that this challenge cannot be met or that the justification of *in bello* discrimination is primarily its usefulness in narrowing the cycle of violence and its relative enforceability in the heat of conflict. Granted that the point of orientation is the general prohibition on murder, most non-pacifists nonetheless assert that some wartime killings are justified, and not merely inevitably tolerated. Recall Walzer's explanation of how soldiers lose their natural immunity in wartime: "That right is lost by those who bear arms 'effectively' because

254. Waldron, "Can Targeted Killing Work as a Neutral Principle?," at 12.
255. Waldron, "Can Targeted Killing Work as a Neutral Principle?," at 14.

they pose a danger to other people. It is retained by those who don't bear arms at all."[256]

Though this traditional criterion of liability to attack is not unanimously accepted, most just war theorists believe there are good identifiable reasons for permitting the killings of at least some combatants in wartime.[257] Figuring out these reasons is the first step toward the type of argument that Professor Waldron cautions against because he believes it leads irresponsibly to an unraveling of our existing restrictions on killing in war, though he admits that philosophers who make these arguments do so mostly in good faith.[258]

Walzer's further comments on the principle of distinction supply the most prominent illustration of the unraveling that Professor Waldron envisions. After explaining how posing a threat can deprive a person of his or her natural immunity from attack, Walzer writes:

> We begin with the distinction between soldiers engaged in combat and soldiers at rest; then we shift to the distinction between soldiers as a class and civilians; and then we concede this or that group of civilians as the processes of economic mobilization establish its direct contribution to the business of fighting.[259]

In the case of targeted killing specifically, however, it is crucial to stress again that it is usually adopted as a means

---

256. Walzer, *Just and Unjust Wars*, at 144–145.
257. Most notably Jeff McMahan, whose work is discussed in the following section, rejects Walzer's traditional criterion of liability.
258. Waldron, "Can Targeted Killing Work as a Neutral Principle?," at 12–14.
259. Walzer, *Just and Unjust Wars*, at 146.

of narrowing the cycle of violence rather than extending it. Targeted killing kills fewer people, whether directly or collaterally, than conventional warfare does. Philosophical arguments for targeted killing admittedly expand the class of individuals who are liable to attack beyond the category of uniformed combatants, but the actual number of people killed in targeting operations is deliberately limited. Assassination is often a substitute for large-scale military operations, or an alternative to pursuing a more costly tactic, in terms of human life, in the course of an ongoing conflict. The very essence of pinpointed attacks is the achievement of necessary military goals with a minimum of casualties, both directly and collaterally. Any argument that regards all wartime killing—of combatants as well as civilians—as an encroachment on the taboo against homicide ought to accord considerable merit to a tactic that drastically reduces the number of fatalities amidst both classes of individuals.

It remains questionable whether civilians, particularly scientists, can ever be legitimate targets of attack, even if their targeting is the most economical means toward achieving military advantage. One final task in advancing our moral reasoning in contemporary cases of targeted killing is to consider the class of civilians who manufacture arms in light of the liabilities and protections accorded them in international law as well as by various theories of just war.

5. Munitions Workers

An atomic scientist is legally a civilian who, at worst, can be described as taking an indirect part in hostilities. Like any munitions worker, his facility is vulnerable to harm during wartime and may be destroyed if it is providing military capability: "[C]ivilians cannot enjoy protection from attack when they enter military objectives (e.g., by working in a military base or in a munitions factory)."[260] But the off-duty munitions worker is protected from harm.[261]

Thomas Nagel and Michael Walzer have argued that combatant status may be partially extended to munitions workers. According to their traditional account of just war theory, combatants lose their immunity from attack because they pose a danger to their adversaries.[262] Both Walzer and Nagel suggest that this threatening nature extends to on-duty munitions workers as well, rendering them liable to attack. Nagel writes that

> the threat presented by an army and its members does not consist merely in the fact that they are men, but in the fact that they are armed and are using their arms in the pursuit of certain objectives. Contributions to their arms and logistics are contributions to this threat; contributions to their mere existence as men are not.[263]

---

260. Dinstein, *The Conduct of Hostilities*, at 129.
261. In principle, even the on-duty munitions worker is protected from disproportionate harm, although, if we assume his facility is a significant military target, his death will usually count as legitimate and proportional collateral harm.
262. Walzer, *Just and Unjust Wars*, at 144–145. Nagel, "War and Massacre," at 140.
263. Nagel, "War and Massacre," at 140.

Similarly, Walzer explains the vulnerability of munitions workers as a partial extension of combatant status to some who are "at least nominally civilians" but who produce the equipment that soldiers specifically require in order to fight.[264] On this understanding, munitions workers are partially assimilated to the class of combatants due to the threat they pose to their enemy, while other civilians, including those who contribute less directly to the war effort, remain immune from attack.[265]

From the perspective of the Law of International Armed Conflict, on the other hand, munitions workers are not assimilated to the class of combatants at all, not even part time. Their civilian contribution does not constitute "direct participation" in hostilities; hence they are not legitimate wartime targets. Causing the deaths of munitions workers is permissible only as foreseeable collateral harm to civilians, assumed to be proportionate in relation to the targeting of their facility as a legitimate military objective.[266]

264. Walzer, *Just and Unjust Wars*, at 145–146.

265. This distinction is widely, but not unanimously, accepted within just war theory. For a prominent critique, see Fabre, "Guns, Food, and Liability to Attack in War."

266. ICRC, "Interpretive Guidance on the Notion of Direct Participation in Hostilities under International Humanitarian Law," at 995, 1009–1010. According to this series of reports on direct participation commissioned by the ICRC, civilian employees are protected from direct attack, though their presence in a military facility exposes them to a greater risk of incidental death, even if they do not take a direct part in hostilities. The guidelines concerning criteria that constitute direct participation remain somewhat vague and controversial (at 995–996, 1012–1019). Nevertheless, the document clearly states that general contributions to the war effort "e.g. design, production and shipment of weapons and military equipment" do not constitute acts of "direct participation" (at 1020–1022).

Yoram Dinstein explains: "A civilian working in a munitions factory does not cease to be a civilian—and does not lose his general mantle of protection—although he is patently running a risk while he is present on the premises of what constitutes a military objective."[267] "'That presence does not permanently contaminate the laborers, turning them *ipso facto* into 'quasi-combatants.'"[268]

Either way, however, both the law and the traditional account of just war theory agree that while at work munitions workers are partly vulnerable, either directly or collaterally, but "[u]pon leaving the factories, civilian laborers shed the risk of being subject to attack. The attacker is forbidden to follow the workforce home and hit civilians there."[269]

In what is by now a well-known critique of mainstream just war theory and international law, Jeff McMahan questions the traditional *in bello* distinction between soldiers and civilians that permits the killing of all combatants during wartime, while leaving all civilians immune from direct attack. McMahan rejects the moralized explanation of this legal requirement according to which the principle of discrimination serves to separate threatening personnel from those who pose no direct threat of harm and who ought therefore to remain protected civilians. Apart from anything else, McMahan argues, "It is, however, a notorious problem in just war theory that there are many people who pose a threat in war who would not be considered combatants by anyone."[270] The orthodox explanation of the legal

---

267. Dinstein, *The Conduct of Hostilities*, at 152. See also 124.
268. Dinstein, *The Conduct of Hostilities*, at 124.
269. Dinstein, *The Conduct of Hostilities*, at 124.
270. McMahan, *Killing in War*, at 12.

requirement of distinction is problematic because not all combatants pose a threat, while some civilians pose grave threats.

More specifically, McMahan supplies an extremely pertinent and timely example of the issue at hand:

> Elderly professors of physics working for the Manhattan project in laboratories at Los Alamos and the University of Chicago posed a far greater threat to the Japanese than any ordinary American soldier, but no one would say that they were combatants. Nor would any defendant of the moralized notion of a combatant be willing to extend combatant status to a computer science professor whose research during a time of war will soon have many applications including improvements in weapons technologies that will be used against her country's enemies.[271]

By contributing to munitions production, one does not forfeit civilian status, even though such contributions may be considerably more threatening to the enemy than serving as a plain soldier at the front. For McMahan, this, among other examples, points to the deficiency in the traditional just war theory notion that posing a threat to others is the correct criterion of liability to attack in war.

Citing Walzer and Nagel as the prominent proponents of the idea that posing a threat establishes combatant status, McMahan continues:

> Various writers in the just war tradition have sought to narrow the gap between the moralized notion of combatant status and the ordinary concept of a combatant by conceding

271. McMahan, *Killing in War*, at 12.

that a limited class of people outside the military count as combatants, while denying that combatant status extends any further among civilians.[272]

But, McMahan argues, they have not gone far enough:

> [E]ven this gloss on the moralized notion of combatant status does not solve the problem. For the work that a computer scientist is doing quietly in her campus office may well produce some medical technology that a wounded soldier needs to live, but it will also provide military hardware that other soldiers will find enormously useful in fighting. Although she is not legally a combatant, it seems that she must be a combatant in the moralized sense and thus must be a legitimate target of attack according to the reigning theory of the just war—despite the fact that few if any of that theory's proponents would accept that this is really an implication of their view.[273]

Scientists are legally civilians.[274] According to McMahan, neither Walzer nor Nagel would be willing to extend his moralized notion of "combatants" far enough

---

272. McMahan, *Killing in War*, at 13.
273. McMahan, *Killing in War*, at 13; see also at 205.
274. Moreover, their civilian contribution is not usually understood by legal experts to qualify as "direct participation." The ICRC report lists scientific research and design, as well as production and transport of weapons, as examples of merely indirect participation "unless carried out as an integral part of a specific military operation designed to directly cause the required threshold of harm" (at 1022). Furthermore, when discussing preparatory measures, the report states that "preparatory measures aiming to establish the general capacity to carry out unspecified hostile acts do not" qualify as direct participation (at 1032). The document's examples of preparations that would *not* entail loss of protection include weapons productions (at 1032).

away from the law in order to include "off-duty" scientists, such as professors on campus, thus essentially leaving the gravest military threats immune from attack. At the same time, they sanction the wholesale killing of all combatants in wartime, however minor the degree of their contribution to the war effort and regardless of the justice of their cause. This, according to McMahan, cannot be morally right, though he concedes that maintaining the traditional distinction between combatants and civilians offers considerable pragmatic-consequential advantages in terms of limiting wartime violence and ought to be legally preserved for that reason.[275]

On deep moral reflection, however, McMahan questions the traditional assertion that posing a threat is the correct criterion for acquiring combatant status. If this were the case, McMahan argues, a computer science professor working to produce new military hardware at her university office would qualify for combatant status by virtue of the threat she poses, and consequently constitute a legitimate target of attack.[276] Walzer and Nagel, he suggests, are involved in an inconsistency when they deny this. Overall, McMahan argues for an alternative criterion for liability to attack in wartime: Moral responsibility for an objectively unjustified or wrongful threat, rather than merely posing a threat.[277] This is the core of McMahan's individualist account of the morality of war, and would presumably

---

275. McMahan, "The Morality of War and the Law of War," at 27–30. McMahan, *Killing in War*, at 234–235.

276. McMahan, *Killing in War*, at 13, 205.

277. McMahan, "The Morality of War and the Law of War," at 21–22. McMahan, *Killing in War*, at 38.

include some scientists developing prohibited weapons as legitimate targets.

In principle (morally speaking), McMahan argues that specific civilians may be liable to attack, even if rarely, in an attempt to avert an unjust threat.[278] Certain civilians may be morally responsible for creating an unjust war or for constituting an unjust threat in the course of war, even if they pose no active immediate threat in battle. According to McMahan's morality of war, removing this unjust threat, subject to requirements of necessity and proportionality, may justify causing harm to specific civilians responsible for instigating this unjust threat.[279] This might license the killing of various physicists and computer scientists if it proves necessary and proportionate in order to avert an unjust threat.

McMahan generally aspires to place greater responsibility on the individual, even young conscripted soldiers, for participating in unjust aggression.[280] He suggests that it is the responsibility of any individual, certainly a well-educated mature adult, to establish the moral nature of the projects in which he engages and to refuse to participate in those that prove to be unjust. When people ignore this responsibility to inquire into the justice of their nation's conflicts and subsequently to refuse to participate in

278. McMahan, *Killing in War*, at 108, 221–235.
279. McMahan, *Killing in War*, Chap. 5. On McMahan's view, cases of morally justified attacks on civilians will be rare, and the laws of war ought not to reflect this possibility. However, in principle, and under certain conditions, some civilians may be morally liable to attack.
280. McMahan, "The Ethics of Killing in War," at 702–708, 722–725; McMahan, "Just Cause for War"; McMahan, *Killing in War*, at 182–188.

injustice, they are thereby, in McMahan's terms, morally liable to be harmed.

McMahan's morality of war paves the way toward legitimizing the assassination of specific civilians, including some professors of physics and computer scientists.[281] On this account, scientists who contribute to an unjust threat render themselves liable to attack; killing them in order to avert the threat is therefore permissible, subject to necessity and proportionality. While the just war tradition regards liability as a function of the de facto threat posed by potential targets, McMahan insists: "The correct criterion of liability to attack . . . is not posing a threat, but moral responsibility for an unjust threat."[282] McMahan's examples are intended to suggest that his revisionist just war theory does better than the orthodox approach in explaining our moral intuitions in the case of scientists and other potentially liable civilians. The revisionist approach is, however, not without its critics, and some general problems with this theory may carry over into the specific case.

McMahan assumes that establishing whether a threat is just or unjust is a matter of discernable fact, accessible to the scientists in his examples as well as to us. Beyond the obvious difficulty in establishing objective justice (did the physics professors at Los Alamos pose an unjust threat to the Japanese?), the degree of moral responsibility attributable to civilians is also problematic, most

---

281. McMahan, *Killing in War*, Chap. 5, esp. at 205.
282. McMahan, "The Ethics of Killing in War," at 722–723; McMahan, "The Morality of War and the Law of War," at 21–22; McMahan, *Killing in War*, at 35, 38.

notably for present purposes in the case of professors. Professors do not instigate hostilities, command them, or carry them out. When professors contribute to a weapons program, they may form part of a threat that could, arguably, render them liable to attack under a traditional criterion of liability. Establishing their moral responsibility for an unjust threat, however, is a more complicated and controversial task. A scientist may intend, for instance, to contribute only to her nation's nuclear energy program rather than to the creation of nuclear weapons. Within a totalitarian regime, she may have little say about what she is required to do. Even in a democracy, there is usually little opportunity of employment for nuclear scientists, arms researchers, or rocket scientists outside government projects.

McMahan concedes that individuals (such as conscripts or coerced scientists) who succumb to overwhelming pressure from a totalitarian regime often possess a full moral and legal excuse for participating in injustice. He maintains, nonetheless, that individuals who contribute to an unjust threat, even under duress, such as scientists who build genocidal weapons for totalitarian regimes, lack justification (as opposed to possible excuses) for their wrongful action and are therefore liable to attack.[283] A scientist in a totalitarian regime might have refused to study nuclear physics to begin with. If compelled to do so or was misled to believe she would work only on civilian nuclear power, the

---

283. For duress and ignorance as an excuse, rather than justification, for participating in injustice, see McMahan, *Killing in War*, at 110–121.

scientist could accept martyrdom instead of building weapons of mass destruction.

Reservations notwithstanding, McMahan's alternative morality of war has gained prominence within contemporary just war theory and offers an important perspective on the issue in hand. By continuing to participate in injustice, whatever the excuse, the scientist renders himself liable to defensive attack by those defending themselves against the threat he has contributed to creating. In cases in which a state openly threatens its adversaries with nuclear aggression, McMahan would insist on its scientists' responsibility to be knowledgeable about, or at least suspicious of, their country's intentions. If they continue to contribute directly to the production of nuclear arms for an aggressive regime they would, on McMahan's revisionist account of just war theory, certainly be liable to attack regardless of their whereabouts if their removal is both necessary and proportionate in countering the threat.

As McMahan himself recognizes, however, there is no principled barrier to reaching this conclusion regarding the liability of weapons scientists from a traditional perspective as well. Walzer comments on the nature of necessity, regarding civilians who directly contribute to the business of fighting (such as seamen on merchant ships or ships carrying military supplies):

> Once direct contribution has been established, only "military necessity" can determine whether the civilians involved are attacked or not. They ought not to be attacked if their activities can be stopped, or their products seized or destroyed, in some other way without significant risk. . . But whenever

seizure without shooting ceases to be possible, the obligation ceases also and the right lapses.[284]

On this traditional account, scientists developing or producing weapons may be construed as direct contributors to the business of war. As Nagel points out, contributions to arms and logistics are contributions to the threat.[285] In Walzer's terms, they produce the equipment that soldiers specifically require in order to fight. Once this direct contribution is established, military necessity may dictate that they be attacked if there is no other way of seizing or destroying their products.[286] If Walzer is correct that wartime necessity may authorize the seizure or destruction of military products by attacking the civilians who produce or transport them, then the targeting of scientists might be similarly necessary for destroying their military knowhow or expertise.

There remains an important legal difference between Walzer's example and the assassination of scientists. The crew on ships carrying military supplies is subject to collateral harm when this is incidentally necessary for seizing their goods. There is no way to sink a merchant ship without endangering the crew, but the members of the crew are themselves collateral to the military value of the target. By contrast, the direct targeting of scientists, even in order to destroy their expertise, cannot conceivably be construed as collateral. Killing the scientist may be a secondary intention in relation to destroying his professional skills or rendering

284. Walzer, *Just and Unjust Wars*, at 146.
285. Nagel, "War and Massacre," at 140.
286. Walzer, *Just and Unjust Wars*, at 145–146.

them unusable, but this killing is nonetheless an intended effect.

As opposed to the Law of Armed Conflict, however, Walzer's and Nagel's respective discussions of direct contribution do not regard the killing of arms transporters or munitions workers as civilian collateral damage. Instead, both partially extend combatant status to direct contributors, rendering them liable to intentional attack.[287] As McMahan points out, they concede that a limited class of people outside the military count as combatants.[288] In fact, Walzer's and Nagel's accounts of munitions workers as partial combatants—taken to its natural conclusion—could license even the killing of off-duty munitions workers, as McMahan rightly observes.[289]

Arguing against the view that "civilians working in munitions factories assume the status of so-called 'quasi-combatants,'" Dinstein points out that if they did, it would be difficult to understand why they may not be attacked before having reached the factory or after leaving it.[290] While combatants are not liable to attack when they are on vacation—when out of uniform and in their homes—they may be targeted on their way to the base or while off-duty and at rest within it. If munitions workers were partly assimilated into the class of combatants, as Walzer and Nagel assert, then it is indeed unclear that this would not license their targeting in their cars to and from work or wherever they are engaged in the business of war, at least in

---

287. Walzer, *Just and Unjust Wars*, at 145.
288. McMahan, *Killing in War*, at 13.
289. McMahan, *Killing in War*, at 13.
290. Dinstein, *The Conduct of Hostilities*, at 124.

exceptional circumstances of necessity. McMahan correctly observes that traditional just war theory, which applies distinction on the basis of threat and partly extends combatant status to munitions workers, ought logically also to extend to nuclear scientists.[291]

Furthermore, the threat posed by a weapons scientist—developing and/or producing long-range missiles, chemical, biological or nuclear weapons—is far greater than that of civilian workers in a bullet factory, both in terms of magnitude of the created threat and in terms of the extent of the workers' contribution to it. Moreover, while munitions workers cease to be threatening when they leave the factory, and soldiers on leave pose no threat to the enemy, this is far from the case with key scientists and top weapon engineers. Scientists carry their knowledge with them in their minds, and their products may be reproduced wherever they go. In the age of personal computers, it is sometimes difficult to distinguish the on-duty from the off-duty munitions worker (when is the scientist at her computer working on the A-bomb as opposed to playing Tetris?). It has become virtually impossible to separate the workplace from the worker or the product from its producer. If even the simplest of munitions workers were partially assimilated to the class of combatants, as Walzer and Nagel suggest, there is then no barrier to targeting enemy scientists directly if and when this is commanded by military necessity.

Partly extending combatant status to the class of munitions workers would generate a morally neutral permission to kill scientists contributing to a credible

291. McMahan, *Killing in War*, at 13; Nagel, "War and Massacre," at 140; Walzer, *Just and Unjust Wars*, at 145–146.

threat, regardless of the justness or injustice of their nation's cause for war. McMahan's account, by contrast, supports only a non-neutral principle that might permit the assassination of a scientist working for an unscrupulous regime but not the assassination of scientists working for a just regime. Walzer's and Nagel's logic would extend symmetrically to the killing of all scientists who produce weapons for their governments, including our own, provided they pose a threat to their adversaries and that there is no reasonable alternative for hampering that threat.

Traditional neutrality with regard to *jus ad bellum* does not, however, entail moral symmetry between individuals who pose a threat and those who do not. Following Walzer's example of civilian ships carrying military supplies, the license to kill arms transporters or manufacturers applies only to those who contribute directly to a threat (whether just or unjust) and whose removal is dictated by military necessity as a last resort. With regard to the production of nuclear weapons specifically, such a rule would not apply equally to atomic scientists working for benign democracies and those manufacturing nuclear weapons for threatening regimes. In keeping with the reigning theory of the just war, nations who threaten their adversaries with weapons of mass destruction may render their scientists vulnerable to attack by virtue of their contribution to that threat if removing them is necessary to countering it. This would not permit the killing of atomic scientists working on behalf of a stable democracy with a provable no-first-use policy for their nuclear arsenal or those working for a regime that would be very unlikely ever to use a nuclear weapon.

It might well apply to scientists working for regimes that threaten to carry out genocidal attacks.

To summarize, both contemporary, leading accounts of just war theory offer interesting insights into recent assassinations of scientists, insights that serve to explain any mixed intuitions in contemporary cases. Civilian immunity notwithstanding, orthodox just war theory, as well as McMahan's individualist morality of war, suggests that scientists who directly participate in the business of war may be liable to attack in exceptional circumstances in which their removal is dictated by military necessity. In an age in which high-ranking munitions workers, weapons developers and manufacturers may be inseparable from their military knowledge or its products, it is arguable that killing them can, in rare cases, be dictated by the urgent military necessity of destroying their intellectual property or expertise. Though admittedly controversial, this suggestion places the killing of scientists on a par with Walzer's more traditional examples of civilians who directly contribute to the business of fighting, such as munitions workers or the crew of merchant ships carrying military supplies.

6. Targeting Scientists—An Exception That Proves the Rule?

The direct targeting of civilians is illegal, and for good reason. Whatever the degree of threat they pose, civilians are defenseless persons rightly protected by the laws of war. Killing defenseless individuals is morally repugnant and reminiscent of terrorism, though it is not always tantamount to it. Assassins, Walzer tells us, ought to be marked off for the better from those who terrorize by killing at random whether or not we support their cause.[292] Gaining moral superiority over terrorists is, however, a small victory for assassins and the nations that dispatch them. Most assassins remain despicable murderers. Any exceptions require overwhelming justification in terms of the liability of the victim and the urgent necessity of their removal in order to outweigh the breach of the relevant moral and legal taboos. That said, however, producing weapons of mass destruction for a threatening regime—or otherwise directly contributing to a potentially genocidal project—would probably serve to overcome these restraints, on any account of the morality of war.

From a purely consequential perspective, assassination is the lesser of two evils when a few acts of killing can substitute for large-scale war. In the Iranian case, whether assassinations aim to prevent future war, or to complement preemptive war by removing the agents who could subsequently rebuild Iran's nuclear program in its aftermath, remains to be seen. The potential success of either of these projects—retarding Iran's nuclear project without resorting to war or enhancing our future military achievements by removing Iran's scientists in advance—also remains an open question that cannot be settled in the realms of philosophy or law.

Assassination is more easily justified in terms of human rights when the status of the victim is assimilated, at least in part, to the class of combatants. This move is admittedly

292. Walzer, *Just and Unjust Wars*, at 199–200.

problematic, as Professor Waldron points out, in terms of loosening the taboo against homicide.[293] Nevertheless, just assassinations are at least possible. No one, I think, would deny that there have been some just assassins in the course of recorded history. Justifying recent assassinations of Iranian scientists specifically would require settling a wide range of surrounding practical issues that remain largely unknown and controversial, such as the identity and precise motive of the perpetrators, the gravity of any Iranian threat, and the projected expediency of assassination in removing or retarding such a threat. In principle, however, these recent cases are potentially justifiable on either account of the just war tradition.

In spite of the rule against targeting civilians, both of the central theories of the morality of war might permit attacks on key scientists in highly constrained circumstances of necessity, such as contending with a genocidal threat. On either account, establishing liability to attack would constitute a justification for killing rather than an excuse. No residual guilt remains to tarnish the hands of those who order and carry out these killings. Specific categories of people (on the Walzer–Nagel account), or particularly blameworthy individuals (on McMahan's account), who are "at least nominally civilians,"[294] may lose their immunity from military attack so that we commit no moral wrong by harming them. Killing them would not be murder.

While these deaths are clearly intentional rather than incidental, they are secondary to the military necessity of

293. Waldron, "Can Targeted Killing Work as a Neutral Principle?";
Waldron, "Justifying Targeted Killing with a Neutral Principle."
294. Walzer, *Just and Unjust Wars*, at 145–146.

destroying their victims' military expertise or know-how; as such they may be morally justified, particularly when deemed essential to averting or retarding a military threat of momentous proportions.

Such justifications, however, if and when possible, constitute exceptions that prove the rule rather than supplanting it. In order to overcome both the legal and moral rule against targeting civilians and the consequential drawbacks of relaxing it, the threat must be grave and credible, and the prospect of impeding it by assassination must be realistic. The scientist's contribution to the materialization of the threat must be crucial, and there must be no realistic possibility of a diplomatic solution.[295] Nuclear projects developed by scientists who are indispensable to them and that place catastrophic threats in the hands of regimes impervious to diplomatic pressure are not hypothetical scenarios, but they are not very common either. Pointing to rare exceptions of urgent necessity, in which targeting key civilians might be morally justifiable, establishes no incongruity between morality and the law. As with political assassination more generally, all the good moral arguments for the rule prohibiting it apply. The laws prohibiting murder, the wartime targeting of civilians, and perfidious killing remain the best legal norms from any moral perspective.

---

295. I draw here on William Tobey's description of the conditions under which nations consider resorting to assassination of nuclear scientists. Tobey, "Nuclear Scientists as Assassination Targets," at 67–68.

CONCLUDING REMARKS

The September 11 attacks led many Americans to believe that al-Qaeda had plunged the United States into a new type of war, already familiar to some of the country's closest allies, most notably Israel. Subsequent debates over terrorism and counter-terrorism often involve a sort of lamentation for the passing of old-fashioned wars.[296] Paul Gilbert's *New Terror, New Wars* suggests that at least when it came to old wars, we knew when they were taking place, who was fighting them, and what they were fighting about. Perhaps most significantly, and the greatest source of nostalgia, is that in the past, a state of war existed between sovereign states, whereas "new wars" exist "between a state, or a combination of states, on one side, and non-state actors on the other."[297] As George Fletcher puts this, we are in "a world beset with nontraditional threats from agents we call 'terrorists.' "[298]

The legal and moral status of these agents is neither on a par with the status of soldiers nor comparable to that of civilian criminals. While it is difficult to specify precise limits for distinguishing irregular combat from some forms of organized crime, it seems clear that organizations dedicated to an ongoing violent struggle against Israel or the United States are not civilian criminal organizations.

296. Fletcher, *Romantics at War*, at 3. Gilbert, *New Terror, New Wars*, at 3, 7–8.
297. Gilbert, *New Terror, New Wars*, at 3. See also Statman, "Can Just War Theory Justify Targeted Killing," at 110; Fletcher, *Romantics at War*, at 3, 46–47.
298. Fletcher, *Romantics at War*, at 6.

Whether we call them "irregulars" or "unlawful combatants" or describe them as "civilians performing the function of a combatant," terrorists are active agents of an armed struggle.[299]

As direct participants in hostilities, terrorists are not entitled to the due process protections of the criminal justice system and are subject instead to the liabilities and vagaries of the wars in which they willingly partake. Trying and sentencing offenders is a job for law courts rather than the army. Targeted killing in the course of an ongoing low-intensity conflict is, by contrast, a form of combat rather than punishment or revenge; as such, it need not comply with any procedural requirements for trying those accused of crimes committed in the past.

At the same time, irregulars who do not abide by the laws of war are not entitled to the specifically conventional protections accorded to lawful combatants, such as the right not to be targeted in civilian locations or to the status of prisoner of war when captured (all are naturally entitled to human rights). Terrorists are legitimate targets for military attack whether they are targeted by name or by deed, at all times and places, subject only to necessity and proportionality.

The legal standard of proportionality in war requires that the military objective be attained at the lowest possible cost to genuine civilians. Due care for civilians during targeting missions involves weighing the value of each target as against the harm to their surroundings and taking relevant precautions concerning the location and

299. HCJ 769/02, esp. Para. 31.

precise timing of attack, selecting appropriate methods and weapons, and possibly introducing a degree of oversight consistent with the supervision of other wartime measures. Beyond conventional tactics, named killing may warrant some institutional guarantees against abuse and ulterior motives because of the individualized nature of the killing and its affinity with assassination. Secondary concerns notwithstanding, named killing exhibits the greatest conformity with the *jus in bello* requirement of distinction.

Like political assassination, targeted killing aims at its victims narrowly and attempts to avoid collateral deaths. Ordinary citizens remain, so far as possible, immune from attack. While targeted killing shares this morally favorable aspect of political assassination, it avoids the normative shortcomings of assassination. First, targeted killing does not take aim at protected civilians who are unengaged in military activity. Second, unlike political assassination, targeting terrorists does not require a complex political evaluation of the victims' cause, determining who is and who is not a political enemy; at most it requires a moral stand against terrorism. Terrorists are targeted for what they do—not for the causes they serve. Targeted killing shares the moral advantages of political assassination—the line it draws between liable targets and ordinary civilians—without retaining its problematic aspects.

UAVs have the capacity to perform this task at a distance, focusing lethal harm at a liable target while minimizing collateral deaths, provided, of course, that we program them to do just this. If we do not, the fault is not in our drones, but in ourselves.

Unlike many conventional weapons (though not unlike long-range missiles and aerial bombing), drones pose no danger to their operators. Some count this as a point in their favor, while others worry about the dangers of riskless warfare. This dispute is largely academic. Either way, no state in its right mind would give up the strategic superiority offered by drones. Not only are drones safe to use, but we also need not worry too much about their proliferation. Drones are primarily weapons of powerful states. While it is true that a single predator may not be all that expensive, running a drone program requires a huge, complicated, massive infrastructure around it. Additionally, drones are far more effective where complete air superiority is established.

Moreover, drones are not only weapons of states but also especially useful in the hands of those states that care about complying with discrimination and proportionality, since drones are very good at that. This type of asymmetry or double standard—enabling law-abiding states to fight safely against terrorists who cannot respond in kind—is a good thing.

The surgical killing of identified enemy combatants is as good as war gets, certainly compared with the common practice of killing young conscripts in battle and incurring large-scale collateral damage. Deliberately killing civilians is a horse of a different color. Targeting civilians is illegal, and rightly so. Beyond plain murder, peacetime assassinations violate state sovereignty. Even in wartime, it often involves perfidy and is always a violation of civilian immunity. All this is more than enough reason to uphold a stringent moral prohibition on targeting civilians and an absolute legal ban on assassination. When civilians are randomly murdered, we call this terrorism, and condemn it without exception, regardless of cause and circumstances. No justification can be offered.[300]

An absolute moral prohibition on assassination, allowing for no exceptions, is more difficult to sustain.[301] Plausible exceptions arise where particular civilians contribute directly to the business of fighting and/or bear responsibility for the emergence of an unjust threat, depending on which version of the morality of war one subscribes to. Even in such cases, I suggested, the threat to be averted must be grave, perhaps of holocaust dimensions. Possibly, the only examples that everyone would accept involve the killing of named Nazis who were nominally civilians during World War II. No rare exception ought to be reflected in our laws of war or peace or acknowledged as the deep morality of war. Paraphrasing on a familiar idea, I readily admit elsewhere that "Nazi cases make bad law."[302] Extreme cases that arouse sympathy are poor bases for general rules. Justifications for killing civilians should not to be concocted, and new, unraveling norms ought not to be introduced.[303] In exceptional emergencies in which the targeting of key civilians may be justified or even warranted as the lesser of evils, hypocrisy and denial are probably the best tributes to the law and moral norms.

300. Walzer, *Just and Unjust Wars*, at 197, 203.
301. Walzer, *Just and Unjust Wars*, at 197, 203.
302. Paraphrasing on "hard cases make bad law," I use this argument to oppose extending the right to take prisoners beyond the current POW regime, in Meisels, "Kidnapped—Kidnapping and Extortion as Tactics of Soft War."
303. Waldron, "Can Targeted Killing Work as a Neutral Principle?"; Waldron, "Justifying Targeted Killing with a Neutral Principle."

3

Against

JEREMY WALDRON

■□■

Debating Targeted Killing. Tamar Meisels and Jeremy Waldron, Oxford University Press (2020)
© Oxford University Press.
DOI: 10.1093/oso/9780190906917.001.0001

PART I: BEGINNINGS

Should governments be permitted to have people killed—
people picked out individually and identified by name? Is it
appropriate for ruling politicians to maintain lists of possible targets, from which individuals may be selected from
time to time to be put to death?

These questions arise in the context of counter-
terrorism operations, where targeted killing has become an
important and controversial strategy. Terrorists attack and
threaten civilians. They kill civilians in shootings, bombings, and other atrocities—sowing fear as well as taking
lives. Think of the thousands of innocent lives in American
cities that were taken in the terrorist attacks of September
11, 2001. The threat is constant and unpredictable; that
is, of course, the point of the terrorist strategy: the idea
is to sow paralyzing fear in the population. For its part,
the state—its armed forces and intelligence and security
operatives—try to prevent such attacks: they build physical barriers, they fortify possible targets of terrorist attack
like stadiums or airports, they accumulate intelligence, and
they insinuate themselves into terrorist organizations,
making it harder for terrorists to plan and conduct their
misdeeds. They listen in on terrorist communications and
disrupt the sources of terrorist funding. It is not easy to
do any of this because many terrorist attacks are conceived

in secret by clandestine organizations based in other countries, and the number of potential objects of attack in a free and open society is very large. But measures like these are indispensable if citizens are to be able to lead their lives in safety.

And then beyond the measures I have mentioned, there is this matter of killing terrorists outright. If state intelligence knows the identity and whereabouts of some of the terrorists or of those who plan, incite, finance, equip, and carry out terrorist operations, is it permissible to have these individuals killed one by one as the opportunity to do so presents itself even when they are not immediately engaged in an atrocity? This is what people have in mind when they talk about targeted killing: hunting down and deliberately killing individuals named, identified, and picked out for death on account of their connection with terrorism.[1] Is this something we should countenance? Is it something we should be comfortable with? Or should we turn our backs on it, as we have turned our backs on other controversial practices associated with counter-terrorism in the recent past—torture, for example, or secret detention? How should we think about targeted killing?

It is customary in a debate like this to ask whether the practice in question is being evaluated from a legal or from a moral point of view. There are ample materials in

---

1. The language of "hunting" was common in the United States after the terrorist attacks of 2001. Donald Rumsfeld asked: "How do we organize the Department of Defense for manhunts?" A 2009 report published by the Joint Special Operations University called for the setting up of a "national manhunting agency" and "building a manhunting force for the future." See Chamayou, *A Theory of the Drone*, 32–33 for these references.

international law. But their application depends on how targeted killing is categorized. Does it present itself as an act of war, in which case we shall have to consider the application of international humanitarian law? Or does it present itself as law enforcement? If so, constraints of a somewhat different legal character come into play—some of them procedural, some of them constitutional, some of them international.

Some authors who write about targeted killing believe it is a sui generis response to a new and distinctive problem,[2] in which case parsing the application of existing law may be more trouble than it is worth. If it is sui generis, perhaps we can argue analogically about the rules that ought to govern it. Both Professor Meisels and I regard this as an area where the application of existing legal norms may be problematic and/or controversial, if only because targeted killing takes place in the context of a new kind of warfare. This means the application of law cannot be undertaken without a moral analysis, as well as a black-letter legal analysis. Certainly there has to be some back and forth between legal and moral arguments as we strain to interpret existing rules to see whether and how they apply to targeted killing or as we advocate for new understandings of legal principles to govern or restrict this practice.

In some ways, though, the legal/moral dichotomy is unhelpful. Outside the scope of pure black-letter analysis, considerations of all sorts are relevant: some of them pragmatic and political, some of them ethical to the point of moralism. We have to consider whether targeted killing is a

2. See, e.g., Anderson, "Targeted Killing in US Counterterrorism Strategy and Law," 3.

wise strategy as well as whether it should be condemned on
ethical grounds. Targeted killing involves the premeditated
taking of a human life, and some will say that the default
position in morals as in law is that such deliberate killing
is forbidden: "Thou shalt not kill." Defending targeted killing means, among other things, showing that it ought not
to be regarded as murder. Accordingly, arguments evaluating it possibly *as* murder are not to be excluded a priori
from this domain of discussion. But they also have to be
complemented with arguments about whether targeted
killing works as a strategy, that is, whether it has the good
consequences that its defenders think it has. Are these distinctions clear? I don't think so, and we don't need them to
be. In a famous exchange with H. L. A. Hart in the 1950s,
Harvard jurist Lon Fuller said that, among legal positivists,

> the word "morality" stands indiscriminately for almost every
> conceivable standard by which human conduct may be judged
> that is not itself law. The inner voice of conscience, notions
> of right and wrong based on religious belief, common con-
> ceptions of decency and fair play, culturally conditioned
> prejudices—all of these are grouped together under the head-
> ing of "morality" and are excluded from the domain of law.[3]

And he said Hart seemed to accept this openness as
well: "When he speaks of morality he seems generally to
have in mind all sorts of extralegal notions about 'what
ought to be,' regardless of their sources, pretensions, or
intrinsic worth." This might be a problem in the context of
the jurisprudential debate about the positivist "separation"

---

3. Fuller, "Positivism and Fidelity to Law," 635.

of law and morality, but it shouldn't be a problem here. Between us, Professor Meisels and I will bring up everything of whatever character that can be said in defense or in criticism of targeted killing.

So the question we are considering should be understood in loose and generous terms. We have a division of labor, Professor Meisels and I. She has presented an array of considerations in support of targeted killing, which need to be taken seriously, though her account is also sensitive to what has been said against the practice. I will present various kinds of considerations that ought to weigh in the balance against targeted killing, though I too am mindful of what can be said on the other side.

For my part, I am not looking for a knockdown argument against targeted killing that results from the deductive application of an accepted principle. I think I can show that a dense array of misgivings accumulates around the practice, which makes it difficult for us to support it. But even if they do not agree with this conclusion, I hope readers will be left with a richer sense of what is at stake. There will be misgivings and reasons for hesitation about the sort of society we are turning ourselves into if we countenance this category of killing. Such considerations may be easy to brush aside if you are a hard man of rough action, angered by what targeted killing is a response to or thrilled by the loosening of ethical constraints that war-making involves. But the misgivings are less easy to brush aside if you pause very long for thought. What we are talking about is not a game—though targeted killing using drones often looks like a video game—but life and death, something that, from any point of view, counts as deadly serious.

Now, all this we might say about any philosophical conundrum set out in the terrain of homicide, like Frances Kamm's "Trolley Problem" or Judith Jarvis Thomson's ailing violinist.[4] Both involve issues about killing, so they too pose questions that are deadly serious. The difference is that targeted killing is not just deadly serious, but deadly serious *in real life*. It is about killings being planned and executed, as I write, by the governments of Israel and the United States. And in the real world they are not all that rare. The philosophers' violinist and trolley problems envisage curiously concocted one-off situations. Maybe that's inevitable when the intuitive method is used in philosophy. I shall use it myself occasionally (for example, at the beginning of Chapter 5). But with targeted killing, the matter goes well beyond a single philosophical puzzle. As a result of this practice becoming a standard method in the armory of the states I have mentioned, we are talking about hundreds or thousands of killings in recent years. That is what has to be either justified (Professor Meisels' agenda) or condemned (mine).

All states are potentially violent,[5] but for the countries that practice it, targeted killing looms quite large in their governments' use and regulation of lethal force. Israel has very seldom used the death penalty, yet it has acknowledged a "policy of liquidating those who plan or carry out attacks,"[6] and the numbers killed in this way are in the hundreds if not thousands.[7] As for the United States, where the

---

4. See Kamm, *The Trolley Problem Mysteries*, and Thomson, "A Defense of Abortion."

5. Weber, "Politics as a Vocation."

6. Melzer, *Targeted Killing in International Law*, 29.

7. See the comprehensive account in Bergman, *Rise and Kill First*.

death penalty still exists, the thousands of lives taken in American targeted killings in recent years greatly exceeds the number of judicially regulated killings in the criminal justice system.[8]

Since these numbers are so large, we need to consider not only the abstract question of moral justification but also the impact of such a practice on the ethos and spirit of our state, our society, and our politics. The two countries I mentioned—the United States and Israel—present themselves as liberal democracies under the rule of law. If it becomes routine in the politics of these countries to have regular high-level meetings of the executive to decide which names and dossiers should be downloaded from a list and assigned to military or intelligence operatives for killing, how long is it before such a practice starts to corrode or undermine the rule of law? The defenders of targeted killing whom I know are quite insouciant about this prospect. They think that if they can find good reasons in favor of this practice and if they can push back against a few objections, we need not worry about knock-on effects. But politicians who acquire a taste for ordering the elimination of "enemies of society" without the inconvenience of judicial process may not find it so easy to limit or curb that inclination when they face pressure from their constituents to address other dangers or

8. The number of those killed in targeted killings by the United States is in the thousands: in 2011 Alston estimated that there had been in excess of two thousand such killings by Americans in Pakistan alone. See Alston, "The CIA and Targeted Killings beyond Borders," 286. The number of judicially approved executions in the United States varies from 52 to 25 per year in the last ten years, while the number of death sentences varies from 118 to 42 in the same period.

insecurities. That adversaries are not simply to be "taken out" is one of the bedrock principles of liberal democracy and the rule of law. The atmosphere of a society in which that principle has been abandoned is likely more brutal and more fearful than a society in which the strongest scruples continue to prohibit political killings. I would like to see more defenders of targeted killing address this possibility for, as things stand, I fear that the case made for targeted killing is too often dismissive of this sort of concern.

PART II: SIDE ISSUES

Most of what I am going to say about targeted killing will proceed on a rather narrow front: I will focus on the killing, and I will focus on the targeting. There are, of course, many other issues one might address. Targeted killing is a complex practice with all sorts of aspects and consequences. It is intensely controversial, along a wide variety of dimensions, including (1) the casualties suffered by innocent civilians in these attacks, (2) the possible targeting by a country of its own citizens, (3) the status and discipline of those who take part in these killings, (4) the use of drones in warfare, and (5) the medium- and long-term strategic consequences of the use of this methodology in the struggle against terrorism.

I will say a word or two about each of these topics but then I will set them aside. I do so not because they are unimportant—there are serious things to say about each of them—but because they do not really go to the heart of our debate in this volume, which, as I said, ought to be the killing and the targeting as such.

1. Collateral Damage

The most important of the side issues we are considering is the issue of "collateral damage," which is a polite term for the unintended (but predictable) killing of civilians not actively involved in terrorist activities. For example, the children or neighbors of those who come under attack are sometimes killed when drones target terrorist operatives in their homes or at social events like weddings. According to Kenneth Anderson, the concern about excessive collateral damage is "the leading objection to drone warfare today."[9] It is certainly one that has been taken quite seriously by the US administration (or at least it was by the Obama administration). Critics concerned about collateral damage seek assurances that untargeted individuals will not be injured or killed in targeted killings.

For their part, defenders of targeted killing say that, with experience, there is less and less collateral damage in operations of this kind,[10] and that in any case the death rate for civilians is arguably much lower than in attacks using the ordinary weapons of war. They say that targeted killing is a more "surgical" form of combat.[11] (Rosa Brooks asks in a recent essay, "Should we prefer untargeted killing?")[12]

---

9. Anderson, "The Case for Drones."

10. For some new missile technology designed specifically to reduce collateral damage, see Gordon Lubold and Warren Strobel, "Secret Missile Targets Terrorist Leaders," *Wall Street Journal*, May 10, 2019.

11. See Blanchard, "This Is Not War by Machine," 124–125.

12. Brooks, "Drones and Cognitive Dissonance," 230, at 234.

Nils Melzer notes the plausibility of the argument "that the carefully prepared use of lethal force against selected individuals is the most discriminate of all means of warfare."[13] This doesn't mean civilians are never killed in these operations—on the contrary, such casualties remain stubbornly high. But the impact on civilian lives and civilian infrastructure is said to be much lower than regular warfare. Using a military model, Sam Issacharoff and Rick Pildes say this:

> The key principles of the law of war are the principles of necessity, distinction, and proportionality—the principles that force should intentionally be used only against military targets and that the damage to individual citizens should be minimized and proportionate. Drones, as against other uses of military force, better realize these principles than any other technology currently available. Indeed, they allow for the most discriminating uses of force in the history of military technology and warfare, in contexts in which the use of force is otherwise justified.[14]

(They talk of drones, but in fact civilian casualties are even less likely with regard to Osama bin Laden–style executions, using death squads on the ground.)

Controversy abounds concerning the methodology that is used to back up these claims. One point concerns the criteria for classifying someone as a civilian casualty in these operations. Targeted killing is often allied with a tactic of "signature strikes,"[15] which target individuals not by

13. Melzer, *Targeted Killing in International Law*, 357.
14. Issacharoff and Pildes, "Targeted Warfare," 1575.
15. For "signature strikes," see Rothenberg, "Drones and the Emergence of Data-driven Warfare," 441, at 450–456.

name but by the physical profile they present at the site of their killing. If a named terrorist is targeted at place P, and he is surrounded there by military-age men who are also blown up when he is, it may all too readily be inferred that they too were terrorists and that P is some sort of terrorist gathering point. The deaths of the other young men killed at P might have been collateral to the killing of the named target, but under this analysis they won't be counted as collateral *civilian* casualties. And if this mode of reckoning seems rather casual, as it often is, then there is a danger that civilian deaths are being seriously undercounted.

In any case, when we hear that targeted killing is a highly discriminate use of lethal force, we should press the question: compared to what? Drones may make an operation with a low (but non-zero) risk of civilian casualties possible, but in the real world such operations are not necessarily substitutes for operations using conventional military force that would have produced larger numbers of casualties. The more dangerous operation with which a targeted killing is being compared might not have taken place at all. The availability of targeted killing and the technology that makes it possible may mean that we undertake operations with a substantial chance of killing some civilians where, in the past, we would not otherwise have undertaken *any* killing operation. In which case, the number of real-world civilian casualties overall goes up rather than down.

Issacharoff and Pildes and others imagine a world in which conventional military operations—bombing raids, for example—are superseded more or less entirely in asymmetric warfare by targeted killings. It is nice to fantasize about such things in a law review article, but there is little evidence that this is happening. Instead what we see is that conventional raids continue, with their blunt force and their indiscriminate tendency to destroy civilian lives and infrastructure, and that targeted killings are *added* to that equation as an additional option. There is no evidence, for example, of the number of bombers or tanks or artillery pieces in our forces being reduced by the availability of drone technology and targeted killing. Yet that is what one would expect from the Issacharoff-Pildes analysis.

One final point about collateral damage. It is not only actual casualties to innocent civilians that we need to be concerned about, but also the general insecurity that the practice of targeted killing gives rise to. Grégoire Chamayou argues that drones "inflict mass terror upon entire populations."[16] This means that even if the kinetic operations themselves are precise, their broader psychological effect is not.[17] Chamayou quotes David Rohde, a *New York Times* journalist held hostage in Waziristan, who reported that both he and his captors found the drones terrifying. "From the ground it is impossible to determine who or what they are tracking as they circle overhead. The buzz of a distant propeller is a constant reminder of imminent death."[18]

Concerns about collateral damage and terrorization are important, and by speaking of them as side issues I don't mean to belittle these concerns. For many people these concerns are key to the case against targeted killing,

---

16. Chamayou, *A Theory of the Drone*, 45.
17. McDonald, *Enemies Known and Unknown*, 204.
18. Chamayou, *A Theory of the Drone*, 43. See also comments about the "bee-like" buzz of drones overhead in Shah, "My Drone War," 100, and Amnesty International, "Will I Be Next?"

especially people who are unwilling to be seen raising any concern at all about the lives of terrorists. The idea seems to be that, if we could be assured of killing only those we were aiming at, then this practice would not be objectionable. I think that is wrong. Targeted killing, in and of itself, is neither a good nor an honorable way for states to fight terrorism. Hunting people down and killing them, even with precision, is not something we should want in the armory of a liberal democratic state.

2. Targeting Citizens

As well as concerns about collateral damage, the Obama administration responded emphatically to concerns about the killing of American citizens. When it came to light that the United States was proposing to target and kill a Yemeni-American (Anwar al-Awlaki), when American courts refused to get involved in reviewing that proposal,[19] and when the citizen concerned was in due course "taken out" by a US drone in Yemen in 2011, a question was raised about whether targeted killing was appropriately applied by a country to its own citizens.[20] I want to treat this too as a

---

19. Al-Aulaqi v. Panetta 35 F.Supp.3d 56 (2013). The refusal was partly based on questions of standing but mostly on the political character of the decision to have al-Awlaki killed. The al-Awlaki killing has one other controversial dimension that we *will* have to explore. Al-Awlaki was not himself a terrorist operative but a preacher and recruiter of terrorism. I will deal with this in Part VI.

20. 18 U.S.C. §1119 makes it an offense for a national of the United States to kill another US national outside the United States. For an attempt to get around this, see Office of Legal Counsel, "Memorandum for the Attorney General."

side issue, predicated as it is on the assumption that the
practice of targeted killing would be more defensible if the
only names on the death lists were the names of foreigners.

In fact most terrorist incidents in the United States
do involve citizens—members of homegrown terrorist movements like white supremacists. I guess there is
always an opportunity to arrest these people and put them
on trial (an option which is less practicable for our forces
in Yemen). This would be reassuring if targeted killing
generally were used only as a last-resort measure of law
enforcement (something we will consider in Chapter 4).
But it is not. The US government and its spokespersons
justify it as a military measure in something called the
war on terror: it is, they say, just like killing a combatant,
albeit an unlawful or irregular combatant. And Professor
Meisels certainly takes this approach. True: some defenders of targeted killing will try to have it both ways as long
as they are able; they slide back and forth between the
military approach and the law enforcement approach.
But when put to the test they seem to prefer the military
analogy.

In any case, as we shall see in Part VI, targeted killing needs to be considered as a tool not only of the United
States but of other governments as well. The United
Kingdom faced a terrorist threat in and from Northern
Ireland, which is a province of the UK, and it larded its
professed policy of treating Irish Republican Army (IRA)
operatives as common criminals with the occasional use
of "shoot-to-kill" as an eradicative measure.[21] Those who

---

21. See the discussion in McCann and Others v. United Kingdom
(21 ECHR 97 GC).

were killed were definitely British citizens (however much they themselves repudiated that allegiance). Or think of the Israeli situation: Palestinian terrorists are in one sense outsiders to Israeli society, but in another sense they are (many of them) subject to Israeli authority in the Occupied Territories. Mostly they are not citizens, but so long as Israel maintains its presence and power in the West Bank and its utter control of conditions of life in the besieged Gaza enclave, its targeted killings are often individuals for whom it has formal state responsibility. We have to evaluate targeted killing in a world where a government targeting its own citizens is not an anomaly, but business as usual in its security policy.

3. The Status of Those Who Do the Killing

How much attention should we pay to the fact that those who carry out the killings are not always people subject to military law? American targeted killings have been carried out not only by military personnel but also by CIA operatives (both in the field and holding a joystick in a remote location to control a drone).[22] Strictly speaking, such intelligence operatives would count as unlawful combatants, unless they were somehow legitimately patched into military units. President Obama reduced this practice; but the word is that under President Trump's administration, restraints

---

22. Ofek, "The Tortured Logic of Obama's Drone War," 36: "We do know from press reports . . . that the unmanned planes usually depart from a secret base in Pakistan but are controlled by civilian officers at CIA headquarters in Langley." See also Jacobsen, *Surprise, Kill, Vanish*.

on non-military participation have been relaxed.[23] There are similarly crossed lines of responsibility in Israel. Many, if not most, targeted killings there are carried out by intelligence operatives.

The importance of this point has to do with the military model of counter-terrorism, and the analogy (which we will explore in Chapter 4) between targeted killing and killing in combat. Military personnel are surely more immersed in and respectful of the ethics and laws of armed conflict than intelligence operatives are. The presence of intelligence operatives may betoken a certain contempt for the laws and customs that govern these practices. Indeed, it shows that targeted killings by the United States and Israeli governments have not in fact always conformed to a strict military model, despite the military justification used by their apologists. Sometimes what is conjured up is an image of a cadre of "hard men" who operate in the twilight with a James Bond type license to kill. Against the exotic appeal of this image, we ought to ask how comfortable a democratic society should be with its undercover operatives killing not just one or two wrongdoers *in extremis*, but hundreds or even thousands of individuals. In Chapter 4, we will consider whether targeted killing is more like combat than like (say) the activity of death squads. Certainly those who defend it as a form of combat need to address the issue of personnel more openly than they have.

23. See Ken Dilanian and Courtney Kube, "Trump Cancels Obama Policy of Reporting Drone Strike Deaths," *NBC News*, March 6, 2019.

4. The Use of Drones

As for the challenges posed by new technology, my argument is not going to focus on unmanned vehicles (drones) alone. Drone killings are a significant part but not the whole, of a broader category of targeted killings, which includes the use of death squads on the ground (like the US Navy SEALs involved in the Osama bin Laden killing), as well as "sniper fire . . . missiles from helicopters, gunships, . . . the use of car bombs, and poison."[24] The Israelis have been particularly versatile in their methods of targeted killing. Their use of drones for assassination only really began in 2000, and at the time it excited grave concern from Israel's American allies.[25] After 9/11, of course, the United States made much larger use of drones for its own targeted killings, but other methods continued to be used as well.

What about the more general challenge posed by the use of drones? It has been said that drones are ushering in a new form of warfare, which challenges traditional notions of reciprocity in combat.[26] There is a lot of silly talk about failure of chivalry and battlefield equality. In fact the age of chivalry has long gone, if it ever existed. Maybe the use of drones makes things worse. But I shall proceed on the basis that the novelty is not the technology; it is the casting-off of some very old constraints.

24. Alston, "Report of the Special Rapporteur," §8.
25. Bergman, *Rise and Kill First*, 508–511.
26. See Chamayou, *A Theory of the Drone*, 153–154 for a suggestion by Albert Camus: "[Y]ou can't kill unless you are prepared to die." And see 161–162 for the suggestion that the privilege of killing depends on reciprocity.

5. Strategic Disadvantages

A number of commentators have encouraged us to think about the incentivizing effects of drone warfare, as well as its kinetic effects. On the one hand, terror from the skies may have a deterrent effect on terrorist operations. On the other hand, civilians may be not just terrified but radicalized by the buzz of drones overhead. After all, terrorists and terrorism don't come out of nowhere. An important element in counter-terrorist strategy surely ought to be the diminishing not the enhancing of factors that motivate people in that direction. So among all the criticisms of targeted killing, we have to consider the possibility that it is, in the final analysis, counter-productive.[27] Maybe targeted killing works as a recruitment tool for terrorist organizations. Remember that unlike regular military operations, terrorism is not a manpower-intensive enterprise. A handful of committed terrorist operatives replenished from time to time is all that the enterprise needs. And the logic of targeted killing cannot possibly be that eventually we will eventually get *every last recruit* and there will be no terrorists left. There is a sort of "whack-a-mole" futility to any such eliminative endeavor.[28]

I don't want to be too glib about this. At its best, counter-terrorism strategy is complex and resourceful. The best methods focus on the disruption of communications and financing for terrorist organizations, and targeted killing may have a part to play in that, making freedom of movement for terrorists and open recruiting and training

27. See Mothana, "How Drones Help Al Qaeda," 82.
28. See, e.g., Maxwell, "Rebutting the Civilian Presumption."

more difficult. The strategic disadvantages are in any case hard to measure.[29] The worry, however, is that our use of this tactic is less sophisticated than that and less well-integrated into some overall strategy. It is often said that the Obama administration shifted to targeted killing in order to avoid the political consequence of being seen as soft on terrorism after its ban on coercive interrogation. If this is right, it is possible that targeted killing is motivated, on the part of our authorities, not by any real strategic analysis, but simply by the political need to be seen to be doing *something*—still something very, very violent—in response to terrorist activity.

***

Each of the issues I have mentioned in this part defines *a* problem with targeted killing as it is currently practiced by the United States and other powers. But important as these problems are, they do not get at *the* problem with targeted killing. Their pursuit should not be allowed to distract us from the main issue, which is the adoption of a new practice of individualized killing by our government. The central issue, from which we must not flinch in our reflections on this practice, is not whether we are killing the right people but whether killings of this kind are appropriate at all.

29. Byman, "Do Targeted Killings Work?": "The number of subsequent attacks carried out by militant groups after a targeted killing has served as a measure of the effectiveness for scholars in the literature." See also Morehouse, "The Claws of the Bear," 273.

PART III: DEPRIVATION OF LIFE

The killing of the person targeted is not the only deprivation of life involved in targeted killing: there are also the unlawful killings committed by terrorists, and there are the deaths of civilians that are the byproduct of targeted killings. There is plenty of killing to go around. Killings by terrorists are murderous atrocities, and they need to be met with resolute resistance and the full force of national and international law. As for collateral damage, this was something addressed in Part II. The only thing to add here is that if the primary attack on human life in a targeted killing is not justified, then incurring the risk of collateral damage cannot be justified either. We should have to abandon the term "collateral damage" and replace it with "reckless and therefore culpable homicide ancillary to deliberate murder." However, the key issue that needs to be addressed in any assessment of targeted killing is, of course, the intentional deprivation of human life of those who are its targets.

No one needs me to tell them that killing is in general prohibited by religious, moral, and legal principles. We talk about the *value* of human life, but actually it is not treated simply as a value to be maximized, for example. "Thou shalt not kill" is perhaps the best-known example of a *deontological* principle, one that constrains action directly with a norm, rather than the upshot of any calculation of the value of consequences.

In fact it is quite difficult for consequentialists, especially utilitarians, to fully explicate the wrongness of killing.[30] When there are things to be said in favor of the state

---

30. Cf. Henson, "Utilitarianism and the Wrongness of Killing" and Glover, *Causing Death and Saving Lives*, 62ff.

of affairs in which a given person no longer exists as well as things to be said in favor of his continued existence, it is hard to get from a consequentialist any decisive understanding of why killing should be regarded morally speaking as out of the question. If we want to do more than talk about consequences, we must associate intentional killing with the desecration of a good that is in some sense holy (the "sanctity of life"), a value that is perhaps incommensurable with gains that people might seek to trade it for, or a value that commands our immediate respect rather than just being factored into our calculations. These are ways of thinking that take us beyond the realm of consequences.

In general, we can say that deliberately putting a person to death "is the ultimate desecration of the individual as a human being. . . . It is the annihilation of the very essence of human dignity."[31] It is the total eradication of an individual from the world—not just the negation of one of his projects (perhaps a bad one, a terrorist project), but the negation of all his hopes, desires, and preferences. It negates the continuity of all his hopes (on earth) and thwarts his present projects, taking away also the possibility of his pursuing any projects at all in the future. The euphemisms that are sometimes used for deliberate killings are telling: A person is said to be "rubbed out," "liquidated," "taken out," "eliminated." More solemnly, the deliberate taking of a human life represents a decision by the living (or by some of the living) that we will no longer share the world with the person whom we have determined to kill. Our target is no longer to be permitted to share a common human existence with

---

31. Kindler v Canada (Minister of Justice) [1991] 2 SCR 779, Cory J. dissenting.

the rest of us. We break into his bedroom, identify him, and shoot him. Or we watch him through a drone as he goes about the business of ordinary life and then fire a missile at him so that he will never have any business or any ordinary life again.

Some will view this sort of language—much of which is taken from the jurisprudence of the death penalty—as overwrought. But for the purposes of this discussion, I am going to assume the truth of the common principle that intentional killing is quite seriously wrong. Please note, however, that such an assumption is not begging the question against the practice of targeted killing. The wrongness of killing anyone (even evildoers) is our default position, not our conclusion. It is where we must start from in any discussion of this kind, and I am not prepared to talk about targeted killing with anyone who treats it more casually than that.

Moreover, I do not assume that the rule about killing is absolute. There are some moral absolutes: the rule against torture is an example, though some moral philosophers strive mightily to show that it must be possible to concoct examples—ticking bombs or whatever—that would justify torture, at least in theory.[32] I have aligned myself elsewhere with the absolutist position so far as torture is concerned:[33] I believe the wrongness of torture is given and that it is decisive, even if the reasoning is hard to put into words. If I were writing half a book on *Torture: For and Against*, my part would be unyielding and categorical, and words like "abomination" would be used.

32. See McMahon, "Torture in Principle and in Practice."
33. Waldron, *Torture, Terror, and Tradeoffs*, 213ff.

But targeted killing is in a different category. Killing is seriously wrong, but it may be permitted in certain circumstances. In Part IV we shall explore attempts to range targeted killing under some of the better-known exceptions to the rule against taking human life. As we shall see, most arguments for its acceptability play out on or adjacent to the terrain of war, which involves some sort of privilege of killing on the part of lawful combatants. Life is cheap, it may be thought, in the law and ethics of armed conflict. That's why we can't just work under the auspices of the Fifth Commandment. It may not even be possible to establish which side bears the burden of argument in this debate. "For," because all killing requires serious justification? Or "against," because it has to be shown that targeted killing is different from the great mass of other killings that war routinely permits. Both sides may have to proceed as though everything is up for grabs. But again, that is not the same as beginning from the position that killing, or the killing of terrorists, really doesn't matter all that much. Nor is it the same as saying that since there are some people whom everyone agrees may be killed, there must be a way of getting other people we fear and condemn into that category also.[34]

Legally, the prohibition on killing is pretty clear. All legal systems have rules against homicide, varying in degree depending on the character of intentionality associated with the causation of death. In all criminal codes, it is one of the two or three most serious offenses. States kill, of course, and this book is in part an exploration of

---

34. See Waldron, "Justifying Targeted Killing with a Neutral Principle."

their right to do so. But constitutionally, a country like the United States treats life as an inalienable and God-given right, and it regulates lawmaking at every level with a principle that people may not be deprived of life without due process of law.[35]

Internationally, the duty not to kill is of very great importance. Article 6 of the International Covenant on Civil and Political Rights lays down that "[e]very human being has the inherent right to life. This right shall be protected by law. No one shall be arbitrarily deprived of his life." There is grudging provision for capital punishment in Article 6, but it must be imposed by a court and only for the most serious crimes. That apart, the right to life in Article 6 is established as more or less absolute, certainly as nonderogable in time of emergency.[36] But it is subject to the laws of war. As Elizabeth Hicks puts it, "a death in wartime will not violate the right to life if it is in accordance with the rules of international humanitarian law."[37]

The importance of the right to life is conveyed in some apt words of Justice Catherine O'Regan in a South African death penalty case:

> The right to life is, in one sense, antecedent to all the other rights in the Constitution. Without life in the sense of

35. As well as the opening lines of the Declaration of Independence, see also the Fifth and Fourteenth Amendments to the US Constitution.

36. See Article 4: 1. "In time of public emergency which threatens the life of the nation and the existence of which is officially proclaimed, the States Parties to the present Covenant may take measures derogating from their obligations under the present Covenant to the extent strictly required by the exigencies of the situation. . . . 2. No derogation from article[] 6 . . . may be made under this provision."

37. Wicks, *The Right to Life and Conflicting Interests*, 1.

existence, it would not be possible to exercise rights or to be
the bearer of them. But the right to life was included in the
Constitution not simply to enshrine the right to existence. It
is not life as mere organic matter that the Constitution cher-
ishes, but the right to human life: the right to live as a human
being, to be part of a broader community, to share in the
experience of humanity. This concept of human life is at the
centre of our constitutional values. The constitution seeks to
establish a society where the individual value of each member
of the community is recognised and treasured. The right to
life is central to such a society.[38]

Justice O'Regan went on to associate the right to life with
the importance of human dignity: "The right to life is more
than existence, it is a right to be treated as a human being
with dignity: without dignity, human life is substantially
diminished."[39] In some other jurisdictions, Germany for
example, the right to life has to be seen through a sort of
Kantian lens of dignity. It does not permit calculations that
would weigh and balance the lives of some (whom the state
might kill) against a greater number of lives (that the state
might save by killing them).[40]

States have a duty to protect life and a duty not to arbitrarily deprive anybody of it. The two duties may have different scope. The protective duty applies to a state's own
citizens. Maybe it has a duty as well to protect the lives of
anyone who is at any given time within its jurisdiction. It
certainly has a protective responsibility for those it might
knowingly endanger—innocent civilians, for example, in a

38. S v. Makwanyane, 1995 (6) BCLR 665, §325.
39. S v. Makwanyane, 1995 (6) BCLR 665, §326.
40. See Aviation Security Act Case, BVerfG, 1 BvR 357/05 (2006).

targeted killing operation (even one undertaken abroad). However, so far as deliberate killing is concerned, the duty extends to the taking of *any* human life. One may not kill anyone, unless the killing fits into one of the narrowly circumscribed categories that make a killing a justified homicide. And, in the case of the American government for example, this is true whether the target of the killing is a US citizen, a US person, or a bona fide foreigner. It is possible that the killing of a US citizen by a US citizen even when it happens overseas constitutes a special legal difficulty. Federal law threatens frightful punishment against any "person who, being a national of the United States, kills or attempts to kill a national of the United States while such national is outside the United States but within the jurisdiction of another country."[41] This section of the US Code occasioned some difficulty in justifying the targeted killing of American citizen Anwar al-Awlaki, who, as we saw in Part II was a propagandist in Yemen for al-Qaeda in the Arabian Peninsula. It was necessary to read the word "unlawfully" into the section just quoted and to hope that the killing of al-Awlaki could be privileged as a lawful killing in combat (despite that al-Awlaki was not a combatant).[42]

Does the right to life apply to terrorists? In the first instance, the answer is "yes." Terrorists are human beings, and the right to life established in the human rights conventions is said to be "inherent" in humanity. Neither international law nor existing doctrines of rights in constitutional law recognize the possibility of any general forfeiture of

41. 18 U.S.C. §1119.
42. Office of Legal Counsel, Memorandum for the Attorney General (July 16, 2010).

rights. It is true that terrorists are wrongdoers; they are themselves murderers, intentionally depriving others of life without a scintilla of remorse or justification. But their own assault on life does not diminish their humanity; indeed, many human rights become important precisely where a person is suspected (rightly or not) of activity of this kind. Neither international human rights law nor—I would venture to say—any respectable moral theory countenances the idea that the normative status of humanity with its attendant rights somehow lapses on account of an individual's wrongdoing. Yair Netanyahu (son of Benjamin Netanyahu, Israeli prime minister at the time of writing) is on record talking about "the monsters in human form known since 1964 as Palestinians."[43] But we are not to describe wrongdoers as monsters or demons, as though they did not belong to our species, as though the general moral attributes of humanity did not belong to them. The best we can say about this young man's characterization is that it is reminiscent of the position of the great English philosopher John Locke, who said the following about malefactors and rights violators. By violating the natural law, "a Man so far becomes degenerate, and declares himself to quit the Principles of Human Nature, and to be a noxious Creature."[44]

> [H]aving renounced Reason, the common Rule and Measure God hath given to Mankind, hath, by the unjust Violence and Slaughter he hath committed upon one, declared War against

43. Isabel Kerschner, "Facebook Blocks Netanyahu Son Saying His Posts 'Included Hate Speech,'" *New York Times*, December 17, 2018.
44. Locke, *Two Treatises*, II §10.

all Mankind, and therefore may be destroyed as a Lyon or a Tyger, one of those wild Savage Beasts, with whom Men can have no Society nor Security.[45]

But even Locke did not follow through on this, for he insisted that the punishment of offenders had to be guided by strong procedural and substantive constraints that would be quite out of place in dealing with lions and tigers, and that destroying them had to be forgone altogether in cases where the public advantage might be promoted thereby.[46]

A better position is that taken by the president emeritus of the Israel Supreme Court in the 2005 case that considered the legality of targeted killing. President Aharon Barak made this observation about terrorists in the course of his opinion:

> Needless to say, unlawful combatants are not beyond the law. They are not "outlaws." God created them as well in his image; their human dignity as well is to be honored; they as well enjoy and are entitled to protection . . . by customary international law.[47]

The reference here to the image of God is striking. It is intended to pull us up short and remind us that, although we are dealing with a wrongdoer who will kill and maim scores of innocent people given the opportunity, still we

---

45. Locke, *Two Treatises*, II §11.
46. See the discussion in Waldron, *God, Locke, and Equality*, 146–147.
47. *Public Committee against Torture in Israel and Palestinian Society for the Protection of Human Rights and the Environment v. The Government of Israel and others* (HCJ 769/02) December 11, 2005, §25.

are not talking about a wild beast or something that may be killed as though its life did not matter. The terrorist is also *man-created-in-the-image-of-God* and the status associated with that characterization imposes radical limits on how lightly we treat the question of what is to be done with him. Barak's characterization presents the respect that humans *as such* are entitled to as something grounded, not in what we happen to care about or in what we happen to have committed ourselves to, but in facts about what humans are actually like, or more accurately, what they have been made by the Creator to be like—like unto himself and by virtue of that likeness sacred and inviolable. We are not just clever animals, and the evildoers among us—even the worst of the worst—are not just good animals gone bad: our dignity is associated with a specifically high rank in creation accorded to us by our Creator and reflecting our likeness to him. Our status even as wrongdoers is to be understood in relation to this, and so is everything we say about justified killing and the punishment of wrongdoers.[48]

In Barak's opinion and in the judgment of the Israeli Supreme Court, this characterization of terrorists did not rule out the possible justifiability of targeted killing, nor did it confer on any killer an immunity against punishment or combat killing. It did mean, however, that these topics needed to be thought through carefully, not casually, because our response to the terrorist puts a human life at stake.

I said earlier that no modern moral philosopher countenances a *general* forfeiture of rights—a loss of normative

48. See Waldron, "The Image of God."

human status—as a consequence of murderous acts of terrorism. Some deploy a limited notion of forfeiture to explain the justifiability of punishment.[49] Even if capital punishment is out of the question (as it is in most advanced democracies), individual rights to liberty are curtailed by arrest and incarceration, and a rights theorist must be able to offer an account of the justifiability of this curtailment. At the same time, any forfeiture theory of punishment has to be able to explain the limits on punishment (proportionality, restrictions on cruelty, etc.); limitations on who may punish; the insistence on procedural due process; the fact that punishment does not affect all or even most other rights of the miscreant (who retains the right of access to law, the right to freedom of worship, in some systems the right to vote); and so on. A theory limited in this way is unlikely to make terrorists fair game for a targeting operation. (I will say more about this when I consider the category of "rough justice" in Part IV.)

Earlier in the present chapter, I acknowledged that the right to life is not absolute. This too has to be understood carefully, in relation to the general point about inalienability. The Law of Armed Conflict privileges killings of combatants by combatants in situations of actual combat. Even in time of peace, an attacker may be resisted with deadly force in self-defense or, by the authorities, in defense of others. In very carefully circumscribed situations, the authorities may use lethal force to see that their orders are obeyed— for example, in the apprehension of a person suspected of committing a serious offense. And as we saw, Article 6 of

49. See, e.g., Wellman, "The Rights Forfeiture Theory of Punishment."

the International Covenant on Civil and Political Rights countenances at least the possibility of capital punishment for heinous and grievous offenses. What it prohibits is "*arbitrary* deprivation of life."

"Arbitrary" is a difficult term to define. At its worst, it can be used to describe any killing we disapprove of. But we can do better than that. Affirmatively, the best legal understanding has to do with the relation between a killing that has been called in question and the carefully defined categories of justifiable homicide sketched out in the previous paragraph. As we will see in the next part, most justifications of targeted killing in the war against terrorism adopt this approach, dispelling the appearance of arbitrary deprivation by drawing analogies to situations in which killing is already permissible, and in which juridical guidelines of necessity and proportionality apply. But there is a negative side as well. Those who drafted and administer Article 6 and its equivalents have in mind kinds of killing of which we have had experience and which are to remain normatively out of the question: summary execution, for example, the use of death squads for political intimidation, collective punishment against whole communities, and the use of lethal force against protestors.[50] In the part that follows, I will explore both sides of this equation: the analogies that make targeted killing look respectable, and the analogies that make it look like murderous havoc. Only if we are willing to stare both possibilities in the face can we say that we are taking seriously the underlying right to life.

---

50. See the cases set out in Melzer, *Targeted Killing in International Law*, 92–100.

PART IV: ANALOGIES

Targeted killing is sui generis—killing named individuals one by one because of their involvement with terrorism. But even if it is unique, we can still ask: is it *like* other forms of killing, permissible or impermissible? The answer might give us a useful analogy, forming the basis for moral or legal categorization.

For example, it is commonly said that targeted killing is like killing in war, and so it should be categorized along with regular combat. We may say: it is so like killing in war that it deserves to be treated like a combat killing in the eyes of the law. Or even apart from legal rules, we may want to say that the analogy with combat is important: moral objections should not be raised against targeted killing since most of us do not object morally to the killing of combatants in war.

Alternatively, it is sometimes said that targeted killing is analogous to law enforcement. Sometimes police officers have to fire on people to defend innocents or to stop miscreants from escaping arrest. Maybe we can justify targeted killing by analogy with these sadly familiar features of law enforcement. Or perhaps targeted killing should be understood as a form of punishment, along the lines of capital punishment.

There's a lot of overlap between the military and the law enforcement analogies in the conceptualization of targeted killing. The two may complement each other in a sort of hybrid model. In this Part I consider how each analogy is supposed to work, the flaws that they respectively reveal in the case for targeted killing, and the viability of a hybrid model. I also have some analogies of my own to pursue—for, remember, analogies can discredit as well as justify. Thus we have to consider, for example, whether targeted killing is like assassination or like the use of death squads by authoritarian regimes. Neither of these analogies flatters the practice, but their availability is something that has to be addressed.

1. Killing in War

The most common analogy for targeted killing is the model of military action. In ordinary warfare we are permitted to use lethal force against our enemies. Since terrorists are our enemies in a violent struggle, why can't we use lethal force against them? Why isn't killing a terrorist just like killing an enemy soldier?

Certainly there are differences. Terrorists are (mostly) not organized under the auspices of sovereign states, let alone under the discipline of the laws of armed conflict. They are not regular combatants. They don't carry weapons openly, nor do they wear uniforms. The warfare they engage in—if indeed warfare is what it is—is quite radically asymmetrical.[51] Not all asymmetrical warfare involves terrorism (though the two are all too often identified, as we shall see in Part VI). Anyway, those who invoke the military analogy maintain that asymmetry does not detract from application of the laws of armed conflict. They say that civil war—or quasi-civil war of the sort involved in the Israel-Palestine conflict—is governed by those laws also. And they

---

51. For asymmetrical warfare, see Halbertal, "Moral Challenges in Asymmetric Warfare."

say that, as in any war, the armed forces fighting against these terrorist factions are justified in responding to armed actions by their adversaries with the lethal means at their disposal.

Now, we have to be careful with this argument. Not all terrorist action against a society involves anything like war against that society. On March 15, 2019, an Australian white supremacist committed an appalling act of terrorism in Christchurch, New Zealand, but New Zealand was not and is not as a result of his actions at war with that individual or his sympathizers (if any). The same can be said of Anders Breivik in Norway. If targeted killing of these individuals were to be justified, it would have to be on some other basis, probably using the law enforcement analogy that we will consider in a moment. A few individuals or an organization consisting of a few individuals armed with firearms and explosives can hardly embroil a whole society in what international law would describe as armed conflict.

These distinctions are not helped by talk of a war on terror, as though a society could go to war against a tactic (as used by anyone). Those who use the military analogy usually rely on a more robust basis for talking of war than that. In the post-1945 world, war is justified only as a means of self-defense and, as the British government noted in a recent document, "in order for the right of self-defence to be invoked against non-State actors, the same level of gravity must be reached as if the armed attack were by another State."[52] The al-Qaeda attack on the United States in September 2011 was certainly comparable to an

52. Joint Committee on Human Rights (UK Parliament), The Government's Policy on the Use of Drones for Targeted

act of war in a conventional sense. So it is arguable that the United States is at war with al-Qaeda and that, in the words of the 2001 Authorization of the Use of Military Force,

> the President is authorized to use all necessary and appro-
> priate force against those nations, organizations, or persons
> he determines planned, authorized, committed, or aided the
> terrorist attacks that occurred on September 11, 2001 . . . in
> order to prevent any future acts of international terrorism
> against the United States by such nations, organizations or
> persons.[53]

It is a pretty indeterminate declaration, but that is under-standable in circumstances in which the United States was still trying to figure out who its adversaries were.

But let me emphasize that the mere fact of a declara-tion of war is not enough. What is up for justification is the killing of certain people regarded as enemies, and, as between states and non-state groups, such killings are priv-ileged only when armed conflict reaches a certain intensity, beyond what could reasonably be dealt with by ordinary law enforcement. Otherwise the category of combatant, crucial for the military analogy, does not really get a grip.[54] Sporadic attacks do not by themselves amount to armed conflict. If we imagine a fifteen-year period in which organi-zation X undertakes one or two armed attacks against tar-gets in country Y, and, in the years intervening, the armed

Killing: Government Response to the Committee's Second Report of Session 2015–16 (October 12, 2016).

53. Authorization for the Use of Military Force, September 18, 2001.

54. McDonald, *Enemies Known and Unknown*, 144.

forces of Y track down dozens of supporters of X around the world at the rate of one or two a month, killing them without substantial risk to Y's own forces—we can describe that in many ways, but it is hardly an image of *combat*. The deaths of those who are killed by Y may be justified in the eyes of those whose society has suffered the attacks, but unless the interaction between the two groups passes "a minimal threshold of intensity and duration," an intensity beyond that of "internal disturbances and tensions, such as riots, isolated and sporadic acts of violence and other acts of a similar nature," the context in which it is proper to talk about the privilege of killing combatants does not apply.[55] Use of the military model to justify targeted killing is not easy or straightforward. We cannot just *say* we are at war with a given organization and then take on the privilege of targeting its members.

Harold Koh, former dean of the Yale Law School and legal counsel in the State Department in the Obama administration, maintained in a speech to the American Society of International Law in 2010 that targeted killing is just a different form of combat.

> [A]s a matter of international law, the United States is in an armed conflict with al-Qaeda, as well as the Taliban and associated forces, in response to the horrific 9/11 attacks, and may use force consistent with its inherent right to self-defense under international law.[56]

55. Alston, "Report of the Special Rapporteur," quoting Additional Protocol II.
56. Koh, "The Obama Administration and International Law."

According to Koh, it is appropriate to lethally target individuals belonging to al-Qaeda as combatants, just as one would target soldiers in an opposing army. As we shall see in Part V, he thinks it does not matter that we target these combatants one by one and name by name. But his argument can't really get off the ground unless an appropriate context of armed conflict is properly established.

The point being made here is not that incidents of targeted killing don't *look* like combat killings. That is no doubt important: As Nils Melzer observes, almost all targeted killings are "carried out while the targeted person is not visibly engaged in active combat."[57] But it is a separate point, and we will explore it in Part V. My present point is that the justifiability of killing on the military model doesn't even arise unless there is already some intensity of fighting in the background.

There is a reason for this, and it is not just a technicality.[58] The privilege of killing in combat represents a concession that international law has made to the exigencies of an otherwise ungovernable situation—large-scale organized fighting, a situation of conflict and horror—in which the prospects for restraint are quite meager. It is partly a matter of recognizing that people, once plunged into a situation of armed conflict, cannot reasonably be expected to refrain from the use of lethal force both defensively and aggressively. This is a dreadful but inevitable acknowledgment: we switch from a categorical prohibition to privileging some

57. Melzer, *Targeted Killing in International Law*, 56.
58. In what follows, I have benefited from many conversations with a graduate student, Marcela Prieto Rudolphy, working at NYU under my supervision. She is not responsible for my formulations here. See also Waldron, "Deep Morality and the Laws of War."

forms of killing, and we try (if we can) to regulate *that*. What happens then is that international humanitarian law responds to the horror of such situations by delimiting both the scope of the acknowledged privilege to kill and the scope of the corresponding liability of those who can properly be regarded as having distinguished themselves, as combatants, from others who may be caught up in the situation. That's the basis of the principle of distinction between combatant and civilian. But it is not just a matter of who is a combatant and who is not. The notion of empowering a combatant to kill other combatants or rendering a combatant liable to be killed by other combatants makes no sense except against the background of the sort of conflict that elicits the reluctant recognition of this privilege. We don't base any of this on moral judgments about who is good, who is bad, and who is deserving of death. We base it on the exigencies of a situation in which the restraint required by the ordinary rules about homicide cannot reasonably be expected to prevail and other bases for restraint must be established.

Unfortunately, most defenses of targeted killing—at least those that use the military model—make no attempt to address this aspect of the situation. For them it is enough that the interaction between soldier and terrorist can be crammed into the categories of international humanitarian law so that the attribution of "combatant" status makes the one liable to be slaughtered by the other. And that is unsatisfactory, for most contexts of targeted killing are contexts in which it is *not* unreasonable for the person or organization with deadly weaponry (drones or a death squad) to refrain for the time being from the use of lethal force.

2. Law Enforcement

If the military model proves unsatisfactory, can targeted killing be justified on a law enforcement model? Not easily, to be sure, because in law enforcement, although we are supposed to hunt down our adversaries, we are not supposed to kill them. But there are exceptions. State officials are authorized to use deadly force in two situations. The first is direct enforcement of the law by police or other officers: firing on people to defend innocents, rescue hostages, or stop miscreants from escaping arrest. The second is the execution of sentences of capital punishment, in those states that allow it. As possible analogies to help the justification of targeted killing, these are quite different, and we will consider them separately.

(I) LAW ENFORCEMENT JUSTIFICATIONS IN THE LAW OF HOMICIDE

Terrorist acts are crimes, and counter-terrorism may be thought of as law enforcement. Does this mean targeted killing should be treated as part of the law enforcement paradigm too?

It may if the killing is calculated to prevent an imminent terrorist act—shooting a man who is about to throw a grenade, for example, or explode a suicide bomb. Such a killing by a police officer would be justified as defense of self and others. However, as a matter of law, such actions are governed by a standard of very strict necessity and immediacy "which allows for no delay in responding to a concrete and grave threat."[59] In the nature of things, most targeted

59. Melzer, *Targeted Killing in International Law*, 59.

killings cannot plausibly be presented as a response to a threat that is imminent in this sense. The planning and deliberation that targeting typically involves happens well away from the time and place of attempted terrorist atrocities. Targeted killing is usually directed at individuals involved in the leadership of terrorist organizations, or those who have committed, incited, or directed terrorist atrocities in the past or are expected to do so in the future. To sustain any sort of analogy with law enforcement prevention, targeted killing requires the development of an extended notion of imminence, sometimes called "elongated imminence."[60] The argument is that the heinousness of these atrocities means we can't afford to wait to prevent them until they are just about to happen. What is really meant, however, is that weapons like drones and the organization of death squads would be mostly futile as counterterrorist measures if conventional notions of imminence were required. "Elongated imminence" often turns out to mean nothing much more than a speculative judgment that the killing of this person right now may make it somewhat less likely that a terrorist atrocity will take place at some undetermined time in the future. Used in this sense, imminence no longer adds any constraint to the more generous notion of counter-terrorist efficacy. And against those who use this analogy, it has to be said that nothing comparable

---

60. Klaidman, *Kill or Capture*, 219, attributes the concept of "elongated imminence" to Harold Koh. See also Yoo, "Using Force," and Holder, "Remarks of Eric Holder at Northwestern," 196. See also Amos Guiora and Laurie Blank, "Targeted Killing's 'Flexibility' Doctrine that Enables US to Flout the Law of War," *The Guardian*, August 10, 2012.

would be countenanced for a moment under the rule of law in regular law enforcement.

Police officers don't just prevent crimes; they apprehend criminals, and sometimes they use deadly force when suspects resist arrest. Can this form the basis of an analogy? Targeted killing operations are sometimes euphemized as "kill or capture" operations. If the threat or use of deadly force is genuinely ancillary to an attempt at capture, accompanied by demands for surrender and so forth, then maybe it is justified on this basis. But with most targeted killings, certainly those involving drones, capture is more or less out of the question. Killing is the raison d'être of the operation and defenders of targeted killing acknowledge this in their use of the military analogy.[61] (Notice, by the way, that the availability of quarter in combat is quite different in its logic from the element of arrest in the law enforcement model. In the latter case, capture is the primary goal and killing is ancillary; in the former case, capture is at best ancillary to an enterprise that is lethal in its whole conception.)

(II) EXECUTION AS JUSTICE
What about the other dimension of the law enforcement model—targeted killing as punishment? We hear the rhetoric of retribution sometimes in cases of targeted killing.

61. Alston, "Report of the Special Rapporteur," §§32–33: "A State killing is legal only if it is required to protect life . . . and there is no other means, such as capture or nonlethal incapacitation, of preventing that threat to life (making lethal force necessary). . . . This means that under human rights law, a targeted killing in the sense of an intentional, premeditated and deliberate killing by law enforcement officials cannot be legal because, unlike in armed conflict, it is never permissible for killing to be the sole objective of an operation."

From time to time, targeted killing is referred to as execution; for instance, an Israeli commentator refers to targeted killing as "a day-to-day execution weapon in the 'war on terror'" and "a covert policy of political capital punishment."[62] So too with the Americans. When the news came that a team of Navy SEALs had shot and killed Osama bin Laden at night in his compound in Abbottabad, Pakistan, President Obama exulted: "Justice was done."[63] And after the killing on January 6, 2019, of Jamal al-Badawi, who masterminded the attack on the USS *Cole* in 2000, President Trump tweeted that the American military had "delivered justice" for those who were lost and wounded in the attack on the USS *Cole*. Rhetoric like this captures the retaliatory aspect of targeted killing.

Is this anything more than vengeful triumphalism? Most countries do not countenance capital punishment, but some do. Even among those who repudiate the death penalty, there is a sense that if execution is ever justified, it is justified for terrorist outrages. The analogy with execution works to a certain extent. Like targeted killing, capital punishment involves the killing of named and identified individuals. A person is identified officially as a wrongdoer, and we arrange for his death specifically. We keep track of him by name and by continuous physical custody, from the time of his sentencing to the time of his death. We target

---

62. Menuchin, "The Case of Israel," 205.
63. Barack Obama, "Osama Bin Laden Dead," White House, May 2, 2011: "And finally, last week, I determined that we had enough intelligence to take action, and authorized an operation to get Osama bin Laden and bring him to justice. . . . [O]n nights like this one, we can say to those families who have lost loved ones to al Qaeda's terror: Justice has been done."

him specifically. We want to be very sure about the person we are executing: he must be the same person who was tried and sentenced to death. *He* is the one who committed a murder and so *he*—the exact same person—must be the one to suffer retribution for that crime. That is the logic of retribution in the criminal justice paradigm.

One difference, of course, in the case of targeted killing is that the targeted person is *not* in our custody from the time that it has been determined he should die to the time of his death.[64] A more important difference is the absence of the due process that the rule of law requires and that a trial provides.[65] That is why targeted killing is sometimes referred to as "extrajudicial killing."[66] It is not just a matter of whether a particular institution—the judiciary—is involved. What's involved here is the absence of process itself, or the use of procedures in the case of targeted killings that are (to say the least) relaxed, considering that someone's life is at stake.

Many of those who work within the law enforcement paradigm say that due process is essential.[67] Michael Gross has suggested that "any party practicing named killing must preserve due process either by maintaining judicial review or by conducting trials in absentia."[68] He notes also,

64. For the extra-custodial aspect, see Melzer, *Targeted Killing in International Law*, 4.
65. For the importance of the procedural dimension, as well as formal and substantial dimensions, of the rule of law, see Waldron, "The Rule of Law and the Importance of Procedure."
66. See, e.g., Murphy and Radsan, "Due Process and Targeted Killing of Terrorists," 408–409. For sustained consideration, see Alston, "Report of the Special Rapporteur."
67. E.g., Gross, "Assassination and Targeted Killing," 324–325.
68. Gross, "Assassination and Targeted Killing," 324–325.

in response to a comment by Professor Meisels, that the fact that this would be difficult is not usually treated as an argument against such a suggestion put forward as a matter of principle.[69] We are not supposed to execute people without trial just because conducting a trial would be difficult or dangerous.

One possible answer to this comes from Nigel Biggar, professor of Moral and Pastoral Theology at Oxford. Biggar has suggested that certain targeted killings may be understood as acts of justice notwithstanding their procedural irregularity. In a letter to *The Times*, he wrote:

> Those who argue that Osama bin Laden should have been brought to trial, rather than killed, tend to suppose that justice only takes place in courts. . . . [W]hen soldiers mount a highly discriminate operation (rather than a more risky missile attack) in order to put an end to the active threat posed by an inveterate and murderous enemy, when they have good reason to allow him no chance of escape, when he does not immediately and unequivocally surrender, and when they therefore kill him, justice is . . . done. If that is indeed what happened in Abbottabad, then justice was done. Rough justice may be rough, but it is still justice.[70]

Biggar is right to insist on the category of "rough justice" and on its possible application in warfare.[71] But justice can

69. Gross, "Assassination and Targeted Killing," 324–325.

70. Nigel Biggar, letter to *The Times* (London), May 10, 2011.

71. See O'Donovan, *The Just War Revisited*, 18, for the suggestion that war itself can sometimes be an act of justice, where no more formal procedure is possible. He compares its roughness to an urgent surgical operation conducted by amateurs with a penknife on a mountainside where qualified surgeons and hospitals are unavailable.

be "rough" in two senses. It can be rough in the sense that there was a rough version of the procedure that justice would ordinarily require. Or it can be rough in the sense that it omits any element of procedure whatsoever and assesses the killing purely on an outcome basis. The killing of Osama bin Laden was like the latter. Bin Laden's remaining alive after the terrorist attacks of September 11, 2001, was an injustice; his being dead in May 2011 is justice, from a consequentialist point of view. However, not only was the execution "rough," but also nothing remotely approaching a trial was held, not even in absentia. Maybe a trial, even a rough version of a trial, was unnecessary because we all know bin Laden was guilty. I guess that is right, though perhaps it is worth reflecting on the fact that one reason we have trials is because sometimes "things we all know to be true" turn out to be false. I wish Biggar had said something to this point. We do sometimes talk of justice in this purely outcome-focused non-procedural way.[72] Whether we should be comfortable with this as a general approach to justice or as an understanding of targeted killing is another matter.[73]

72. Toward the end of the Second World War, the Allies pledged themselves to "pursue [Nazi leaders] to the uttermost ends of the earth . . . in order that justice may be done." But Churchill and other British politicians thought that summary execution would be a better way of doing justice than a formal trial. See Ian Cobain, "Britain Favoured Execution over Nuremberg Trials for Nazi Leaders," *The Guardian*, October 25, 2012.

73. Cf. Holder, "Attorney-General Eric Holder Speaks at Northwestern," 232. Too often, the logic of rough justice is John Yoo's statement to the effect that applying procedural guarantees to al-Qaeda terrorists "would gravely impede the killing or capture of the enemy" (cited in McDonald, *Enemies Known and Unknown*, 70).

I am not saying that the target of attack ought to receive the full panoply of procedural safeguards afforded in a criminal trial.[74] In the years following 9/11, the Americans set up military commissions to determine the guilt or innocence of those whom they had detained in the war on terror, and it was acknowledged that the commissions would follow procedures that were less rigorous than those laid down for either criminal trials in civilian law or courts-martial. In the case of *Hamdan v. Rumsfeld*, the US Supreme Court accepted that the exigencies of the war on terror might require the attenuation of some procedural safeguards, though it insisted that the latitude here was quite narrow and that the case for exigency had to be exactingly established.[75] The Court countenanced, in effect, a sort of "due process lite" for terrorist trials, including the rudiments of the right to an impartial tribunal, the right to challenge evidence, and the right to put one's own side of the story that English jurisprudence describes as "natural justice." Debate about this limited version of procedural due process continues. But it is not engaged at all in the case of targeted killings. The problem with targeted killing is not due process lite; it is due process zero. Whatever process there is in the case of these killings is purely political: a determination of the strategic desirability of each particular killing and a demand for assurance that few or no innocent civilians will be killed or wounded in the attack.

74. See the discussion in Holder, "Attorney-General Eric Holder Speaks at Northwestern," 195, addressing different forms of due process for different circumstances.
75. Hamdan v. Rumsfeld 548 U.S. 557 (2006).

3. A Hybrid Model?

Both opponents and defenders of the current practice of targeted killing observe that it spans and blurs the line between the armed conflict model and the law enforcement model. As we saw at the beginning of this section, the naming and targeting elements seem redolent of the law enforcement model, while the peremptory killing and lack of due process are associated more with the armed conflict model. Philip Alston calls the blurring of these categories "highly problematic."[76] But others defend it as a rational response to the realities of modern conflict.

Sam Issacharoff and Rick Pildes say the blurring is a virtue. Their view rests, partly, on *structural* grounds as a response to changes in technology and in the nature of modern warfare. "We are now moving to a world that implicitly or explicitly requires the individuation of enemy responsibility of specific enemy persons before the use of military force is considered justified."[77] They say too that "there is a great deal about the preexisting laws of war that seems poorly addressed to the current circumstances.[78] What circumstances? Issacharoff and Pildes cite the asymmetry of most modern warfare, the involvement of ill-defined nonstate forces comprising irregular and sometimes stateless combatants whose military doctrine involves violating principles of distinction between combatants and civilians both as to their own targets and as to their own visibility. Issacharoff and Pildes also mention the availability of new

76. Alston, "Report of the Special Rapporteur," §3.
77. Issacharoff and Pildes, "Targeted Warfare," 1523.
78. Issacharoff and Pildes, "Targeted Warfare," 1534.

technology, including large and powerful databases and (obviously) drones capable of "surgical" targeting. In what they call an "inadequately appreciated transformation," these "unavoidable structural forces . . . drive uses of military force against modern terrorism [that] come to depend on individuated judgments of responsibility"[79] Modern targeted killing makes "fine-grained distinctions among and between enemy soldiers."[80]

Issacharoff and Pildes take this analysis one step further when they argue that, as governments "individuat[e] the responsibility of specific enemies and target[] only those engaged in specific acts or employed in specific roles," they are making "what appear to be (and in reality, are) quasi-adjudicative judgments based on highly specific facts about the alleged actions of particular individuals."[81]

> [O]nce warfare interjects the question of why a particular enemy is being targeted, and whether the targeting corresponds to the threats presented by a particular individual, the inquiry starts to take on the feel of individualized adjudication. . . . A tremendous premium is immediately placed on what we might call "adjudicative facts"—is this the person who did X?[82]

---

79. Issacharoff and Pildes, "Targeted Warfare," 1534, 1523, and 1531.
80. Issacharoff and Pildes, "Targeted Warfare," 1534, 1569. See also Blum, "The Dispensable Lives of Soldiers," 74, for the view that the "changing nature of the battlefield" is creating a military environment that "is becoming increasingly dependent on case-by-case judgments."
81. Issacharoff and Pildes, "Targeted Warfare," 1524.
82. Issacharoff and Pildes, "Targeted Warfare," 1530.

And so, blurring the lines between the law enforcement and military models is not only inevitable but also desirable.

Should this convince us? I think not. It remains the case that the decision to kill is made in the executive branch in the absence of anything remotely recognizable as due process. Or if it is a fragment of due process, it is more like the decisions that are made in a prosecutor's office than in a court of law.[83] Is this just a matter of which institutions are involved?

> If government is making such quasi-adjudicative judgments of individual responsibility before using military force, should it be required to use the more traditional institutions and processes through which similar ascriptions of individual moral and legal responsibility are traditionally made—namely, the criminal law?[84]

The answer given by Pildes and Issacharoff is a clear no. The adjudicative function need not be performed by any particular institution.[85] The important thing is that *some* sort of legalization—a phrase they use is "legal-style guidance"[86]—bleeds into military practice:

> The military . . . is already in the process of trying to generate procedural protections, analogous to those used in more traditional adjudicative settings but adapted to the unique context of military force, that provide sufficient accuracy and legitimacy to ensure that individuated attributions of

83. Brennan, "The Efficacy and Ethics of US Counterterrorism Strategy," 36.
84. Issacharoff and Pildes, "Targeted Warfare," 1570.
85. Issacharoff and Pildes, "Targeted Warfare," 1537.
86. Issacharoff and Pildes, "Targeted Warfare," 1581.

responsibility are being made through credible processes and structures to make them as accurate and fair as possible.[87]

Should we really be as easy-going as this about due process when life and death are at stake? Even if one were to accept the idea of "rough justice" or "due process lite," there is nothing here corresponding *even roughly* to the natural justice requirement of *audi alteram partem* (listen to the other side). Here is what we know about process in the United States. The president and a committee of his high national security advisors maintain one or more "kill lists" of persons whose continued existence is deemed to be not in the best interests of the United States. The lists contain names, photographs, and dossiers,[88] drawn from received intelligence. Names on these lists are ranked according to the prioritization of their destruction. From time to time, as the opportunity presents itself, names are plucked from the list and assigned to officials who arrange for the killing of the named individuals. If there is any sort of devil's advocate element in such protocols, it has to do not with a defense for the potential target but with the danger of collateral casualties—innocent civilians.[89] That is certainly an important consideration. But we wouldn't regard it as a remotely adequate substitute for due process in any other case that involved the taking of a suspect's life.

There is a chilling note in the Issacharoff and Pildes's defense of the hybrid model. They say it is "inevitable that

87. Issacharoff and Pildes, "Targeted Warfare," 1532.
88. Jo Becker and Scott Shane, "Secret 'Kill List' Proves a Test of Obama's Principles and Will," *New York Times*, May 29, 2012: "The mug shots and brief biographies resembled a high school yearbook layout."
89. See Issacharoff and Pildes, "Targeted Warfare," 1591–1592.

the boundaries between the military system and the judicial system will become more permeable than in the past. . . . The considerations that have traditionally informed one will spill over into the other—and vice versa."[90] If I understand this, we should expect the hybridization to work in both directions—some proceduralization of the military domain (as we have just seen) but also some militarization of the way regular criminal proceedings are conducted. Issacharoff and Pildes's "vice versa" seems to mean not only that "military force inevitably begins to look justified in similar terms to the uses of punishment in the criminal justice system,"[91] but also that criminal justice will start to become more militarized. There has always been a concern in regard to irregular tactics of this kind that they will blow back and undermine the integrity of the institutions we have already.[92]

We will look at this again in Part VI, in our discussion of the extension of the logic of targeted killing into areas of enmity other than counter-terrorism. Right now, the point is *contagion*: by loosening our inhibitions on the government killing its individual enemies, we may upset other

90. Issacharoff and Pildes, "Drones and the Dilemma of Modern Warfare," 392.
91. Issacharoff and Pildes, "Drones and the Dilemma of Modern Warfare," 391.
92. This concern was voiced by Edmund Burke in his apprehensions about the effect on England of the unchecked abuses of Warren Hastings in India (Burke, "Speech in General Reply"). It was also voiced also by Arendt, *The Origins of Totalitarianism*, 185–186, 215–216, and 221, who offered the tradition of racist and oppressive administration in the African colonies as part of her explanation of the easy acceptance of the most atrocious modes of oppression in mid-20th-century Europe.

inhibitions that have long been regarded as key to our system of justice. To put it bluntly, we are facing the possible emergence of extrajudicial killings in areas where we would once have hoped and expected that the rule of law would prevail.

Like Nils Melzer, I think the hybrid model "does not withstand closer scrutiny."[93] As Blum and Heymann observe, "More than any other counterterrorism tactic, targeted killing operations display the tension between addressing terrorism as a crime and addressing it as war."[94] If they cannot maintain the due process lite position, defenders of targeted killing have no choice but to revert to Harold Koh's position, noted earlier, that combatant targets are owed no process whatsoever.[95] But if the combat model is in itself unsatisfactory—as I think it is—then the practice is not redeemed by importing an essentially notional element of adjudication into the process.[96]

***

The two models we have considered and the hybrid version are cited to justify targeted killing. Between them, they try to reconcile us to targeted killing as a practice conducted

93. Melzer, *Targeted Killing in International Law*, 66. See also Kretzmer, "Targeted Killing of Suspected Terrorists," 201–204.

94. Blum and Heymann, "Law and Policy of Targeted Killing," 145.

95. Koh, "The Obama Administration and International Law": "[A] state that is engaged in an armed conflict or in legitimate self-defense is not required to provide targets with legal process before the state may use lethal force."

96. On Koh's comment that "drones can deliver justice," see McKelvey, "Defending the Drones," 203.

by the state in our name by casting it in a good or at least a familiar light. In fact, targeted killing doesn't fit either of these models—or not exactly. Other analogies are available, which may fit a bit better. But they make targeted killing look even less reputable, and they are much less likely to reconcile us to it.

***

4. Assassination

A term that American defenders of targeted killing strive to avoid is *assassination*. (In other countries there is less inhibition.) Targeted killing originates as a decapitation method, a way of going after high-level terrorist organizers—sometimes in circumstances where the targets are not themselves combatants, but political, ideological, or religious leaders. As Miller puts it:

> Targeted killing is a species of assassination; specifically, it is assassination that takes place in the overall context of a war— but not necessarily or even typically in a theatre of war—and consists only of the killing of political leaders who are also in the chain of command of the military forces engaged in the war in question.[97]

However, the term is often avoided because of American administrative regulations prohibiting state agencies from engaging in killings under that description. Pursuant to

97. Miller, "The Ethics of Assassination and Targeted Killing," 317.

the report of the Church Committee in 1976 investigating abuses by US intelligence agencies, an executive order of the Reagan administration stipulated: "No person employed by or acting on behalf of the United States Government shall engage in, or conspire to engage in, assassination."[98]

Although Reagan's executive order provided no definition of "assassination" and little to no guidance for interpretation, at least three definitional distinctions have been put forward. First, a further executive order—the so-called Parks memorandum of 1989—distinguished targeted killing from assassination by saying that the ban on assassination was only against "covert acts of murder for political reasons."[99] This puts a lot of strain on the word "political," which it may not be able to bear in the context of counter-terrorism.

A second distinction takes us back to the war model. According to Seamus Miller, "One way of differentiating targeted killings from assassination is to restrict the former to armed conflicts."[100] In connection with this we might pursue a distinction between political and military leaders. But this leaves unclear how to categorize the killing of someone like Anwar al-Awlaki, whom we have mentioned a few times already. Al-Awlaki was not a combatant in any sense of that term, although he was an effective propagandist for jihad.

A third approach is to distinguish assassination as necessarily involving killing by treacherous means, for example by somebody in disguise. (Some Israeli targeted killings

---

98. US Executive Order 12333 (1981) §2.11.
99. This further order—Executive Order 11905—was signed in 1976 by President Ford. See Banks, "Regulating Drones," 136–138.
100. Miller, "The Ethics of Assassination and Targeted Killing," 315.

involve stealth and covert operations.) Whether killing by
drone is relevantly analogous to this, from a moral point of
view, is an open question.

On the whole, I disagree with the definitional approach.
It is a bit panic stricken in its assumption that, if targeted
killing *were* to be identified with assassination in some
or all cases, then that would be a way of losing the argument. I think it is a mistake to try either to define targeted
killing as justified by definition or to assume that assassination is always wrong. It is better to acknowledge the
obvious resonance between assassination and at least some
cases of targeted killing and to treat as an open question
whether assassination in these circumstances can possibly
be justified.[101]

For assassination is not always seen as a bad thing.
In any argument of this kind, we have to face the inevitable Hitler hypothetical: "Arguably the assassination of
Hitler by Colonel Graf Claus von Stauffenberg and his co-
conspirators in 1944 would have been morally justifiable,
even if not legally allowed."[102] However, it is not enough to
just pull out the Hitler card. I have encountered respectable scholars who think that asking, "What about Hitler?"
clinches the argument on targeted killing. But the Hitler
example has to be integrated into the argument in a way
that speaks to both the nature and the quantity of the cases
we are concerned with. Natural law adherent Michael Moore

101. Blum and Heymann, "Law and Policy of Targeted Killing,"
147, have no hesitation in describing targeted killing as "the deliberate
assassination of a known terrorist."
102. Miller, "The Ethics of Assassination and Targeted Killing," 312.
For a similar hypothetical about Stalin, see Altman and Wellman, "From
Humanitarian Intervention to Assassination."

draws an important "distinction between justifying an individual decision to target a particular terrorist for assassination, on the one hand, and justifying the general practice of targeted killings, on the other."[103] Our task in this book is to think about the justification of an entire practice, not an incident. If we really want to work with the Hitler hypothetical, then the question we have to ask is this: Beginning from the Hitler example, what generalization—on the scale of hundreds or thousands of killings—is envisaged? For what other cases, not quite like Hitler's or differing from Hitler's in substantial respects, is targeted killing appropriate? And how far down the terrorist chain of command does the Hitler analogy descend?

5. Death Squads

In El Salvador in the early 1980s, during that country's civil war, the government set up "death squads" (*Escuadróns de la muerte*) and maintained "death lists," from which victims would be selected to be killed.[104] The victims targeted by these procedures were usually leaders of or known participants in political opposition at the state or national level. The killings were brutal, and they were partly intended to terrorize the populations among whom the individual targets lived and worked, to frighten them away from political opposition. This we may think of as *the classic case* of the death squad. Is it a helpful analogue for understanding the American or the Israeli practice of targeted killing? It is not

---

103. Moore, "Targeted Killings and the Morality of Hard Choices."
104. For a good account, see Americas Watch 1993 report, *El Salvador's Decade of Terror*.

going to be helpful in legitimizing the practice, but it may be of some assistance in explaining the sense of unease that surrounds it in certain circles.

"Death lists" and "death squads" are not the terminology used by officials to characterize the practices I want to address. Our death lists are sometimes called "kill lists," which is not much better,[105] or "kill-or-capture lists" (a phrase in which "the capture part has become largely theoretical").[106] *Der Spiegel* reports that in Afghanistan the American death list is referred to euphemistically as the "Joint Prioritized Effects List."[107] The death squads are sometimes called "hit squads,"[108] though usually the language of "squads" is avoided altogether.

Is it a fair analogy?[109] Some have thought so. Seamus Milne of the *Guardian* talks of drone crews as "hi-tech

---

105. Jo Becker and Scott Shane, "Secret 'Kill List' Proves a Test of Obama's Principles and Will," *New York Times*, May 29, 2012.

106. See Steve Coll, "Kill or Capture," *The New Yorker*, August 2, 2012.

107. "Obama's Lists: Dubious History of Targeted Killings in Afghanistan," *Der Spiegel*, December 28, 2014.

108. Are, *Analyzing the Drone Debates*, 3.

109. In 2004, there were credible reports of the United States having helped implement what was called the "Salvador Option" in Iraq under the auspices of its counter-insurgency program in that country. (The claim is that the United States helped organize and train squads of Shia special police commandos or militia-men who killed or captured and tortured large numbers of Sunni insurgents.) See Mona Mahmood and others, "From El Salvador to Iraq: Washington's Man Behind Brutal Police squads," *The Guardian*, March 6, 2013. See also Roland Watson, "El Salvador-style 'Death Squads' to Be Deployed by US against Iraq Militants," *The Times* (London), January 10, 2005. See generally Bennis, "Drones and Assassination," 54–56.

death squads,"[110] and he said this about special forces on the ground in Afghanistan:

> What emerges is both the scale of covert killings by US special forces—running 20 raids a night at one point in Afghanistan—and the unmistakable fact that these units are operating as death squads, whose bloodletting is dressed up as "targeted killings" of terrorists and insurgents for the benefit of a grateful nation back home.[111]

Conservative law professor Robert Delahunty worries about the administration's brushing aside objections to the practice. Referring to former State Department legal advisor Harold Koh, he has said that

> [i]f Koh returns to the legality of targeted killing of al Qaeda and Taliban terrorist suspects, he should deal far more adequately with the human rights objection that targeting an un-uniformed combatant is akin to outlawing and sentencing him without trial—something more like killing individuals by *paramilitary death squads* than ordinary military combat.[112]

Delahunty thinks there may be persuasive answers to that objection. But he acknowledges the problem is a serious one and deserves something more than Koh's rather shallow response.

Talk of "death squads" makes our national security and military apparatus sound sinister and brutal. In a

110. Seamus Milne, "Comment: The US drone campaign is fuelling, not fighting, terror," *The Guardian*, May 30, 2012.

111. Seamas Milne, "UK Up to Its Neck in US Dirty Wars," *The Guardian*, December 5, 2013.

112. Delahunty, "Obama's War Law," 83 (my emphasis).

2016 paper, I considered the analogy at length and asked whether American practices of targeted killing were redeemed by the many differences that distinguish them from the classic case of death squads in (say) El Salvador in the early 1980s.[113] Some differences, I said, were trivial, albeit colorful. We think of the classic death squad as a poorly disciplined bunch of brutal and unshaven men in sweaty uniforms, cruel and sadistic in their actions beyond perhaps what their assignment requires. But deodorant and air-conditioning take us only so far. It is true that no one accuses drone operators of sadism,[114] and the brutality that their actions involve is simply the brutality of the kinetic means they use for sudden and lethal strikes.

What about the contrast between our targeted killings and the endemic indiscipline of classic death squads? Here the picture is not so straightforward. For a while, American drone operators were acting outside the military chain of command, involving intelligence operatives rather than or as well as military personnel. And in Israel, a great many targeted killings are carried out not by members of the Israel Defense Forces but by intelligence operatives. Strictly speaking, such operatives count as unlawful combatants,

---

113. Waldron, "Death Squads and Death Lists."

114. There was a recent report on the brutality of SEALs teams compared with their army counterparts in Afghanistan, indicating that those involved in targeted killing find it harder to return to duties that require more sensitivity and conciliation than those who have mostly not been so involved. See Nicholas Kulish, Christopher Drew, and Matthew Rosenberg, "Navy SEALs, a Beating Death and Claims of a Cover-Up," *New York Times*, December 17, 2015. For more recent worries, see Barbara Starr, "Top US Navy SEAL Tells Commanders in Letter: 'We have a problem,'" CNN, August 1, 2019.

unless they can be deemed part of legitimate military units. True, this is not the sort of indiscipline we envisage in the classic paradigm. Still it may be important because it illustrates the point that targeted killings by our government have not always conformed to a strict military model.[115]

In the classic case of death squads, the killings are "politically motivated murders" of regime opponents carried out in the regime's own territory.[116] This is a striking difference. As far as I am aware, targeted killings by American forces have never taken place in American territory and, even when directed at American citizens, they have taken place in foreign countries. American use of targeted killing has not been pursuant to any agenda associated with political authoritarianism as it is in the classic cases. In Israel, obviously, the situation is more complicated—if only because of the ambiguous jurisdictional and political relationship between the West Bank and Israel proper.

Moreover, the contrast between the killing of terrorists by US death squads and the killing of political opponents in the classic model is complicated by two points. First, targeted killing is used by the United States not just to eliminate members of bona fide terrorist organizations like al-Qaeda, but also to eliminate insurgents rising up against our forces or against the regimes that we have been trying to establish in Afghanistan and Iraq. So, for example, though

115. See also Kenneth Anderson, "More Predator Drone Debate in the *Wall Street Journal*, and What the Obama Administration Should Do as a Public Legal Position," *The Volokh Conspiracy*, January 9, 2010: "The reasons for using civilian agents versus military personnel are complicated—sometimes involving deniability."
116. Sluka, "Death from Above," 2.

the Taliban has had strong connections with al-Qaeda in the past, the use of targeted killings against Taliban leaders is related mainly to their violent attempt to overthrow the US-sponsored regime in Kabul (initially to resist its own overthrow) or to establish pockets of resistance to its authority. In that endeavor, the Taliban sometimes uses methods that can be labeled terroristic, and the same can certainly be said about ISIS and other insurgent forces in Syria and Iraq. But whether or not these violent insurgents can plausibly be *labeled* terrorists, they are plainly not terrorists in a sense that would distinguish them importantly from political opponents of regimes we are supporting or political opponents of our presence in the countries where they operate.

When unfavorable comparisons are made in regard to features of American practice or policy, one often hears the indignant complaint: "Are you calling these practices *morally equivalent*?" People say this without much idea of what "morally equivalent" means. If they mean, "Is the one set of practices as bad or as evil as the other?" one can answer, "Probably not." *Tens* of thousands of people were killed by El Salvadorian death squads, and only thousands have been killed so far by America's targeted killings, and the terroristic and authoritarian elements were no doubt much worse in the former case. But if the "moral equivalence" question means something like, "Does the one set of practices raise the same sort of concerns as the other?" the answer may be, "Yes." For in both cases there are concerns of exactly the same kind about the state's relation to these killings: the killings are extrajudicial, they stand in a problematic relation to privileged killings in combat, and they betoken a form of state practice—drawing up lists of enemies and trying to kill them off one by one—that is radically at odds with how a democratic constitutional state is supposed to operate. Because our practice is much more like such activities than we ought to be comfortable with, the classification of targeted killing in the same category as the classic case of death squads may be instructive in reflections upon our own practices.

For suppose we were considering *classic* death squads on the El Salvadorian model and wondering how to categorize *them*. I don't think we would for a moment countenance an argument that the classic use of death lists and death squads could be put into either of the two categories we considered at the beginning of this chapter: law enforcement or legitimate acts of war or any hybrid of the two. Classic death squad practice would strike us as a distinct form of the relation between state and deadly force—and a distinctly disreputable form. Since that is so, then it is at the very least an open question whether *our* practices of targeted killing should be put into that distinctive category too.

PART V: NAMED AND TARGETED

Enough of analogies. Let us go now to the core of the argument and consider the very idea of *naming and targeting* individuals for death. Targeted killing is, as Blum and Heymann put it, "an entire military operation that is planned and executed against a particular, known person."[117] The logic of targeting killing is that the existence

---

117. Blum and Heymann, "Law and Policy of Targeted Killing," 147.

of a certain named individual is deemed incompatible with the best interests of the state.

Hunting down someone whose name we know is a familiar feature of law enforcement operations, though such operations seldom end in that person's death. But I want to consider the role of naming and targeting primarily in the context of the military analogy because that is where the issue has been most directly addressed by defenders of targeted killing. So our discussion in this chapter picks up from our consideration of the military analogy in Part IV.

Targeted killing looks different from the usual image of combat. Traditional combat involves mass and anonymous killing. "In military hostilities," writes Nils Meltzer in his study of targeted killing, "the killing of human beings is [usually] understood as an impersonal act motivated by the military necessity of achieving victory over the adversary in an inter-collective confrontation."[118] Or as Michael Gross puts it: "Soldiers are vulnerable solely because they are members of their nation's armed services. Their vulnerability has nothing to do with the threat they pose personally. Instead, they are part of a collective, organizational threat that waxes and wanes during warfare."[119] Considered in itself, a targeted killing looks like the "conceptual antithesis" of the "depersonalized, inter-collective warfare" that traditional hostilities involve.[120] But defenders of the practice say that naming an individual enemy and hunting him down—hunting *him* in particular—does not really differ in any important moral

118. Melzer, *Targeted Killing in International Law*, 434–435.
119. Gross, "Assassination and Targeted Killing," 329.
120. Melzer, *Targeted Killing in International Law*, 435.

or legal respect from the acts of killing that are clearly privileged already in the course of ordinary armed conflict. Crudely, the argument goes: "If you're allowed to kill someone *anyway*, what does it matter whether you know their name or not?"

Accordingly, many defenders of the practice we are considering refuse to accord any validity to questions that focus on the sheer fact of naming. In his March 2010 talk to the American Society of International Law, Harold Koh considered a number of possible objections and he answered some of them. He was quite dismissive of the one we are considering in this chapter:[121]

> [S]ome have suggested that the very act of targeting a particular leader of an enemy force in an armed conflict must violate the laws of war. But individuals who are part of such an armed group are belligerents and, therefore, lawful targets under international law.

For a precedent, he cited the targeting and killing of a high-ranking Japanese officer, Admiral Isoroku Yamamoto, in the Second World War. Koh said:

> During World War II . . . American aviators tracked and shot down the airplane carrying the architect of the Japanese attack on Pearl Harbor, who was also the leader of enemy forces in the Battle of Midway. This was a lawful operation then, and would be if conducted today.[122]

---

121. Koh, "The Obama Administration and International Law."
122. See the description in Miller, *Cartwheel: The Reduction of Rabaul*, 44.

A great many defenses of targeted killing refer to this example in one way or another. Sometimes the case of Admiral Yamamoto is cited as though it were a legal precedent establishing the lawfulness of this sort of targeted killing.[123] This is nonsense. The fact that something was done once before doesn't establish the lawfulness of its being done now. The matter was never tested in a court.[124] It is said that the legality of the attack on Yamamoto was uncontroversial at the time, so we can project that clear sense of lawfulness from the 1940s onto targeted killings in the present day.[125] In fact the decision to kill Yamamoto *was* quite controversial in 1943. Naval historian Craig Symonds says it was controversial on tactical grounds because it might disclose the codes the Americans had broken, but it was also controversial as a matter of principle.[126] He writes that Admiral

123. Daskal, "The Geography of the Battlefield," 1213: "[T]he main precedent upon which the United States relies to justify its lethal-targeting operations is the killing of Admiral Isoroku Yamamoto, the commander of the Imperial Japanese Navy's combined fleet in World War II, who was shot down over the Pacific while en route to several forward-operating bases." See also Turner, "An Insider's Look at the War on Terrorism," 487: "To mention but one precedent, during World War II the United States intentionally targeted an aircraft carrying Admiral Yamamoto."

124. Intriguingly, however, there is one Ninth Circuit case concerning the targeted killing of Admiral Yamamoto. Barber v. Widnall (Secretary of the Air Force) 78 F.3d 1419 (USCA 9th Circuit) concerned a pilot who wanted to receive some of the credit for shooting down the admiral's aircraft.

125. Delahunty and Yoo, in "What Is the Role of International Human Rights Law in the War on Terror?," 808, say of strikes like that against Yamamoto that "their legality has been accepted without significant controversy." Blum and Heymann, "Law and Policy of Targeted Killing," 150, talk of "the uncontroversial targeted killing of Japanese Admiral Isoroku Yamamoto."

126. Craig Symonds, *World War II at Sea*, 410–414.

Nimitz questioned its legality, and the story goes that the query went up to Roosevelt who made the final decision. Symonds adds: "And finally, there was the moral issue. Men died in combat every day, but to target a specific individual like this seemed more like assassination. Did the United States want to do that?"[127] The late John Paul Stevens, until recently an associate justice on the US Supreme Court, was one of the codebreakers who secured the information that formed the basis of the Yamamoto attack. He too was troubled by the prospect at the time and talked of it later. According to Diane Amann, "Stevens affirmed that the Yamamoto incident led him to conclude that '[t]he targeting of a particular individual with the intent to kill him was a lot different than killing a soldier in battle and dealing with a statistic.'"[128] Others maintain that the legality of the attack would be controversial today, taking place as it did so far from any active center of combat. Imagine a British strike in 1982 against an Argentine general as he flew to Mendoza or some other spot in Argentina remote from the Malvinas.[129] Or maybe the parties involved should have worried (as some worry today about the killing of Osama bin Laden) that the primary motive for targeting Yamamoto was retribution—he was the architect of the attack on Pearl Harbor—rather than military necessity.[130]

127. Craig Symonds, *World War II at Sea*, 411.

128. Amann, "John Paul Stevens, Human Rights Judge," 1583. See also Jeffrey Rosen, "The Dissenter: Justice John Paul Stevens," *New York Times*, September 23, 2007.

129. O'Connell, "The Choice of Law against Terrorism," 361.

130. Afsheen and Murphy, "The Evolution of Law and Policy for CIA Targeted Killing," 441: "President Franklin D. Roosevelt . . . ordered Admiral Yamamoto killed not because he was any Japanese sailor, but because he was the author of '*tora, tora, tora*' on Pearl Harbor. President

The action against Yamamoto was code-named "Operation Vengeance."

Perhaps the best one can do with the Yamamoto "precedent" is to say that most targeted killings today are not killings of such high-rank individuals. So it is hard to see how the Yamamoto case is supposed to help. In the words of Jennifer Daskell, the public defense of current American practices does not include any historical examples "in which a state has tracked down and killed a low-level soldier far from the battlefield, even in a state-to-state conflict where combatants are relatively easy to identify and are clearly legitimate military targets."[131]

Yamamoto or not, Harold Koh is adamant (or he certainly was in his 2012 address) that the mere fact of naming, dossier building, particular identification, and individualized hunting does not detract from either the legality or the morality of deadly force when it is directed against a person who, as an enemy combatant, is liable to be killed anyway. There may be reasonable questions to raise about civilian casualties, the proper identification of targets, the sovereignty of other countries, and the proportionality of this sort of attack—but not the naming as such. That, in Koh's opinion, is a nonstarter.

Obama, more recently, ordered Osama bin Laden killed not because the Saudi was any member of al Qaeda, but because he was the author of 9/11 who continued to command the terrorist organization."

131. Daskal, "The Geography of the Battlefield," at 1213. See also Jane Mayer, "The Predator War: What Are the Risks of the C.I.A.'s Covert Drone Program?" *New Yorker*, October 26, 2009: "These strikes are killing a lot of low-level militants, which raises the question of whether they are going beyond the authorization to kill leaders."

In response to Koh's speech, Philip Alston, at the time UN Special Rapporteur on Extrajudicial, Summary or Arbitrary Executions, said that this particular line of argument was a red herring. Responding to Koh's consideration of the naming and targeting objection, Alston said: "I am not aware of any reputable author who might have made such an argument and the proposition, as stated, is clearly without foundation."[132] Alston thought there were other, much better arguments to use against targeted killing. But I find Koh's dismissal of the naming objection too quick, and Alston's concession too hasty.

The core of the case made by Koh and others in defense of targeted killing is that if it is lawful to target a person impersonally as a member of a military force, it must be lawful also to target that person by name. If the former does not make us uneasy, there is nothing about the latter that should give us pause. Is this right? Here is a hypothetical example that troubles me. It doesn't settle anything, but it generates some misgivings in my thinking.

> Suppose you are a company commander in regular warfare, and you have been ordered to attack a defended position. The position is held by a few score enemy soldiers and you are commanded to attack it with a company of men. Just before the jump-off time, a civilian official hands you a list of names and photographs of twelve members of the defending force and instructs you to ensure (if at all possible and of course within the laws of war) that these enemy combatants are killed in the course of the operation. Would you simply accept the list, shrug, and say, "Sounds odd, but people are going to be killed anyway; these twelve are enemy soldiers defending

132. Alston, "The CIA and Targeted Killings," 321.

> this position, and they can have no complaint if they are targeted with lethal force"? Or might alarm-bells go off in the mind of the company commander, along the following lines?
>
> Why am I being given this list of names? I know they are all combatants, but why are these particular ones being singled out? Is it because they are high-ranking officers? Is it because they are troublemakers and their surviving the campaign will make post-bellum governance more difficult? Are they communists or fanatics of some other kind? Are they Jews? Is someone taking the opportunity presented by otherwise legitimate combat to settle a score that has nothing to do with the present conflict? What's going on?

Part of the commander's concern may be about the prospect for quarter so far as the named individuals are concerned. He may worry: "Am I being told not to accept the surrender of any of the individuals on the list?" But even if quarter is not ruled out, the mere fact of the list and its presentation to the company commander by a civilian would feel odd. It would feel like some sort of abuse of military privilege, a distorting of military ethos. If that's the case, then we can't say that the mere fact that the names on the list are legitimate combat targets *anyway* answers all of our concerns. There is something about the targeting of named individuals that gives us pause, particularly if it is adopted as a regular practice.[133]

133. Daniel Statman (in a private communication) offers the following response: "I would definitely feel uneasy about such an order simply because it would *make no sense*. I would immediately ask my officer: 'Why these people?' If the answer was that they are known to be the best soldiers or the best sergeants of the enemy, I would say fine and feel no uneasiness. If the answer was 'This is top secret, we can't tell you why,' I would imagine that these targets have some special and secret role in the enemy efforts and hence it is important to kill them.

What is it that nourishes this intuition (if that is what it is)? There may not be anything in international humanitarian law that formally forbids targeting soldiers by name. Actually, there *is*, in the military doctrine of some countries. Israel's Manual on the Laws of War stipulates both that "[a]n attempt on the lives of enemy leaders (civilian *or military*) is forbidden" and more generally that "[a]s a rule, it is forbidden *to single out a specific person* on the adversary's side and request his death."[134] I am not saying that either of these is altogether complied with, although Israeli generals, politicians, and intelligence chiefs have argued long and hard about how far up the leadership hierarchy of terrorist and insurgent groups targeted killing should be taken.[135] The first of the Israeli rules I mentioned is tantamount to a prohibition on assassination. Now, as we saw, the United States is also subject to an order prohibiting assassination,[136] but the practice today is to say that a targeted killing cannot count as an assassination if that leader

Again, no special sense of uneasiness. Now imagine a more realist example: We're fighting against an enemy brigade that has an excellent commander. The rest of the high-ranked officers in the brigade are mediocre so there is good reason to believe that if the commander is killed, it will be much easier for us to win the battle. So I get this order (not from a 'civilian official,' but from my superiors in the military) that we should make a serious effort to target this commander. I confess that this would cause me no uneasiness."

134. Israel Defense Forces, *Manuel on the Laws of War*, cited by Melzer, *Targeted Killing in International Law*, 48–49 (my emphasis).

135. The matter is discussed throughout Bergman, *Rise and Kill First*.

136. Executive Order 12333, December 4, 1981, superseding a similar prohibition, Executive Order 11905 (1976).

is also a member of the enemy's armed forces. The Israeli rule, as framed, seems to reject that.

Anyway, I do not assume in my hypothetical example that the names are all high-ranking officers. Some may be private soldiers. The question is, whatever we think about assassination, would we not feel uneasy about these men being singled out by name to be killed? I am not a great believer in the intuitive method in moral philosophy. But I do think an "intuition pump" like my hypothetical example shows that this issue of naming and targeting is worth lingering over.[137] So, let us linger.

One concern is that singling someone out by name for death amounts to a form of outlawry.[138] Another is that it is uncomfortably like what we prohibit in the United States as a bill of attainder. Neither analogy is perfect, but acknowledging the imperfections does not dispel the misgivings they generate.

First, *outlawry*. In the Lieber Code of 1863, a set of instructions governing the conduct of US armies in the field devised by German-American jurist Franz Lieber, we are told:

> The law of war does not allow proclaiming either an individual belonging to the hostile army, or a citizen, or a subject of the hostile government an outlaw who may be slain without trial by any captor, any more than the modern law of peace allows such international outlawry; on the contrary, it abhors such

137. The term "intuition pump" was coined by Dennett, "The Milk of Human Intentionality," 429.
138. For an explicit acknowledgment that targeted killing might involve something like outlawry, see Issacharoff and Pildes, "Targeted Warfare," at 1589.

outrage. The sternest retaliation should follow the murder committed in consequence of such proclamation, made by whatever authority.[139]

Now the targeting envisaged in my hypothetical example is not exactly like that. The list of names is passed on quietly to the company commander: there is no proclamation. And there is no general proclamation of outlawry in targeted killing.[140] Also I said in my example that there was no suggestion that the laws of war should otherwise be violated in targeting these individuals: if they ask for quarter they must be given it. Suppose though that the position is being attacked by helicopter, and lack of cover means that the defenders can be individually identified from the air. May the attacking force go ahead and "pick off" the named individuals?

In making an argument against targeted killing, Michael Gross offered this commentary on the Lieber Code's prohibition:

Lieber assumed it was impossible to make the argument for targeted killings without giving way to the charge of outlawry. Given the conditions of warfare in his day and, indeed, in most of the modern period he was probably right. Soldiers wore uniforms and insignia, and were easy to identify. Naming names added nothing to their vulnerability nor did it render any person a more legitimate target. On the contrary, it

139. Lieber Code, §148, quoted by Gross, "Assassination and Targeted Killing," 326.
140. Cf. HCJ 769/02, §25: "Needless to say, unlawful combatants are not beyond the law. They are not 'outlaws.'"

only presupposed an element of moral culpability that Lieber
found loathsome.[141]

Gross suggests that Lieber would have been concerned
about the element of "hunting" that targeted killing often
involved. Suppose the defenders flee from the position we
are attacking. It is 1865 and the war is nearing its end.
But it's not over yet. The twelve named individuals flee
towards their homes, but they are still in uniform. With
our list in hand, we hunt them down. Gross worries that
"named killing . . . undermines the relative peace charac-
terizing civilian centers of population by threatening to
bring the battle field home."[142] To make the comparison
fair, perhaps we should contrast the impersonal killing
of unknown soldiers fleeing the battlefield toward their
homes with the targeted killing of soldiers heading in the
same direction whom we identify and pursue by name.
Maybe the defenders of targeted killing are right that
there is no difference. With Gross, though, I think that
there is.

The second source of misgiving is that targeted killing
has features uncomfortably like those prohibited in the
constitutional rule about bills of attainder.[143] In England,
attainder was a process used to condemn the bloodline
of prominent traitors, so that their descendants could
not inherit their titles or estates. Henry VII arranged for

141. Gross, "Assassination and Targeted Killing," 328.
142. Gross, "Assassination and Targeted Killing," 328.
143. See US Constitution, Article I, Section 9. The prohibition
on bills of attainder was one ground put forward by the petitioner in
Al-Aulaqi v. Panetta 35 F.Supp.3d 56 (2013), quoted in Knuckey (ed.)
Drones and Targeted Killings, 259 at 274.

the attainder of more than one hundred men who had opposed his taking the throne. A bill of attainder was a legislative means of doing this. While the American framers were not concerned about families losing titles of nobility, they did worry about the use of the device against individuals opposing the Revolution. Ryan Alford describes it:

> The reasons for the Framers' uncompromising approach to attainder in the Constitution were demonstrated during the ratification debate in Virginia. Edmund Randolph (later the first Attorney General of the United States) condemned the attainder of the vicious Tory bandit Josiah Phillips, who had been accused in 1778 of numerous counts of arson and murder, and for (in the words of the bill) having "levied war against this Commonwealth." "[W]hereas the . . . usual forms and procedures of the courts of law would leave the said good people for a long time exposed to murder and devastation," he was attaindered by the General Assembly. Randolph believed that "a man, who was then a citizen, was deprived of his life thus," and he promised that "if I conceived my country would passively permit a repetition of it . . . I would seek a means of expatriating myself from it." When the counterargument was made that Phillips was "a fugitive murderer and an outlaw . . . [and] the enormity of his crimes did not entitle him to [due process]," John Marshall replied: "Can we pretend to the enjoyment of political freedom or security, when we are told that a man has been, by act of Assembly, struck out of existence without being confronted with his accusers and witnesses, without benefit of the law of the land?"

Alford says that Randolph and Marshall's interventions were decisive. Given this background, it is "beyond peradventure that the Framers never intended to invest the president with the power to order a citizen's execution without trial."[144]

The arguments we develop from these considerations—the ban on attainder and the prohibition of outlawry—may not be conclusive, and there is plenty to distinguish the modern practice of targeted killing from the abuses that Lieber and Randolph identified.[145] All I am doing at this stage is answering Koh's argument that there is *nothing whatever* in the element of particularizing by name individuals targeted for death to give us pause in our evaluation of the practice.

***

As we explore the nature of these misgivings further, we need to ask: How much do our worries depend on the fact that people are being targeted *by name*. Can a legitimate concern possibly be based on that feature alone? Or is the concern about what we *do* with the names. After all, the target's name is just one element in hunting him down and killing him. There is also his photograph, the dossier that has been assembled with information about his life, his hometown, his family and his associates, his movements, his role in the organization we are fighting, and his past misdeeds. His name operates as sort of a nexus, a point of

144. Alford, "Targeted Killing and the Rule of Law." See also Finkelstein, "Targeted Killing as Pre-emptive Action," for concerns about attainder in this context.
145. For a response to the argument about attainder, see Dehn, "Targeting Citizens in Armed Conflict."

access to his place in the immense databases used in the war against terrorism.[146]

It is worth spending some time on the very idea of a proper name (if that is what seems important) or certainly on the idea of referring to an individual—*picking him out* as a target. *Proper names* and *reference*: these are both important topics in the philosophy of language, and some of that philosophical understanding may be of use to us here. If the next few pages seem picky and abstract, please bear with me, for they may help us distinguish between targeted killing and ordinary combat.

Reference—referring to an individual—is characteristically a speech act. (Not always; sometimes one refers just by pointing.) Usually, reference is a way of using language to focus the attention of one's audience on a particular individual and making that individual the subject of some attribution or command. One says: "Look at *him; he* is a terrorist," or "*That's* who I am talking about," or "*That's* the person I want you to kill." In these locutions, we use pronouns (with demonstrative emphasis) or demonstrative terms like "that." But we can also refer to particular individuals by using their names: we use "Osama bin Laden" to pick out a person about whom we want to say certain things or concerning whom we want to have certain outcomes (like death) brought about. Indeed, it seems that a term like "Osama bin Laden," like any other proper name, just *is* a device for referring.

In addition to pronouns and proper names, we sometimes use descriptive phrases to refer. We may pick out the

---

146. See McDonald, *Enemies Known and Unknown*, 162–163, for the importance of this technology.

individual Osama bin Laden using a phrase like "the patriarch in the mansion in Abbottabad." If we say (in 2011),
"The patriarch in the mansion in Abbottabad has a long gray
beard," we may be using the *italicized* phrase to direct our
audience's attention to an individual, and the underlined
phrase to say something about that particular person. Or
at least that's how definite descriptions are sometimes
used. It is possible that the italicized phrase is also used
mainly to convey information—along the lines of "there
is someone in the Abbottabad mansion who is a patriarch
and has a long grey beard." There used to be a controversy
about this in philosophical logic.[147] But it is now generally
accepted that a phrase like "the patriarch in the mansion
in Abbottabad" *can* be used to refer and often is, even if it
sometimes can also have a non-referential use.

Now here I want to go out on a limb philosophically.
The difference I have just been talking about—roughly,
between what philosophers call referential and attributive
uses of definite descriptions[148]—conceals another distinction, quite important for our purposes. When we use a
descriptive phrase to refer to someone, the reference may
be, as I shall say, *tighter* or *looser*. We may use the phrase
"the patriarch in the mansion in Abbottabad" to refer to
Osama bin Laden. But what if he dies or leaves Abbottabad?
If bin Laden takes off for his hometown of Riyadh, do we
expect the listener to track him over to Saudi Arabia? Or
do we expect the listener to focus his attention on *the next
patriarch* who occupies the mansion in Abbottabad. The

147. For the so-called Strawson/Russell debate on this, see Russell,
"On Denoting," and Strawson, "On Referring."
148. See Donnellan, "Reference and Definite Descriptions."

former would probably apply to those who are targeting bin Laden for death: for them, "the patriarch in the mansion in Abbottabad" was just a way of beginning to focus on him; once that gets underway, they want the focus to remain on *him*, wherever he goes. I call this *tight* reference: the focus is drawn tightly on the individual whom the descriptive phrase identified, and that focus remains even after the descriptive phrase ceases to apply.[149] But, in other uses, the descriptive phrase may be used to refer in a way that is referentially looser than that. One says (in a feudal spirit) to a young man in a village near Abbottabad: "Go pay your respects *to the patriarch in the mansion in Abbottabad*." The italicized phrase picks out a person, but if the role is occupied now by some person other than bin Laden, then perhaps it is the *someone else* to whom the young man should go and pay his respects (if he wants to get ahead in the neighborhood). I would argue that this is still a referential use of the phrase. But it is a looser kind of reference, not tied as tightly to the particular flesh and blood individual. Loose reference edges toward an attributive use of the descriptive phrase, for it turns out that the content

---

149. Philosophers sometimes use the phrase *"rigid* designation" to mean a form of reference that goes way beyond tight reference as I have understood it. I have imagined Osama bin Laden moving from place to place in the actual world. They imagine possible worlds in which that individual (bin Laden) has other qualities altogether: he never was involved in 9/11, he never grew a beard, he converted to Christianity, etc. They say that for metaphysical reasons we need referential devices of this sort to keep track of individuals across possible worlds. Happily, we don't have to worry about possible worlds or rigid designators in the present context. The *locus classicus* for talk of rigid designators is Kripke, *Naming and Necessity*.

of the descriptive phrase matters as much as the focus on a
particular individual.

Do proper names have any content of this kind? (Bear
with me a little bit longer.) Can they be used for loose reference? Some philosophers say that the meaning of a proper
name is some definite description or cluster of definite
descriptions associated with the name that identifies its
bearer; for example, "Aristotle" means the same as "the
philosopher who taught Alexander the Great *or* the writer
of the *Nichomachean Ethics*."[150] But most theorists shy away
from descriptivism and maintain that a proper name is
really devoid of meaning, save that its function is to desig-
nate a particular individual.[151] So the meaning of "Aristotle"
is Aristotle the man, and it would continue to pick him out
even if (as it turned out) he stopped writing about ethics
and had had no interaction with Alexander the Great. In
between there are metalinguistic theories which say that a
proper name is a conventional designator associated with
an individual by his being conventionally called *that*. Maybe
"Osama bin Laden" means "the man with the label 'Osama
bin Laden' conventionally attached to him."[152] Other conventional designators—like social security numbers—also
operate to pick people out. Perhaps they do so more reliably
and uniquely, but they don't quite work through people
being *addressed as* "403-99-7893" or whatever.

150. Russell, "On Denoting." For the cluster-of-descriptions view,
see Searle, "Proper Names."
151. In one account, that of Mill, *A System of Logic*, 34, a name is
defined simply as "a word that answers the purpose of showing what
thing it is that we are talking about but not of telling anything about it."
152. Cf. Dickie, "How Proper Names Refer," 45: "A semantic theory
should treat 'a is F' the way it treats 'the bearer of "a" is F.'"

It is time now to focus this discussion of the philosophy of language on our real interest, which is targeted killing. Is it significant, I asked, that targeted killing involves tracking and hunting down people *by name*, as opposed to the sort of impersonal anonymous killing involved in ordinary combat?

Names are not used in ordinary military killings. We set out to destroy that nest of machine-gunners on the hill we are attacking. If our leaders know the enemy order of battle, they (and we) may be vaguely aware of the unit that those we are firing on belong to—which battalion or which regiment—and glimpses of their uniform may tell us something about their individual rank. Names may be embroidered on battle tunics. But little of this matters. We target people on the basis of what they are *doing* in the current engagement. It is their place in the engagement or the campaign that legitimizes the use of lethal force. We don't need to know who they are; the description of what they are doing is sufficient.

We do refer to a soldier when we try to kill him: "Take *him* out," we say, or "Shoot *that guy over there with the machine gun*." But does this sort of combat killing involve loose or tight reference? Well, we try to shoot this person because he is operating a machine gun and holding up our attack. We aim at him in that capacity; if he falls back or is relieved from that capacity, we will probably aim at the person who takes his place. It is, so to speak, the function we are aiming at not the person per se. It still is natural to say, even in this case, that we are referring to someone in particular when we aim our fire at an enemy soldier. "Shoot him. Shoot *him*. *That man* over there. *He* is the one who is holding up our attack." But the reference here, I think, is loose referring rather than tight referring. We don't usually say, of a soldier on the other side, "Shoot *him*—and I mean HIM, wherever he goes, whatever he does." We say: "Shoot him, the person currently doing *this* or occupying *that* role or function or position." The latter is the language of a soldier; the former is that of an assassin.

Targeted killing, I believe, involves tight reference. One identifies an individual, usually by name, to be killed and we expect that individual to be hunted down and shot. Even if he is identified at first by a description—say, in a dossier (with bio, photograph, and whereabouts, but incomplete as to his name)—the description helps us to find our way to him, and then *he* is the target. That is characteristic of tight reference. If we have to choose between the description that led us to him and the man himself, we follow the latter. *He* is the one we want to kill.

In my view, this puts considerable pressure on Harold Koh's position that targeted killing is just an instance of ordinary combatant killing, where names just happen to be involved. The logic of targeting is quite different in the two cases. One is governed by function and context. The other is just the tracking down for death of a particular individual. Koh's position comes close to treating liability to be killed as a status taken on by and then permanently associated with a person as such. A person acquires that status by being a combatant, and in that capacity he is liable to lethal force. So far, agreed. But, I want to insist, it doesn't follow that he has become an outlaw and that *he* may be hunted down by anyone and killed. Having been identified as a combatant and become "killable" as such, it is not true that he can be killed now for any reason. I know we do talk loosely of combatant *status*, but in international humanitarian law the key to a person's liability to lethal force is *context*, not status alone.[153] Or at least status, if we want to keep using that term, is always tied to context: it is temporary and it is conditional. The context relative to which a status of killability is assigned may be a particular battlefield or series of battles. And perhaps the status persists as the person concerned moves from one battlefield to another in a long campaign or up to and down from the front line. But if he is home on extended leave, visiting his mother, is he still a legitimate target? More so than any other military age male in the civilian population?[154] I don't think so. Naming an individual enables us to track that individual from context to context, whereas regular military targeting is context dependent.

I am told by defenders of targeted killing that tracking down and killing combatants in this way is a perfectly familiar aspect of modern warfare. It is not. Apart from wanting to finesse the objection we are considering in this chapter, it would never occur to anyone involved in discussions of the ethics of armed conflict to say that it was perfectly permissible for our forces to fan out and track down individual enemy soldiers to their homes and kill them there. But in the

153. See Finkelstein, "Targeted Killing as Pre-emptive Action," 169, for "the potential moral risks in *status* rather than *conduct*, based killing," i.e., "[n]aming a target in advance, and then killing him based on his status."

154. See McMahan, "Targeted Killing," 139, for the suggestion that the targeted killing of a terrorist when he is not actually blowing things up is morally quite like the killing of a combatant while he is asleep. McMahan seems to approve of killing in the latter case and therefore, by analogy, in the former.

context of arguing about targeted killing, they insist that we do this all the time. I rarely impute bad faith to my opponents, but this insistence is quite implausible, and in my view it is made up just in order to bolster the argument in defense of targeted killing. Certainly we should avoid any implication that, once a person has been designated as a combatant, they become fair game to combatants on the other side who suddenly have an unfettered license to kill them.[155] In the Law of Armed Conflict, it always matters what description such a person is killed under, at least if the killing is intentional. I may not open fire on a combatant if my main reason for doing so is some personal grudge or retaliation for something he did in the past. I may not do it for political reasons or for reasons of crime control unrelated to the military campaign.

Issacharoff and Pildes say that in decisions to target, dangerousness may be a decisive consideration.[156] But dangerousness can be political as well as lethal. It can refer not just to the likelihood that that the target will kill someone but also to the general threat posed by the target in various ways to the order that the state constitutes and the values it is defending. A name becomes a sort of clearinghouse for all the information that might bear on a decision—strategic, political, and legal—to have someone killed. I am not saying the question faced by the US president and his counselors is simply, "How convenient would it be, politically, to have NN killed?" But it may be closer to that than we ought to be comfortable with.

***

155. Melzer's language, in *Targeted Killing in International Law*, 429.
156. Issacharoff and Pildes, "Targeted Warfare," 1533.

Professor Meisels has acknowledged that "[t]errorist leaders are pursued individually and targeted by name." She acknowledges too that many people thinking that "lifting the targeted 'veil of ignorance' from the personal identity of the enemy-victim . . . dramatically transforms the morality of war."[157] But, she says, it might change the situation without worsening it. "Why should we accept that killing anonymous soldiers, purely because they represent 'the enemy,' is legitimate . . . whereas targeting particular 'named' culprits in the course of a war against terrorism is morally abhorrent?" A similar point is made by Daniel Statman, who concedes the importance in principle of a distinction between anonymous killing in traditional combat and killing by name, but argues against the proposition that anonymity is a necessary condition for the privilege of killing in war and that "the license to kill soldiers from the other side rests precisely on the fact that their personal merits or demerits are ignored."

> To kill by name is to kill somebody simply because he is who he is, regardless of any contingent features he possesses or actions he has committed. This type of killing is, indeed, deeply problematic from a moral point of view.[158]

However, he insists that the sort of targeted killing we are talking about in this book is not really killing *by name*. Instead, it kills people by *role*, as perpetrators of terror, not by their personal identity.[159] And that, he

157. Meisels, "Targeting Terror," 301.
158. Statman, "Targeted Killing," 190.
159. Statman, "Targeted Killing," 190.

says, is actually better than impersonal killing in traditional warfare: "With targeted killings, human beings are killed . . . because they bear special responsibility or play a special role in the enemy's aggression"[160] The deliberation that takes place prior to any particular targeting means that only the truly dangerous, the truly guilty, are picked out for death.

This way of defending targeted killing resonates with some well-known revisionist positions in the jurisprudence of armed conflict generally. In an article on "The Ethics of Killing in War," Jeff McMahan (one of our most thoughtful philosophical writers about the laws of war) argues that there is no moral justification for the usual principle of discrimination that crudely puts combatants and civilians in different categories so far as liability to deadly force is concerned.[161] He thinks one can make a moral case for saying that not all combatants but only those who are genuinely implicated morally in a just war should be liable to deadly force. This is because he believes that, in the eyes of critical morality, "it is moral responsibility for an unjust threat that is the principal basis of liability to [be the target of] defensive (or preservative) force."[162] And he certainly thinks some combatants, like conscripts on either side or soldiers fighting on the right side in a just war, cannot be regarded legitimate targets. (The flip side of this is that McMahan also believes that certain civilians *are* properly

160. Statman, "Targeted Killing," 191.
161. McMahan, "The Ethics of Killing in War." See also the discussion in McMahan, *Killing in War*.
162. McMahan, "The Ethics of Killing in War," 722.

liable to intentional attack—for example, civilians who share responsibility for an unjust war.)[163]

A surprising number of moral philosophers accept McMahan's outlook,[164] while the very best-known just war theorists oppose it.[165] One of the most powerful objections to his position has to do with administrability.[166] Not only do norms *in bello* have to be administered among people who disagree about justice and guilt in relation to the armed conflict in question, but they also have to be administered quickly by unit commanders and their men in fraught and dangerous circumstances. A deep or refined moral principle might require a delicate inquiry into the moral status of every person or unit fired upon. But that would be utterly unworkable. Some crude criterion such as the wearing of uniforms has to be used instead, even though this is massively over- and under-inclusive by moral standards, even though it places what may seem to a philosopher to be undue emphasis on trivial conventions like uniforms or insignia. McMahan himself has acknowledged that these points require him to distinguish between the actual laws of war (which he says ought to remain the same) and the

163. For McMahan's own take on targeted killing using some of these revisionist criteria, see McMahan, "Targeted Killing."

164. Besides McMahan, see, e.g., Rodin, *War and Self-Defense*;, Lazar, "Evaluating the Revisionist Critique of Just War Theory"; and Frowe, *Defensive Killing*.

165. Michael Walzer remains a firm defender (against McMahan-style revisionism) of the moral equality of combatants and the importance of the traditional principle of distinction set out in successive editions of his classic book, *Just and Unjust Wars*. See also Shue, "Do We Need a 'Morality of War'?"

166. See the discussion in Waldron, "Deep Morality and the Laws of War."

"deep morality" of war (which is what he claims to be talking about).[167]

Actually, the defender of targeted killing has a partial retort to the objection about administrability. The defender can say that our practice of targeted killing has shown that McMahan-type revisionism *is* administrable, at least in the technological circumstances of asymmetric warfare, where the burdens of discrimination are placed upon high-level committees rather than unit commanders on the battlefield. But this is a partial answer only. Since drone warfare will never be the whole of modern warfare, we have to understand that there is nothing to stop the logic of targeted killing from infecting practices of civilian/combatant discrimination generally. This back and forth certainly gives the lie to Koh's suggestion, discussed earlier, that targeted killing is just business as usual under the ordinary unrevised laws of *ius in bello*.

PART VI: GETTING OUT OF HAND

Targeted killing would not be needed in a perfect world. It is supposed to be a response to the novel circumstance of terrorism—a new kind of threat to the security of modern societies—and it has to be evaluated in the first instance in relation to this novel threat in the real world we live in.

Unfortunately, we may not pick and choose which features of the real world are to be taken into account in our evaluation of this practice. We must also consider

167. McMahan, "The Ethics of Killing in War," 730.

the possibility that, in the real world, the practice will be abused, or, even if it is not exactly a question of abuse, that it will be used in circumstances way beyond those that originally elicited it—in short, that targeted killing will get out of hand. We are not entitled to affect naivety about this prospect while instructing everyone else to be hard-headed about what is needed to meet the terrorist menace. Even if the justification of targeted killing is officially confined to counter-terrorism, defenders of the practice have to reckon with the fact that governments may end up using the word "terrorist" for anyone they would like to have killed, rather than using it as a firm constraint on the practice. The concerns that I will address in this chapter may seem exaggerated, but there is precious little in the rhetoric of official and academic defenses of targeted killing to justify any confidence that these possibilities will be approached carefully and scrupulously.

I hinted at these possibilities in Part IV, in our discussion of death squads. That unsavory analogy reminds us that there have been (and are) societies where political leaders find it helpful to have individuals "disappeared." It was always a mark of democratic rights-respecting regimes that they would treat such a practice as being out of the question, rather like torture. For us now, the question is whether targeted killing can be defended for the specific issue of counter-terrorism without weakening that earlier categorical response.

It is not just opportunism we should be worried about. Governments acting, as they see it, for the public good might feel called upon to use targeted killing as a routine military tactic. They may use it against insurgents who, though engaged in asymmetric warfare, do not commit war crimes or terrorist atrocities. They may use it against political opponents who have teetered for decades on the edge of rebellion. In law enforcement campaigns that have a warlike aspect (or at least a martial theme)—the "war on drugs," for example—targeted killing may be used against hard-to-catch criminals, masterminds, kingpins, "Public Enemy Number 1" and the like.

These are not only abstract possibilities. The terms currently used to justify targeted killings are already being extended into some of these areas.[168] The clearest instance of this extension is the broad use of "terrorist" to refer to any insurgent movement, irrespective of whether it follows the laws and customs of armed conflict, irrespective of whether it uses violence against civilians. The term "terrorist" is notoriously ill-defined[169] and those who justify targeted killing with respect to terrorism need to contemplate the possibility that the practice may, in certain hands, follow the careless application of the expression. Indeed certain regimes may value the flexibility of the term "terrorist" precisely in order to be able to defend the more extensive use of targeted killing. Or the practice may be justified as a response to "militants" or "extremists" or "jihadists," which are terms often used as synonyms for "terrorists" and

168. My concern does not depend on the slipperiness of words in general; it also reflects the instability of the analogies that are used in justifying targeted killing—from one kind of war-making to another, or from one kind of law enforcement to another.

169. For a sampling of the controversy, see Waldron, "Terrorism and the Uses of Terror" and Coady, "Defining Terrorism."

which are at least as vague and extendable as "terrorists" might be.[170]

I suppose these may be described as "slippery slope" arguments.[171] Their form is: once we start justifying targeted killing for certain good purposes, there is no way to stop the practice being used for bad purposes. And what is the bottom of the slippery slope?—a general abandonment of the Rule of Law, a brutalization of our society in its dealings with wrongdoers, and a broad weakening of moral and legal inhibitions against murder. I don't intend any of these possibilities to be treated as a *reductio*. I do intend them as warnings, and as the basis of a hard question that needs to be put to targeted killing's defenders: what provision do they make in their arguments for the possibility that this practice may get out of hand?

The usual response is to assert either that the slope is not all that slippery or that there are ways to stop the slide on the way down. Neither Professor Meisels nor the authors ranged on her side of the debate favor the use of targeted killing as a general political tactic, either for dealing with insurgencies, political adversaries, or ordinary crime control. However, they say that any practice is liable to abuse, and we shouldn't let that possibility distract us. They say

170. Nancy Youssef and Gordon Lubold in "ISIS Fighters Held in Syria Complicate U.S. Withdrawal," *Wall Street Journal*, March 6, 2019 move effortlessly between "Islamic State members," "extremist fighters," and "terrorists."

171. For the general concept, see Schauer, "Slippery Slopes." See also Blum and Heymann, "Law and Policy of Targeted Killing," who observe that "[t]here are slippery slope concerns of excessive use of targeted killings against individuals or in territories that are harder to justify."

that as supporters of targeted killing they are ready and willing to hold the line against any deployment of it other than against terrorists. Experience tells us, however, that it is harder to hold such a line when the use of a tactic like this has already been permitted. For no matter what dissimilarity there is between its use and its abuse, abstractly an example has been set and it is *out there* to exploit.

So let us consider the ways in which targeted killing may get out of hand, and the many modes of its extension into other areas of law and practice. I am going to start with what the defenders of targeted killing think is the easiest case and then chart the route to cases where even they should be more worried.

1. Terrorism—The Central Case

I begin by focusing on the use of targeted killing against those who slaughter civilians to sow fear and insecurity for political purposes—terrorists in the strictest sense. The use of targeted killing is surely most defensible when it is an immediate response to the prospect of terrorism, that is, when the killing is undertaken to prevent a terrorist attack *right now*—for example, by a suicide bomber about to explode his device. Here, the person targeted is attempting to commit mass murder and apart from killing him there may be no other way of stopping him, no other way of saving the lives he means to destroy.

In fact very few instances of targeted killing are just like this. The targeting, planning, and technology that the practice involves takes time and it means that targeted killings are usually more distant than this from immediate acts of terrorism. Individuals are targeted because they have engaged in terrorist action in the past and they are expected to do so again in the future. As noted in Part IV, almost all targeted killings are "carried out while the targeted person is not visibly engaged in active combat."[172] Though targeted killing is defended as a response to imminent threats, the use of the technology that it involves would be frustrated if we were not allowed to work with ideas of "elongated" or "continuing" imminence.[173] Naming, as we saw, enables us to do that; instead of having to wait until someone comes into view with his finger on the button of an explosive device, we use an individual's name to trace him from his involvement in a particular terrorist incident in the past to his present availability as a target based on a likelihood that he will be involved in some other attack in the future. The name operates as a nexus to connect these various events and possibilities and in that way establishes that the person concerned is a terrorist, as a matter of enduring identity. We elongate our sense of his terrorist activity to match the elongation of response that counter-terrorist techniques require. Thus even when we begin by focusing our arguments on the narrowest cases of terrorist attack, we see the beginnings of an understandable tendency to expand the range of those we target beyond direct kinetic involvement.

And the elongation doesn't stop there. There are different kinds of complicity in terrorism. People may be said to be involved and thus liable to be a target for many reasons other than direct action, past, present or future. They may be targeted because they are working to arm those who

---

172. Melzer, *Targeted Killing in International Law*, 56.
173. See Klaidman, *Kill or Capture*, 219.

engage in such actions (building the vests, for example, that suicide bombers use), or recruiting terrorists, inciting and encouraging terrorist acts, or managing the organizations responsible for them. Some of these individuals may never have touched an explosive. Consider the killing of Anwar al-Awlaki, the American citizen operating in Yemen, to whom I have alluded a couple of times. A case can be made that al-Awlaki was a bad person whose activities certainly endangered the interests of the United States: he was an able preacher, propagandist, and recruiter and he certainly incited terroristic actions. But it would be difficult to classify him as a combatant. Targeting him was more like targeting a high civilian official in a regular war.

People may be targeted just on account of their membership of a group which also includes terrorists as its members: the killing of police recruits by Israeli forces at a graduation ceremony in Gaza simply because they were employed by the Hamas administration there is an extreme example of this.[174] There is a whole range of potential targets connected to terror by something other than their immediate involvement. The German Constitutional Court has recently expressed concern about American attacks, organized from German soil, against people who are targeted

174. Taghreed El-Khodary and Ethan Bronner, "Israelis Say Strikes against Hamas Will Continue," *New York Times*, December 27, 2008: "Israeli officials said that anyone linked to the Hamas security structure or government was fair game because Hamas was a terrorist group that sought Israel's destruction. But with work here increasingly scarce . . . , young men are tempted by the steady work of the police force without necessarily fully accepting the Hamas ideology. One of the biggest tolls on Saturday was at a police cadet graduation ceremony in which 15 people were killed."

simply because they are "supporters" of organizations like ISIS and AQAP.[175]

Targeting people within any of these ranges can be rationalized in a number of different ways. The central case we began with is preventive: one puts a stop to an immediate threat right now by killing the person about to perpetrate it. But the preventive rationale for targeting someone may also be that his death will incapacitate a terrorist organization at least temporarily by disrupting its operations: he may be an organizer or a facilitator. Or targeting someone may be intended as a way of deterring terrorist atrocities, preventing them indirectly. Or—as is often the case with deterrence arguments—targeted killings may be associated covertly with a retaliatory or retributive response. I am not saying that these accounts of how targeted killing is supposed to work are necessarily misconceived. What I am emphasizing is the existence of a certain momentum to extend the range of the practice beyond the cases where its rationale as a counter-terrorist measure is most persuasive and makes most plausible contact with official justifications.

2. From Terrorism to Insurgency

What I am talking about is the *metastasization* of targeted killing: the way it grows up and out in the body politic beyond the circumstances to which it was supposed originally to be narrowly confined. The metastasization begins in earnest with the shift from terrorists to insurgents

175. Jürgen Bering, "Legal Explainer: German Court Reins in Support for U.S. Drone Strikes," *Just Security*, March 22, 2019.

as appropriate targets.[176] There is sometimes a fine line between terrorism and insurgency and there are precious few governments facing an armed uprising among their own people who do not refer to the insurgents and their leaders as terrorists. Indeed, many countries with restive minorities, whose agitation challenges the country's official sense of itself, will be tempted to call the minority agitators "terrorists" before they even take up a weapon. It is just such a good way of discrediting them.

Nonetheless "insurgent" and "terrorist" are not synonyms. Back in the day (the 1970s), we used to debate endlessly whether various self-styled liberation movements around the world should be described as "terrorists" or as "freedom-fighters." It escaped our notice at the time that a movement could be both—terrorist in its tactics and freedom-fighting in its aims. But we were right to insist that not all freedom-fighting insurgents were terrorists.[177] "George Washington's motley army"[178] in 1776 comprised rebels but not terrorists. Certainly the two ideas are sometimes factually entangled. The reason Americans fought against the Taliban insurgency in Afghanistan was not that the Taliban was itself an organizer of international terrorism, but because the Taliban regime in Afghanistan

176. "Insurgents are organized bodies of men who, for public political purposes, are in a state of armed hostility to an established government." Wilson and Tucker, *International Law*, 66, cited by Powers, "Insurgency and the Law of Nations," 65.

177. Sitaraman, "Counterinsurgency, the War on Terror, and the Laws of War," 1747–1748: "Counterinsurgency's strategy is . . . starkly different from the strategy that undergirds the laws of war and the debates on legal issues in the war on terror."

178. Ketchum, *The Winter Soldiers*, 14.

provided a safe haven for organizations like Al Qaeda, which are real terrorist organizations even if the Taliban is not. So Taliban members—insurgents certainly—are judged as complicit in terrorism for that reason.[179] And it has to be said that even in its insurgency, the Taliban was not above using car bombs to terrorize civilians. It is a complex entanglement. Also, insurgent methods of rule in the territories they control may be hideous, and that too may be folded into the extension of targeted killing beyond terrorism in the strict sense. Few observers will be inclined to disagree with the targeted killing in November 2015 of ISIS executioner Mohammed Emwazi, even though it was a response not to terrorism but to egregious human rights violations.[180] Because they recoil from Emwazi's deeds, friends of mine think it is offensive to even question the applicability to him of the label "terrorist." That is understandable, but it means that outrage as such rather than scrupulous focus on counter-terrorist activity is becoming key to the way the justificatory debate is conducted.

It is not even clear that insurgent action has to involve attacks on civilians before it is described as terrorist. When an irregular unit attacks a US naval vessel or blows up a marine barracks or lays down and sets off an improvised explosive device as an army column passes by, is that terrorism? Most politicians instinctively say yes, but in effect they seem to be using a sense of the term that covers any

---

179. Blanchard, "This is not war by machine," acknowledges that the fight against the Taliban is a fight against an insurgency. See Bennis, "Drones and Assassination in the US's Permanent War," 56 on the counterinsurgency/counter-terrorism toggle.

180. McDonald, *Enemies Known and Unknown*, 236.

form of asymmetric warfare. The US just announces that a given body of insurgent combatants are terrorists, citing nothing more than their use of improvised explosive devices and their unpredictable attacks on our troops. In early 2019, President Erdogan of Turkey just announced that Kurdish separatists were terrorists, and the Indian government has made similar pronouncements about Kashmiri separatists. Calling these opponents of the regime terrorists is the go-to tactic in any political or military campaign against them. They may be called terrorists because they use improvised weaponry or because they are not properly dressed up as an identifiable armed force. It is difficult to wage war against insurgents in an asymmetric struggle because they can melt away easily into the general population; calling the group "terrorists" is often a cry of frustration, though it is also the angry threat of a "gloves-off" approach.

The tendency to denounce insurgents as terrorists is long-established. Nelson Mandela was described as a terrorist by the South African regime in the 1970s and 80s and remained on US terrorist watch-lists until 2008.[181] As it clung to the remnants of empire, Britain faced insurgencies in Palestine, Cyprus, Aden, India, Kenya, Malaya, and elsewhere. At one time or another, the British government denounced as terrorists those who emerged to become leaders of these countries: Menachim Begin, Jomo Kenyatta, and Archbishop Makarios are well-known examples. The temptation to respond to insurgency by targeting individuals whom the regime can get away with describing as

---

181. Olivia Waxman, "The U.S. Government Had Nelson Mandela on Terrorist Watch Lists Until 2008," *Time*, July 18, 2018.

terrorists would no doubt be irresistible if it were not for the presence of strong legal norms prohibiting assassination. Think of the use that might have been made of such tactics in the conflict in Northern Ireland. We know the British government was comfortable framing and imprisoning innocent people in the struggle against terrorism and would no doubt have been comfortable hanging them, had hanging been available.[182] If targeted killing had been respectable as a state practice in the 1970s, it would almost certainly have been used to eliminate IRA and Sinn Fein leaders, including some who are currently Stormont and Westminster politicians.

I have little sympathy with the indiscriminate use of this label. But semantics is not the issue. The opportunistic availability of the label reflects the fact that there is no canonical definition of "terrorism." But it is also a consequence of disingenuousness in the defense of targeted killing. And I raise it in this part because I have yet to hear any defender of targeted killing express apprehension about the looseness of this term which, as we have seen, looms so large in their defense of the practice.

3. Ordinary Warfare

The looseness of "terrorism" is not the only basis for the metastasization of targeted killing. As we saw earlier, one

182. See John Robbins, "Birmingham Six Member Paddy Hill on Why the Challenges Facing the Wrongly Convicted Are More Severe Than Ever," *The Independent*, March 12, 2016, quotes Master of the Rolls Lord Denning's comments to the effect that the use of the death penalty ought to have been available for the murders allegedly committed by these in fact innocent men.

defense of the practice is that targeted killing is no different from any justified killing in war. We are told that anyone who might legitimately be killed in ordinary military operations might eo ipso be targeted legitimately as a named and identified individual. This—you will remember—was Harold Koh's argument, discussed at the beginning of Part V.

Well, this defense of targeted killing—that it is simply warfare, waged legitimately on a smaller and more precise scale—must be available in principle to all armed forces, including our adversaries. As the laws and customs of armed conflict are traditionally understood, military practices are assessed under the auspices of *ius in bello* (justice in war), and *ius in bello* is a domain of normative assessment that is supposedly detached from any assessment of the justice of a nation's participation in a conflict, at least in traditional approaches to the laws of war. The laws regarding the actual conduct of war are neutral as between aggressors and defenders, as between those who go to war unjustly and those who are engaged in a just war. Soldiers of both the unjust aggressive side and the just defending side engaged in fighting are legally liable on an equal basis to deadly force at the hands of the other side's combatants; soldiers of either side are entitled to quarter and other protections; forbidden munitions, such as poisonous gas, are forbidden alike to attackers and defenders; civilians may not be attacked whether they are civilians in the aggressor country or not; and so on. A practice of killing that is legitimate under the laws of war is necessarily legitimate in the hands of bad guys and the good guys.

In international humanitarian law, the success of an argument such as Koh's must mean it would have been legitimate for Iraqi leaders in 2003 to maintain dossiers on named members of American units—whether high-ranking officers or ordinary soldiers and Marines—and to hunt them down individually, whether on the front line or on leave so long as the conflict lasted. All countries maintain armed forces and are prepared in certain circumstances to use them, and it is part of the logic of Koh's argument that targeted killing is a use to which the armed forces of any country may legitimately be put. My opponents will say that I am ignoring the special context of the war on terrorism. But that is not how *ius in bello* works, and it was not the gist of Koh's argument. I have great respect for those who try to defend targeted killing, but it is unedifying to watch them scrambling opportunistically back and forth between Koh's ordinary warfare argument and the special case for counter-terrorist operations, depending on which critical arguments they feel the need to respond to at any given time.

I am not saying we cannot make distinctions between countries that use and those that abuse the practice of targeted killing. We can make such distinctions, just as we distinguish between those who murder prisoners and those who do not, and those who target civilians and those who do not. And we do this whatever *they* say about their infringement of these rules. A practice that is neutrally available in *ius in bello* may nevertheless be hedged around with all sorts of qualifications that severely limit its use. But the justice or importance of the cause for which war is being waged in this manner cannot be among the conditions that limit its use.

I suppose we might take the opportunity of a defense of targeted killing to open up the whole question of the independence of *ius in bello* from *ius ad bellum*. This could be done retail, confining the legitimation of targeted killing to asymmetric warfare waged against non-state terrorist actors (on the ground that it was a uniquely troubling use of force). Or it might be done wholesale, along lines urged by Jeff McMahan and other laws-of-war revisionists.[183] I talked about this in relation to Daniel Statman's view in Part V. Probably such revision could not be confined to particular cases, however, for it is part of the usual argument for targeted killing that it is nothing but an application of central principles of *ius in bello* (legitimacy of targeting combatants).

Or we might try to undermine the neutrality point in a different way. We might associate American use of targeted killing with some sort of non-proliferation principle. This practice is to be used by us, but it is too dangerous to be used by just any country.[184] It might be like nuclear weapons: *we* have nuclear weapons, *we* have used them against enemy cities, and *we* reserve the right to use them again; but we regard it as a matter of grave concern when other countries, whom we do not trust as we trust ourselves, acquire this capability. I'm not sure this was ever plausible, even for nuclear weapons, from a moral point of view. In any case, I don't find it even practically plausible for targeted killing.

---

183. See McMahan, "The Ethics of Killing in War," and McMahan, *Killing in War*, and the discussion, supra, in Part V.

184. See Zenko and Kreps, "Limiting Armed Drone Proliferation," 126–127. Compare the argument in Falk, "Why Drones Are More Dangerous Than Nuclear Weapons."

Given the way that our use of death lists and death squads is justified, it would be hard to deny other sovereign states the power to fight in this way when fighting was required or to execute their enemies in similar ways.

4. Crime Control

Some of the prospects for the metastasization of targeted killing take us out of the realm of military justification altogether and into the realm of crime control. Consider, for example, the relation between what Americans call the "war on drugs" and what they call the "war on terror." Both phrases identify a rather diffuse threat to society—fear and insecurity on the one hand, narcosis and social dysfunction on the other. Both are exasperatingly difficult to respond to. Both generate politically compelling demands that "something" must be done. And both are associated with simplistic rhetoric maintaining that if only the kingpins were eliminated the problem would evaporate.

There are recent reports about the United States having a "hit list" of Afghan drug lords. Though these "hits" supposedly take place in an active combat zone, they have sparked criticism that drug lords, even when they finance the Taliban, do not fit neatly within the concept of "combatant" and "should instead be treated with law enforcement tools."[185] There are reports too of China considering using armed drones to kill a drug lord in Myanmar.[186] Seamus Miller discusses the 1993 case of Pablo Escobar, Colombian

185. Craig Whitlock, "Afghans Oppose U.S. Hit List of Drug Traffickers," *Washington Post*, October 24, 2009.
186. Bergen and Rowland, "World of Drones," 302.

drug cartel head, apparently executed by Colombian police, trained by the Americans in techniques of manhunting and targeted killing.[187]

In his recent book *The Counterrevolution*, Bernard Harcourt has traced the story of increasing militarization of policing in the United States. He asserts that policing strategy is more and more taking on the character of counter-insurgency, using some of the tools and embodying many of the attitudes that counter-insurgency strategy involves. And all this without the sense of there being any real insurgency to confront.

> We are now witnessing the triumph of a counterinsurgency model of government on American soil in the absence of an insurgency, or uprising, or revolution. The perfected logic of counterinsurgency now applies regardless of whether there is a domestic insurrection.[188]

He does not suggest that targeted killing, as such, is being used domestically, or at least not systematically. But logically and ideologically, the ground is prepared for it, and if it is used domestically, the case against it will more difficult to make, for there will be less that is jarring analytically about the extension of this tactic from counter-terrorism to counter-insurgency to the maintenance of order at home.

187. Miller, "The Ethics of Assassination and Targeted Killing," 314. See also Stimson Center, "Recommendations and Report," 115 note 6 and 131. For a defense of targeted killing in this context, see Tesón, "Targeted Killing in War and Peace," 422. See also Chiesa and Greenawalt, "Beyond War: Bin Laden, Escobar, and the Justification of Targeted Killing."
188. Harcourt, *The Counterrevolution*, 12.

Once again, it may seem hysterical to raise these possibilities. But some of this metastasization is already occurring. And the logic used in arguments for targeted killing encourages the spread. For example, sometimes it is said that targeted killing should be available as a last resort against terrorists in cases where arrest and trial are dangerous or impractical. In an essay I quoted from earlier, Daniel Statman said we are entitled to regard the US campaign against al-Qaeda as war because of "the impracticality of coping with this threat by conventional law-enforcing institutions and methods."[189] Confined to terrorist suspects, this rationale may seem alright, but not if it tends over time to give rise to a general permission to kill whenever one finds it difficult to arrest a dangerous criminal of any kind.

5. Economic and Technical Warfare

Professor Meisels devotes her final section to a discussion of a campaign of targeted assassination by Israeli forces against scientists working for the Syrian and the Iranian governments. Though these were covert operations,[190] they are now more or less acknowledged by the Israeli authorities. It is natural to see some continuity between this sort of targeted killing and the targeted killing of terrorists. Israeli society, after all, is understandably terrorized as much by the one kind of threat as by the other. The animus against Jews and against Israel as a nation informs both phenomena. In general, societies are said to be terrorized by nuclear threats: think of the phrase "the balance of

189. Statman, "Targeted Killing," 183.
190. Bergman, *Rise and Kill First*, 578–580.

terror," used in the United States to describe nuclear deterrence during the Cold War. However, despite the semantic connection—terrorism and terrorization—there can be no question of extending the justifications of targeted killing (such as they are) to just *any* phenomenon that people are greatly afraid of. There lies a recipe for *wholesale* metastasis. In the modern era, foreign and security policy have to be conducted through regular channels—through diplomacy and networks of alliances, all under the auspices of international law.

***

The slopes I have identified in this chapter vary in their slipperiness. They vary as to probabilities, as to circumstances, and above all as to the good faith of the kinds of state actors we are considering. So here is a question:

Defenses of targeted killing focus mostly on its use by the United States in the global war on terrorism and, to a lesser extent, on Israel's use of targeted killing against its adversaries in the Middle East. The United States and Israel have their problems at the level of policy and leadership, but both are still acknowledged as liberal democracies and (within limits determined by Israel's continued rule in the West Bank) as rule-of-law states. Their respective uses of targeted killing have attracted criticism, but it is, I think, fair to say that until recently both states have used the practice in response to bona fide threats, and they have used it with some degree of restraint. So, since in the real world the use of targeted killing by these nations is the focus of controversy, is it appropriate to limit our discussion to these two cases? Are we entitled to put aside the prospect of the practice getting out of hand, when that prospect involves assessing how targeted killing is likely to be used by other less scrupulous states (Russia, China, Turkey, for example)?[191] In 2013, I was a member of a team that won an Oxford Union debate (by a margin of 2:1) on the question, "This house believes drone warfare is ethical and effective."[192] My contribution was to argue that we had to consider the ethics and efficacy of drone warfare in the hands of rogue states as well as (say) the United States. This blindsided our opponents in the debate who had concentrated entirely on the American use of the practice. Was this a fair strategy?

Obviously we ought to consider everything we can. Perhaps as a matter of the ethics of honorable argument, those who take the "for" side should feel obligated to respond to the gravest threats that their opponents have identified, and those who take the "against" side in the debate should respond to the best case that can be made by *their* opponents. That is why I have tried to take on the most powerful argument made by the defenders of the practice that targeting people by name is no different from targeting combatants as such in regular warfare. But even if we do focus on the use of targeted killing only by the United States and Israel, for example, the prospects for metastasization are

191. For concerns about proliferation, see Byman, "Why Drones Work," 54, and Stimson Center, "Recommendations and Report," 113 note 6. See also Zenko and Kreps, "Limiting Armed Drone Proliferation," 124.

192. See the debate at https://www.youtube.com/watch?v=cpt-web6N6Y. See also the discussion in Benjamin Wittes, "Defending Drones at the Oxford Union," *Lawfare*, April 27, 2013.

there already. There is already blurring of the line between terrorists and insurgents; there is already movement into the crime control area; assassination is already being used in scientific and technological policy. We daren't look away.

I finish this chapter with a point about the purpose of political philosophy. Our task is not just to see whether a given practice can be justified but also to consider ways in which it might be abused. In the liberal tradition—what Judith Shklar called "the liberalism of fear"[193]—we are supposed to do this with all state practices. It is surely incumbent on us to consider this possibility with regard to a newly legitimized lethal practice or a new variation on established lethal practices. True, terrorist atrocities over the last twenty years have heightened our fear of the worst that can be done to us by individuals and groups other than the state. And an increase in the power of the state may be necessary to prevent or diminish the prospect of that horror. But the existence of a threat from terrorist attack does not diminish the threat that liberals have traditionally apprehended from the state. The former complements the latter; it does not diminish it, and it may enhance it. It has always been part of the liberalism of fear that new powers given to the government are liable to expand and perhaps be abused.[194]

We have seen this happening, moreover, in other aspects of policy in war on terror, and the unravelling of other constraints. Who would have thought we would have been debating *torture* in the early years of the twenty-first

193. Shklar, "The Liberalism of Fear."
194. These last formulations are adapted from Waldron, *Torture, Terror, and Trade-offs*, 40 and 43.

century? And who can deny that the kind of mentality that allowed *that* to get out of hand might also land us in a situation where targeted killing might begin to seem an all-purpose tool of government, to be used whenever governments feel that their back is against the wall and that there are enemies of the state that need to be dealt with decisively. There is a danger that legitimizing targeted killing in the hands of scrupulous states makes it more likely that unscrupulous states will resort to it or that their abuse of this method anyway will find new forms of defense. There is a danger that it will help upset the international constraint on the use of these methods. How comfortable should we be with evil or rogue regimes purporting to "follow" (as they will call it) the example we have set? I don't think any responsible defense of targeted killing should seek to evade this question. And even though it doesn't settle the matter, I insist on its being confronted here.

CONCLUSION

In politics and in the pursuit of national security, the stakes sometimes seem very high. The stakes include the viability of national policy, the safeguarding of innocent lives, and the survival in office of not-so-innocent politicians. Political leaders have to deal with things like accumulated grievances, minority discontent, and political insurgencies. Some such situations may pose grave threats to values like national identity and public order. Sometimes it may seem better to "eliminate" or "take out" those who are leading the agitation that is posing the problem—posing this threat to the life of the nation—than to continue risking the values that the government stands for. Such a tactic may seem less costly and more decisive than what can be achieved through the uncertain and long drawn-out procedures of ordinary scrupulous law enforcement or less costly and more decisive than what can purchased in ordinary politics, in the uncertain currency of negotiation, compromise, the addressing of grievances, and so on.

Assassinating one's enemies (especially those who can plausibly be designated "enemies of society") is one of the standing temptations of politics. If it has been held at bay in the practice of some advanced democracies over the past hundred years, it has been held at bay only partially and uncertainly, through fragile structures of law, ethics, and humanity that place firm restrictions on what a state can do so far as the use of lethal force is concerned. Indeed, until now in democratic states we have proceeded on the basis that this temptation is not just to be held at bay, but that it must also be put literally "out of the question." In the words of the philosopher Bernard Williams, "I mean by that, that *there is no question of it,* and it would be thought outrageous or insane to mention it as an option. The situation is not one of those in which such options are mentioned and then, all things considered, laid aside."[195] I believe Williams glossed this once by insisting that what we don't want are politicians facing difficulties with some opponent to go round saying, "*Of course we could have him killed, but that's out of the question.*" That would be one thought too many. I fear that the adoption and establishment of targeted killing as a

195. Williams, "Politics and Moral Character," 59.

respectable state practice—as one among many state practices involving the use of lethal force—is a step toward a situation in which killing opponents who can be defined as enemies of the state is no longer out of the question in that very strong sense.

My part of this book has not presented a "slam-dunk" case against targeted killing. My argument has been suggestive in character, with an accumulating array of misgivings about this practice and the way it is defended. My opponents will say, in a realistic spirit, that such misgivings are to be expected, and they are not incompatible with targeted killing's being justified. Surely any practice along these lines, justified or not, will generate some uneasiness, reflecting the fact that competing moral considerations are having to be balanced against one another. There will always be what philosophers call "a moral remainder," and, to adapt another observation from Bernard Williams, only someone who feels uneasy about targeted killing when it *is* justified has much chance of holding the line against it when it is not justified.[196] But the doubts I have tried to develop in this part of the book are not just considerations of mild regret comprising a moral remainder in Williams's sense. They are alarm bells, and their form is something like: "Do we really want to go down this path? Are we happy with what this is going to do to the sense of restraint that democracies have traditionally relied on?"

Or we can face up to the gradual evaporation of that sense of restraint. We begin with justified public anger and insecurity about terrorism. Something has to be done, we

---

196. Williams, "Politics and Moral Character," 59.

say. So we look around for people to attack—our perceived enemies, those who organized the attacks upon us, people whose death is supposed to slake our anger and make us sleep better at night. We congratulate ourselves on not being troubled by fantastic moral scruples, on being hard enough to countenance what is necessary in protecting our society. And then another threat emerges—a threat of a slightly different kind. Again, there is a suggestion that if only we would hunt down those who are posing the problem and kill them, we would be better able to manage our situation. Again, there are scruples and there is resistance to such a course of action, but they turn out to be easier to kick aside now by the fact of our having kicked them aside already in the war against terrorism. And then there is another threat, of a slightly different kind . . . And so it begins: we transform ourselves into a society in which the killing of opponents, as well as enemies, has become one of the ordinary routines of our statecraft.

4

Reply to Professor Waldron

TAMAR MEISELS

■□■

THE LATE ISRAELI COMEDIAN SHAIKE Ophir had a sketch called "The English Teacher," in which he played an Arab teacher teaching *Hamlet* to his class. At one point the teacher attempts to explain the difference between a monologue and a dialogue. "Do you know what the difference between a dialogue and a monologue is?" he asks his pupils. "In a monologue, there is *one* person talking to himself," he answers. "In a dialogue," he continues, "There are *two* persons talking to themselves."

I trust this has not entirely been the case with our debate, but there is a grain of truth in every joke. Professor Waldron and I have proceeded thus far by developing our own distinctive approaches to the issue in hand, not worrying too much about mirroring each other's arguments point by point. We each had our own argument to make, in our own way. We have mostly entrusted the reader with the task of creating a good dialogue out of our two distinct essays. At the risk of repetition, we now welcome the opportunity for a chat and direct engagement.

Debating Targeted Killing. Tamar Meisels and Jeremy Waldron, Oxford University Press (2020)
© Oxford University Press.
DOI: 10.1093/oso/9780190906917.001.0001

1. DEPRIVATION OF LIFE

First and principally, I wholeheartedly agree with professor Waldron that the general point of orientation for any discussion of deliberate killing is "thou shalt not kill." Great vigilance is required with regard to human life, even in wartime. The Israeli High Court of Justice has said as much on numerous occasions. Indeed, the burden of proof falls to those, like myself, who defend targeted killing (any killing) both in principle and case by case.

That said, we also agree that the laws and customs of war represent an exception to the general prohibition on murder. The Law of Armed Conflict privilege a specific set of killings, performed by a particular class of designated agents during wartime. Even this limited license to kill does not render all these privileged killing *morally* "alright." Nonetheless, many of us accept that some wartime killings are morally justified as self-defense (or defense of others) and not merely legally permissible.

Self-defense has a wider meaning in wartime than it does in domestic criminal situations where law enforcement agents are close at hand. Outside a war-like context, or that of an armed struggle, targeted killing is rarely justifiable. A good argument for targeted killing would show that it is an instance of wartime self-defense, or at least analogous to it. *If* there are good reasons underlying the rules that privilege killing in combat, then perhaps these same reasons also justify targeted killings. This would be a good argument by analogy.

2. ANALOGIES

Professor Waldron and others highlight the many differences between targeted killing and regular combat. Targeted killing does not usually take place on the battlefield and is often carried out amidst civilians; neither perpetrator nor victim are necessarily and straightforwardly regular "combatants," and the target is listed and hunted down individually, by name, based on his previous deeds and offenses. Many of these features seem to resemble police action more closely than acts of war. In cases of law enforcement—albeit against well-identified, hardened criminals—we ought indeed to worry very seriously about deploying police hit teams and government death squads, about state-instigated extrajudicial killings and assassination.

It strikes me, however, that all this important work by analogy is slightly misconstrued and out of focus or at least premature. The initial issue in hand is decidedly *not* whether we can construct an analogy between targeted killing and anonymous killing on the battlefield. Not at all (*pas du tout!*). The initial question is whether counter-insurgency/terrorism—the war on terror—ought to be regulated by the Laws of Armed Conflict, or by a set of rules roughly or partly analogous to domestic law enforcement procedures. Is fighting the Hamas government in Gaza, al-Qaeda, the Taliban, or the Islamic State an armed struggle, or is it more like the NYPD trying to maintain law and order?

My unequivocal starting point regarding counter-terrorism was the existence of a continuous armed conflict. In the words of Justice Barak, "It is not police activity. It is an armed struggle."[1] This is an observation—a considered evaluation of timely events—*not* an argument by analogy.

What is the appropriate legal framework for regulating international/non-international armed struggles? I think the Law of Armed Conflict—corresponding to traditional *ius in bello* rules—fits the bill. Otherwise, we leave the door open to philosophers and lawyers who would argue that our laws and moral codes of war are antiquated, out of step with deep morality, and that the Geneva Conventions are obsolete and inadequate for dealing with asymmetrical conflict against terrorists.

Precedents and analogies enter my argument only after the terms of discussion have been set. Absent a settled normative framework, or context (war/peacetime), any test for the relevance of similarities and differences remain utterly contestable and irresoluble, because there is no anchor, no settled regime of set standards, against which to test our conflicting analogies. To state the obvious example of this point: There is no civilian/combatant distinction for killing in peacetime.

Once at war, on the other hand, many cases of targeted killing fall quite neatly under our old-fashioned rules of conduct, with no need for analogies whatsoever. Targeting insurgents at their headquarters or offices, in training camps, alongside their bodyguards, or in their cars with co-militants are all instances of killing on-duty, irregular

---

1. HCJ 7015/02 Ajuri v. IDF Commander. As noted, the armed conflict with al-Qaeda et al. has been categorized by the US Supreme Court as a *non-international* armed conflict. Maxwell, "Rebutting the Civilian Presumption," at 49; Blum and Heymann, "Law and Policy of Targeted Killing," at 157.

combatants. To the extent that these killings are regulated by pre-existing laws of war, there is no need to argue by analogy with anything at all. Nothing hinges on the label "terrorism," and even the derogatory term "unlawful combatant" is redundant here. Active partisans, freedom fighters, guerrilla leaders—call them what you will—have always been fair game when engaged in the business of war.

Beyond irregulars, military commanders—colonels, generals, admirals—are liable to wartime attack.[2] Moreover, high-ranking officers are often specifically sought after as valuable targets, and sometimes their armies instruct them to remove their ranks before going into battle.

What about the targeting of Admiral Yamamoto in 1943? Of course this occurrence cannot in itself be taken as anything like a precedent, establishing a new legal rule of conduct. Professor Waldron cites historical sources indicating that the attack on Yamamoto did not represent universal agreement and practice even in its time, and that it was legally and morally controversial (though practices may not require unanimous agreement in order to be widely accepted).

Anyhow, the singularity of the Yamamoto case speaks for itself: It features mostly solo in arguments favoring targeted killing (including my own), as a fairly unique historical example of named killing. I use it (together with the very different example of Manfred von Richthofen) mainly to point out that there is no explicit legal prohibition on personalized killings of combatants in war. I think I am on solid ground in noting that individuated killing in wartime

2. Walzer, "Targeted Killing and Drone Warfare."

is not clearly illegal or historically unheard of, but this is admittedly a far cry from recommending it as the respectable thing to do right now.

So what work can Admiral Yamamoto do for us? This is precisely the sort of point at which arguments by analogy properly begin. Some instances of targeted killing may not fall clearly under previously well-established rules or precedents (if they did, there would be no need for analogical reasoning). Contemporary named attacks by the United States and Israel do not necessarily target high-ranking individuals;[3] targets are not shot down in bomber planes or on traditional battlefields, instead they are often attacked "off-duty" in a civilian location. Moreover, as Professor Waldron notes, targeted killing is swiftly becoming the norm rather than an exceptional incident.

Can the reasons underling Roosevelt's decision to attack Yamamoto back in 1943 equally justify an executive order to target a terrorist in the 21st century? (Were these reasons *merely* vengeance and boosting morale amongst American troops?) More generally, do the reasons that support our old rules and practices of killing *in war* apply just as well to the named killing of terrorists in contemporary armed conflicts? I listed justifying features such as wartime necessity, national self-defense, and defense of compatriots; the target's direct participation in armed conflict;

---

3. A good example of analogical reasoning here is "the Syrian cook question," posed by the IDF: In regular warfare, all combatants are legitimate targets, even an army cook. How far can we expand the category of legitimate targets within paramilitary organizations by analogy with our Syrian cook? (Bergman, *Rise and Kill First*, at 150–151). To restate, analogies function within our chosen normative framework, not as a means of selecting it.

his/her legal status—their legal liability to attack—the threatening nature of belligerent activity; the lethal danger posed; and the threat to be averted. I argued by analogy that the relevant reasons justifying killing in traditional war apply equally (if not more so) to killing terrorists or insurgents—high ranking or lowly—whether by name, function, or deed.

3. NAMED AND TARGETED

Professor Waldron attributes greater weight to some of the differences between killing in combat, on the one hand, and named killing. on the other hand, such as anonymity, context, and location. Perhaps he is right. But times (as Dylan sings) they are a-changin'; contemporary wars are different. Irregular warfare has long existed side by side with conventional combat but has since become commonplace. Old-fashioned battlefields with machine-gunners lined up on a hill are now few and far between.[4] Most armed conflicts since 1945 have been civil wars (without benefit of uniforms or the Lieber Code) or international low-intensity conflicts involving insurgencies; and the overwhelming majority of wartime casualties following World War II have occurred within these types of conflict. If we are to continue to take the laws of war deadly seriously—and I am in complete agreement with Professor Waldron that we should—they must apply sensibly to the wars we are actually fighting. A little nostalgia can be a dangerous thing. We do well to remember—just before we pack up our drones—the

4. Cf. Waldron in this volume, at 226.

vast number of anonymous casualties incurred *on all sides* in the untargeted good old-fashioned wars we enjoy at the cinema. Targeted killing is a good alternative to burning cities, mass killing fields, and aerial bombardments. Where true peace (not appeasement) is sincerely available, I readily concede it is the preferable option.

What's in a name? Professor Waldron is ill at ease about marking individual combatants for death (by listing their names, details, or photographs), even if the killings themselves are not formally forbidden by international humanitarian law. Targeting terrorists, however, is justified in terms of an individual's specific function, role, or threat, which render him/her liable to attack. Like Waldron's machine-gunner, "We aim at him in that capacity; if he falls back or is relieved from that capacity, we will probably aim at the person who takes his place. "[5]

I already mentioned a succession of Hamas leaders targeted by Israel, most notably Sheik Yassin followed closely by his successor, one Dr. Abdel Aziz al-Rantisi.[6] Philosophy of language and proper names aside, Hamas abruptly stopped naming individuals for the job in question at that point.[7]

Earlier, in the mid-1990s, Israel targeted top explosives expert Yahiya Ayyash (when his Israeli mobile phone mysteriously exploded), and then proceeded to blow up his replacement, Mohi al-Dinh Sharif—"engineer number 2"—when he was driving his car into a garage in Ramallah.[8] As

---

5. Waldron in this volume, Sec. 5. "Named and Targeted," at 226–227.

6. Bergman, *Rise and Kill First*, at 549–556.

7. On Philosophy of language, proper names and reference, see Waldron in this volume, at 222–228.

8. Bergman, *Rise and Kill First*, at 444, 472–473.

for tight and loose references, we say, "target the political leader of Hamas" (or their leading bombmakers) or shoot "the regional commander of al-Qaeda," and to me these references imply the basis—*a very good basis*—for liability to lethal attack; though names, dossiers, and photographs remain important means of identification. "We aim at him in that capacity," and after we have relieved him of that capacity—at least in the Israeli case—"we will probably aim at the person who takes his place"![9]

4. GETTING OUT OF HAND

I am in complete agreement with Professor Waldron about the importance of a careful and strict definition of "terrorism."[10] Defining "terrorism" is, however, totally irrelevant and unimportant *in this context*. In keeping with traditional just war theory and international law, liability to lethal attack is determined by military engagement rather than moral judgment of specific cause or even tactics. The same criterion of liability to attack applies neutrally to French partisans, Hezbollah guerrillas, Taliban insurgents, or jihadist terrorists.

Moreover, *jus in bello* remains entirely independent of *jus ad bellum*. Defending targeted killing involves no wavering back and forth between just war theory and international law on the one side, versus Jeff McMahan's revisionist morality of war on the other.[11] If, however—as

---

9. Cf. Waldron in this volume, Sec. 5. "Named and Targeted," at 226.
10. Meisels, *The Trouble with Terror*, Chap. 1.
11. Cf. Waldron in this volume, at 245–247. See also previously: Waldron at 233.

indicated in my part of the book—some overlapping consensus on targeted killing can be reached between these two very different normative theories, this points in favor of the practice rather than against it.

Professor Waldron is still rightly concerned about hunting combatants back to the home-front, thereby disrupting its relative peace.[12] When it comes to irregulars, and particularly terrorist, however, it is usually the target himself who takes the battlefield home.

What about proliferation? On all accounts, Israel is a veteran at targeted killing, and a good case study for considering its possible abuse. Some of the assassinations attributed to Israel along the years admittedly accede the legal limits of combatant status and direct participation: scientists working on genocidal projects and the odd leftover Nazi war criminal are cases in point. In all this time, however, Israel has never resorted to, or ever contemplated, using targeted killing against domestic criminals or political opponents or in the war on drugs.

Professor Waldron also warns about the situation getting out of hand with a seemingly open-ended list of targets, including terrorists by association.

> People may be targeted just on account of their membership of a group which also includes terrorists as its members: the killing of police recruits at a graduation ceremony in Gaza

---

12. Waldron in this volume, at 219: "It is 1865 and the war is nearing its end . . . twelve named individuals flee towards their homes, but they are still in uniform. With our list in hand, we hunt them down . . . ."

simply because they were employed by the Hamas administration there is an extreme example of this.[13]

These were clearly not named killings (perhaps Professor
Waldron means this was a signature strike), and the attack
was carried out indisputably within a wartime situation or
armed struggle. More importantly, the wartime affiliation of
police units is an old legal question, having little to do with
the label "terrorism" or its affiliates.

Police are an interesting category within the Law of
Armed Conflict. Whether members of law enforcement
agencies may be subsumed in the course of war under the
heading of members of armed forces, and therefore be considered legitimate targets for attack, depends on whether
the armed law enforcement agency has been officially
incorporated into the armed forces or is in fact involved in
hostilities.[14] Israel argued that Hamas police served as an
auxiliary paramilitary unit, and consequently its members
were de facto military objectives, and therefore legitimate
targets under international law.[15]

13. Waldron in this volume, at 239.
14. Dinstein, *The Conduct of Hostilities*, at 95. Dinstein, "Legitimate
Military Objectives," at 154.
15. Halbertal, "The Goldstone Illusion," at 2, addresses the accusation
that Israel's targeting of Hamas police constitutes an attack on
noncombatants: "It is also clear that applying the international law of war
to this new battlefield is fraught with problems. . . . There is no question
that, in an ordinary war, a police force that is dedicated to keeping the
civilian peace is not a military target. . . . What happens in semi-states
that do not have an institutionalized army, whose armed forces are
a militia loyal to the movement or party that seized power? In such
situations, the police force might be just a way of putting combatants on
the payroll of the state, which basically assigns them clear military roles."
See also Gross, *Moral Dilemmas of Modern War*, at 256.

How comfortable should we be with evil or rogue regimes resorting to targeted killings? Not at all, but then I am not usually comfortable with any lethal measures in the hands of evil or rogue regimes. Nor am I convinced that refraining from targeted killing under justified circumstances would have any restraining effect on rogues or tyrants.

Ultimately, the end is in the beginning. For the most part, it boils down to whether we are at war or in peacetime. I have unreservedly defended the named killing of irregular combatants during wartime. Later I offered a possible moral justification for rare instances of targeted killing outside the framework of formally recognized conventional war, in the case of nuclear scientists. There are no combatants outside the Law of Armed Conflict,[16] and even in the course of hostilities or an ongoing proxy war, scientists are legally civilians. Any deliberate killing of civilians by our governments warrant all the suspicions and concerns raised by Professor Waldron throughout.

Nonetheless, neither Professor Waldron nor I aligned ourselves with an absolutist position so far as assassination is concerned. The final section of my argument strongly suggested that if assassination of civilians can be justified under certain circumstances, scientists developing weapons of mass destruction for the Iranian and Syrian governments might very well be just the right kind of case. Justification for such killings would have to be the exception, and never the new norm. In peacetime, the prohibition on murder, the traditional liberal fear of government, and further concerns besides will usually prevail.

16. Cf. Shue, "Do We Need a 'Morality of War'?," 85–111, at 100–101.

5

Reply to Professor Meisels

JEREMY WALDRON

■□■

PROFESSOR MEISELS AND I HAVE ALREADY responded to each other's arguments, inasmuch as defending targeted killing necessarily involves rebutting moral and legal criticisms put forward against it, and opposing targeted killing involves rebutting arguments brought forward in its favor. This is as it should be. There is no one-sided burden of proof in this debate, and we enter it from each side in the midst of ongoing controversy. Inevitably, then, this opportunity for reply will consist mainly in each of us re-emphasizing themes we have already set out, which we think have not been given the attention they ought to have received in the main arguments of the other. (There is one exception: since Meisels' argument about the killing of nuclear scientists introduces a set of considerations that I barely addressed in my main contribution, I would like to say something about those considerations here, at the end of my remarks.)

Let me proceed by mentioning three different themes in the critique of targeted killing that ought to have received more attention from Meisels: the first concerns the particular nature of the hunting and killing that is involved in the practice we are discussing; the second concerns likely abuse

Debating Targeted Killing. Tamar Meisels and Jeremy Waldron, Oxford University Press (2020)
© Oxford University Press.
DOI: 10.1093/oso/9780190906917.001.0001

of the authority to order targeted killings; and the third addresses the effectiveness or otherwise of this practice.

1. HUNTING AND KILLING

Targeted killing is not just killing; it involves the investment of considerable time and effort in the active and sustained hunting down of a known individual until he can be found in a position that enables him to be put to death. I worry that Professor Meisels does not take the *hunting down* element seriously enough. She often writes as though targeted killing was just a matter of knowing the name of a combatant who is killed by the military in the course of ordinary hostilities. But it is not. It is an entirely different sort of enterprise.

There is some recognition of this in Meisels' refreshing willingness to use the term "assassination" to describe targeted killing (e.g., in the opening lines of her contribution), for assassination certainly involves careful preparation and hunting, quite unlike ordinary military action. But she does not address one other point that poses a startling difference between combat killings and the manhunting that targeted assassination involves. A lot of the targeted killing perpetrated by Israel and the United States is undertaken by intelligence operatives.[1] Meisels says very little about this and almost nothing about the problems it poses for her laws-of-war analysis. Sometimes targeted killing is undertaken by soldiers, disciplined by the chain of military command and subject to the laws of

---

1. See Bergman, *Rise and Kill First* and the new book on targeted killing by the CIA, Jacobsen, *Surprise, Kill, Vanish*.

war. But often it is not; does she not think it matters? Does Meisels think that civilians (which is what Mossad or CIA operatives are) should have the same privilege of killing as soldiers have? I am not putting this forward as a knock-down argument against targeted killing. But it reinforces the point that the use of drones and death squads to hunt down individuals and kill them is really quite different from combat.

That the ethos of hunting is a problem is indicated also by the space that Meisels has to devote to the issue of context and location. She faces up to the objection that targeted killing characteristically involves killing people far from any battlefield, when they are not actively engaged in terrorist activity. She acknowledges that defenders of targeted killing have to deal with the "objection that their targeting is often carried out in civilian settings (e.g., at their desks, in their cars, or even in their beds), and that this fact distinguishes their killing from legitimate combat on the battlefield (p. 33)." My point is not just that the killing *happens* to take place there. Military or intelligence operatives spend a lot of time tracking each target down from terrorist camp to village, from planning meeting to family wedding. Meisels acknowledges that this is irregular, to say the least, and that it seems to represent a form of killing not covered by the customs of armed conflict. "Assassinating terrorists in non-military settings admittedly defies such conventions." She acknowledges the existence of a rule that says that "soldiers may not be killed in civilian locations, e.g., when on leave out of uniform, back home, or vacationing with their families." But she says this is just a convention, and if the convention is not reciprocated—which in the case of terrorism is true more or less by definition—then we revert back to the default position, which is that combatants are liable to be killed *anywhere* by virtue of their status. "Terrorists who do not maintain conventional rules—specifically those rules that confine fighting to the battlefield and uphold civilian immunity—are not entitled to the same protection."

But is it just a matter of defeasible convention? The norm about killing taking place in the context of armed conflict goes to the heart of the rationale of our recognition of a privilege of killing. As I said in my main argument, we acknowledge a privilege to kill in situations of high-intensity conflict because it is not reasonable to expect soldiers to refrain from the use of deadly force in such a context. But what about low-intensity conflict? There is surely a point at which the level of hostilities is too low to engage the laws and privileges of war. If a group engages in very sporadic terrorist activity, we have to think hard about whether that sort of hostile action (and the sporadic response to it) rises to the level of armed conflict for the purposes of engaging the rules of war. This is too close to the foundations of the laws of war to make reciprocity a factor. That the terrorists fail to think responsibly about whether the appropriate level of armed conflict has been reached does not mean that we are excused from doing so.

Anyway, my main point is that this insensitivity to context quite sharply distinguishes targeted killing from regular killing in war. And no defense of targeted killing can be adequate if it fails to probe the significance of this.

2. THE POSSIBLE ABUSE
OF TARGETED KILLING

I devoted a considerable part of my argument to the tendency of targeted killing to expand from the narrow context of the killing of an individual terrorist operative in a situation of imminent danger to a much wider range of targets, situations, and problems.

Meisels addresses some of the dimensions of this metastasization, but not all. As we have just seen, she is interested in killings that go beyond situations of imminent danger, as that term is usually defined. That is the issue of context we have just discussed. She is interested also in the reach of targeted killing into terrorist organizations in a way that goes beyond the operatives who actually make use of deadly force—the targeting of recruiters, organizers, motivators, figureheads, and so forth.

She is also prepared to acknowledge the worry that the power to target and terrorists and put them to death might be abused or that there might be mistakes. Sometimes the wrong names will be on the death lists. Fair enough. Beyond that Meisels tells us that considerations like "suspicion of government power, fear of its abuse, [and] lack of transparency" are secondary arguments. What is the point of this categorization? Either it is a concern or it is not. In liberal political philosophy, these "secondary" arguments are tremendously important. Consider the arguments traditionally made against secret police or (in the liberal tradition) against standing armies.[2] Meisels acknowledges

2. See Shklar, "The Liberalism of Fear."

this when she says that an argument's being "secondary" doesn't make it any weaker. But then I fail to see why calling the objection about the possibility of abuse a secondary argument should entitle her to move on with her defense of targeted killing as though the objection didn't matter.

Meisels barely touches on the prospect that targeted killing may be extended to settings that have nothing really to do with terrorism. She acknowledges the difficulty in defining "terrorism," but not the point that the term may be used (and misused) to bridge this extension. There is no discussion in Meisels' account of the misuse/ extension of the term "terrorism," although she must know it is very common indeed. Often governments describe insurgents as terrorists even though the insurgents attack only soldiers of the regime and not civilians. Now, since Meisels' argument depends mostly on assimilating targeted killing to regular warfare, it doesn't matter that it may be used against insurgencies. "Whether terroristic in the strictest sense or otherwise engaged in insurgency, irregular enemy forces and their militants are legitimate wartime targets because of the paramilitary function they perform." However, since, some of her arguments for modifying the regular laws of armed conflict have to do with the special horror of terrorism, then probably more attention needs to be paid to the blurring of this line.

The closest Professor Meisels comes to addressing these possible abuses of what she thinks is the legitimacy of targeted killing is when she says:

> Politicians may be insincere or misuse their power to advance partisan political ends rather than purely security-oriented

goals under the guise of preventing terror attacks on civilian populations. Again, political leaders might misuse, or over-use, targeted killing to pacify an outraged terrorized public or be adopted out of sheer vindictiveness. (XREF)

She says quite rightly that we do not want a situation "in which it is legal and legitimate to go around eliminating political opponents, however bad they may be." But although these concerns are genuine, she seems to think they can be brushed aside. Her strategy seems to be one of acknowledging and then dismissing these concerns, in a way that is really quite reckless. "Imminent terrorist threats requiring immediate action might supersede our concerns about government abuse," she says. And she adds: "[I]n the name of 'national security' or personal safety, we resign ourselves to these negative side effects." If so, we are guilty of wishful thinking, for nothing in our experience justifies the claim that the threat from terrorist action diminishes the risk of abuse of political power.[3]

3. EFFECTIVENESS

The strategy Meisels ends up adopting with regard to the possibility of abuse is that the risk is worth it. But is it? Surely we should say it is worth it only if targeted killing is effective in countering terrorism. I don't think she makes a good case to that effect. She acknowledges that targeted killing is "not an overall political solution." At best it is necessary for "conflict management." And even then, she says,

3. See also Waldron, *Torture, Terror and Trade-offs*, 39–44.

"it is difficult for anyone, even military experts, to establish absolutely the utility of targeting individual terrorists."
Still, she says, we do not need to be absolutely sure. And the
conclusion she rests with is that "targeted killing is our best
shot at combating terrorism at the lowest cost to innocent
human life."

Once again, I don't think this is adequate. It is altogether too casual for an argument that is supposed to justify our risking the likelihood of abuse of this power. It does
not take proper account of the possibility that targeted
killing may make things worse rather than better. And it
involves no comparison with other methods of protecting
against terrorism. President Barack Obama famously maintained that doing nothing in response to terrorism was not
an option.[4] But the United States was already doing a whole
lot: disrupting terrorist communications; disrupting the
flow of money to finance terrorist operations; arresting,
detaining, and trying terrorist suspects; hardening possible targets of terrorist activity; enhancing the sharing
of intelligence with other governments; and so on. A case
specifically for the necessity of targeted killing would have
to compare its efficacy to that of these other means. Such
calculations are extraordinarily difficult, but it is not appropriate to respond to such difficulty by simply announcing
that it has "a reasonable chance of success."

Meisels also talks a little about the success of targeted
killing in protecting Israel. She says:

> Those of us who support it believe that a sustained policy
> of targeting terrorists, particularly leaders, can dramatically

4. "Obama's Speech on Drone Policy," *New York Times*, May 23, 2013.

reduce terrorist hostility and save many lives. Israel's success in overcoming Palestinian suicide terrorism in the early 2000s is a strong case in point, whatever one's view on the surrounding political issues may be. (XREF)

A responsible assessment of this dramatic success would also mention the Israeli use of physical barriers separating Israel proper from Gaza and the West Bank. Targeted killing by Israeli security forces began well before 2000, but the numbers only began to decline dramatically after significant portions of the "wall" were built. And certainly the Israeli government attributes the decline in terrorist attacks to the effect of the barrier, not the effect of targeted killings.

I did say in Part II of my contribution that I would treat effectiveness per se as a side issue. I raise it here, however, because it seems to be the key to some of Professor Meisels' arguments. It was she who said that the risk of abuse is worth tolerating if (and I presume "only if") targeted killing is effective in suppressing terrorism. She can hardly put this forward as an argument and then go straight on to say that its effectiveness is unknown and at best it is just a form of conflict management.

4. KILLING OF NUCLEAR SCIENTISTS

The final topic I want to discuss is the killing of nuclear scientists in Iran by Israeli intelligence operatives. As I have said, I appreciate Professor Meisels' willingness to introduce these cases into our discussion.

Meisels is certainly right to acknowledge that any attempt to justify the assassination of Iranian nuclear scientists requires "settling a wide range of surrounding practical issues that remain largely unknown and controversial, such as the identity and precise motive of the perpetrators, the gravity of any Iranian threat, and the projected expediency of assassination in removing or retarding such a threat." The gist of her position, however, is that nuclear scientists are (or are like) particularly dangerous munitions workers, and that, although munitions workers are not to be made targets of intentional deadly attack under the laws of war as they stand, nevertheless the laws of war might be amended—and perhaps ought to be amended—to make such individuals liable to deadly force. Meisels is not arguing, I think, that because there is a case for changing the laws of war therefore we ought to treat killings like this as licit. Rather she is saying that the case against killing these scientists is quite weak given that it rests upon laws of war that lack solid moral foundation. That is a fair argument to make.

However, the fatal flaw in its application to the case of assassination of nuclear scientists by Israeli forces is that Israel is not at war with Iran, and so no real or notional modification of the laws of war in the direction of exposing munitions workers to deadly force could possibly be relevant. She acknowledges this, and it is important because, as she says, the "privileges of belligerency . . . apply only in wartime." The best that might be said for her argument about the killings of scientists is that it presents itself as a form of pre-emptive attack. But the pre-emptive distance (between the killing and the event that is apprehended) is huge.

At the beginning of her contribution to the book, Meisels hints at an argument for killing scientists that is supposed to be based on Michael Walzer's discussion of supreme emergency in *Just and Unjust Wars*.[5] I am skeptical about any such argument, and I do not believe that Walzer was commending it to us.[6] In any case, Meisels does not really elaborate this in the final part of her paper. And just as well, because it too is vulnerable to the point that we are not talking about a wartime situation. She would be taking Walzer's doctrine, such as it is, way out of the realm of its applicability. At best it would be a "supreme emergency" exception to the laws of peace, that is, to the regular law forbidding murder.

In the end, the case is one of assassination pure and simple, and that's where the argument has to be made. The rule against murder has to be breached, and the key to her argument seems to be that nuclear programs of countries like Iran pose "catastrophic threats" and constitute "rare exceptions of urgent necessity" to the rule about killing. Meisels thinks she can engage in this consequentialist reasoning because an absolute ban on assassination is hard to justify. As I have found in my work on torture, an absolute ban on anything is hard to justify in an age where many moral philosophers believe that non-consequentialist constraints represent outdated moral taboos. Be that as it may, Meisels is definitely interested in the consequentialist case for assassination. Indeed, she wants to make a very ambitious consequentialist argument: she says that such killings can not only be justified by good consequences, but that

5. Walzer, *Just and Unjust Wars*, 250ff.
6. See Waldron, "Reflections on 'Supreme Emergency.'"

consequences can also establish a justification such that "[n]o residual guilt remains to tarnish the hands of those who order and carry out these killings." No regrets, not even for putting civilians to death in peacetime! With these simplistic moral categories, perhaps it is all too easy to justify targeted killing. But resting her case there involves selling short what I am willing to acknowledge is a much more complex argument in her contribution to this controversy.

BIBLIOGRAPHY

Newspaper, magazine, and website articles are cited fully in the footnotes and are not included in the bibliography. This is true also of statutes, treaties, and cases.

AFSHEEN, JOHN RADSAN and RICHARD MURPHY, "The Evolution of Law and Policy for CIA Targeted Killing," *Journal of National Security Law and Policy*, 5 (2012), 439–464.

ALFORD, RYAN, "Targeted Killing and the Rule of Law," *Cato Unbound*, June 2011.

ALSTON, PHILIP, "Report of the Special Rapporteur on Extrajudicial, Summary or Arbitrary Executions, Addendum: Study on Targeted Killings," UN Human Rights Council, 14th Session (2010), available at https://www2.ohchr.org/english/bodies/hrcouncil/docs/14session/A.HRC.14.24.Add6.pdf.

ALSTON, PHILIP, "The CIA and Targeted Killings beyond Borders," *Harvard National Security Journal*, 2 (2011), 283–446.

ALTMAN, ANDREW, "Targeted Killing as an Alternative to War: The Problem of the Fair Distribution of Risk," Paper presented at ELAC Annual Conference (Oxford, 2014).

ALTMAN, ANDREW and CHRISTOPHER HEATH WELLMAN, "From Humanitarian Intervention to Assassination: Human Rights and Political Violence," *Ethics*, 118 (2008), 228–257.

AMANN, DIANE MARIE, "John Paul Stevens, Human Rights Judge," *Fordham Law Review*, 74 (2006), 1569–1605.

AMERICAS WATCH, *El Salvador's Decade of Terror: Human Rights Since the Assassination of Archbishop Romero* (New Haven: Yale University Press, 1993).

AMNESTY INTERNATIONAL, "Will I Be Next? US Drone Strikes in Pakistan," in Knuckey (ed.), *Drones and Targeted Killings*, 319–331.

ANDERSON, KENNETH, "Targeted Killing in U.S. Counterterrorism Strategy and Law," Brookings Institution, May 11, 2009, available at https://www.brookings.edu/research/targeted-killing-in-u-s-counterterrorism-strategy-and-law/.

ANDERSON, KENNETH, "More Predator Drone Debate in the Wall Street Journal, and What the Obama Administration Should Do as a Public Legal Position," *The Volokh Conspiracy*, January 9, 2010, available at http://volokh.com/2010/01/09/more-predator-drone-debate-in-the-wall-street-journal-and-what-the-obama-administration-should-do-as-a-public-legal-position/.

ANDERSON, KENNETH, "Targeted Killing and Drone Warfare: How We Came to Debate Whether There Is a 'Legal Geography of War,'" WCL Research Paper No. 2011–16 (2011), available at http://ssrn.com/abstract=1824783.

ANDERSON, KENNETH, "The Case for Drones," *Commentary*, June 2013.

ANDRADE, DALE, *Ashes to Ashes: The Phoenix Program and the Vietnam War* (New York: Lexington Books, 1990).

ARE, JAMES DESHAW, *Targeted Killing, Remote Warfare, and Military Technology* (New York: Palgrave MacMillan, 2014).

ARENDT, HANNAH, *The Origins of Totalitarianism* (New York: Harcourt, Brace, Jovanovich, 1973).

BANKS, WILLIAM, "Regulating Drones: Are Targeted Killings by Drones Outside Traditional Battlefields Legal?" in Bergen and Rothenberg (eds.), *Drone Wars*, 129–159.

BAR ZOHAR, MICHAEL and MISHAL, NISSIM, *Mossad – The Greatest Missions of the Israeli Secret Service* (Harper Collins, 2012).

BENNIS, PHYLLIS, "Drones and Assassination in the US's Permanent War," in Cohn (ed.), *Drones and Targeted Killing*, 51–62.

BENVENISTI, EYAL, "The Law on Asymmetric Warfare," *Tel Aviv University Law Faculty Papers.* Working Paper 143, available at http://law.bepress.com/taulwps/art143.

BERGEN, PETER and DANIEL ROTHENBERG (eds.), *Drone Wars: Transforming Conflict, Law, and Policy* (Cambridge: Cambridge University Press, 2015).

BERGEN, PETER and JENNIFER ROWLAND, "Decade of the Drone: Analyzing CIA Drone Attacks, Casualties, and Policy," in Bergen and Rothenberg (eds.), *Drone Wars*, 12–41.

BERGEN, PETER and JENNIFER ROWLAND, "World of Drones: The Global Proliferation of Drone Technology," in Bergen and Rothenberg (eds.), *Drone Wars*, 300–341.

BERGMAN, RONEN, *Rise and Kill First: The Secret History of Israel's Targeted Assassinations* (New York: Random House Penguin, 2018).

BLANCHARD, CHARLES, "This Is Not War by Machine," in Bergen and Rothenberg (eds.), *Drone Wars*, 123–128.

BLUM, GABRIELLA, "The Dispensable Lives of Soldiers," *Journal of Legal Analysis*, 2 (2010), 69–124.

BLUM, GABRIELLA and PHILIP HEYMANN, "Law and Policy of Targeted Killing," *Harvard National Security Journal*, 1 (2010), 145–165.

BOLTON, ROGER, *Death on the Rock and Other Stories* (London: W. H. Allen, 1990).

BRENNAN, JOHN, "The Efficacy and Ethics of US Counterterrorism Strategy," in Knuckey (ed.), *Drones and Targeted Killings*, 29–45.

BRENNAN, JOHN, "Strengthening our Security by Adhering to our Values and Laws," in Jaffer (ed.), *The Drone Memos*, 161–166.

BROOKS, ROSA, "Drones and Cognitive Dissonance," in Bergen and Rothenberg (eds.), *Drone Wars*, 230–252.

BUGNION FRANCOIS, "Just War, Wars of Aggression and International Humanitarian Law," *The International Review of the Red Cross*, 847 (84) (2002), 523–546, available at http://

www.icrc.org/eng/assets/files/other/irrc-847-2002-bugnion-ang.pdf.

BURKE, EDMUND, *The Writings and Speeches of Edmund Burke*, volume 11: *Speech in General Reply* (London: Cosimo Classics, 2008).

BYMAN, DANIEL, "Do Targeted Killings Work?" *Foreign Affairs*, 85 (2006), 95–111.

BYMAN, DANIEL, "Why Drones Work: The Case for Washington's Weapon of Choice," in Knuckey (ed.), *Drones and Targeted Killings*, 46–56.

CHAMAYOU, GRÉGOIRE, *A Theory of the Drone* (New York: New Press, 2013).

CHIESA, LUIS and ALEXANDER GREENAWALT, "Beyond War: Bin Laden, Escobar, and the Justification of Targeted Killing," *Washington and Lee Law Review*, 69 (2012), 1371–1470.

CLAUSEWITZ, CARL VON, *On War*, trans. Michael Howard and Peter Paret (Princeton: Princeton University Press, 1976).

COADY, C. A. J., "Defining Terrorism," in Primoratz (ed.), *Terrorism: The Philosophical Issues*, 3–14.

COHN, MARJORIE (ed.), *Drones and Targeted Killing: Legal, Moral, and Geopolitical Issues* (Northampton, MA: Olive Branch Press, 2015).

CORN, GEOFFREY, "Back to the Future: De Facto Hostilities, Transnational Terrorism, and the Purpose of the Law of Armed Conflict," *University of Pennsylvania Journal of International Law*, 30 (Summer 2009), 1345–1354.

DASKAL, JENNIFER, "The Geography of the Battlefield: A Framework for Detention and Targeting Outside the 'Hot' Conflict Zone," *University of Pennsylvania Law Review*, 161 (2013), 1165–1234.

DASKAL, JENNIFER and STEPHEN VLADECK, "After the AUMF," *Harvard National Security Journal*, 5 (January 2014), 115–146.

DAVIDSON, EUGENE, *The Nuremberg Fallacy* (Columbia: University of Missouri Press, 1998).

DEHN, JOHN, "Targeting Citizens in Armed Conflict: Examining the Threat to the Rule of Law," *Cato Unbound* (2011).

DELAHUNTY, ROBERT, "Obama's War Law," *Engage: Journal of the Federalist Society Practice Groups*, 11 (2010), 80–87.

DELAHUNTY, ROBERT and JOHN YOO, "What Is the Role of International Human Rights Law in the War on Terror?" *DePaul Law Review*, 59 (2010), 803–849.

DENNETT, DANIEL, "The Milk of Human Intentionality," *Behavioral and Brain Sciences*, 3 (1980), 417–457.

DERSHOWITZ, ALAN, "Killing Terrorist Chieftains is Legal," *The Jerusalem Post*, April 22, 2004.

DICKIE, IMOGEN, "How Proper Names Refer," *Proceedings of the Aristotelian Society*, 111 (2011), 43–78.

DINSTEIN, YORAM, "Legitimate Military Objectives under the Current Jus in Bello," *International Law Studies*, 78 (2002), 139–171.

DINSTEIN, YORAM, *The Conduct of Hostilities under the Law of International Armed Conflict* (Cambridge: Cambridge University Press, 2004).

DONNELLAN, KEITH, "Reference and Definite Descriptions," *Philosophical Review*, 75 (1966), 281–304.

DWORKIN, GERALD, "Non-Neutral Principles," *Journal of Philosophy*, 71 (1974), 491–506.

EICHENSEHR, KRISTEN, "On Target? The Israeli Supreme Court and the Expansion of Targeted Killing," *Yale Law Journal*, 116 (8) (June 2007), 1873–1881.

FABRE, CECILE, "Guns, Food, and Liability to Attack in War," *Ethics*, 120 (2009), 36–63.

FALK, RICHARD, "Why Drones Are More Dangerous than Nuclear Weapons," in Cohn (ed.), *Drones and Targeted Killing*, 29–50.

FINKELSTEIN, CLAIRE, "Targeted Killing as Pre-emptive Action," in Finkelstein et al. (eds.), *Targeted Killings*, 156–182.

FINKELSTEIN, CLAIRE, JENS OHLIN, and ANDREW ALTMAN (eds.), *Targeted Killings: Law and Morality in an Asymmetrical World* (Oxford: Oxford University Press, 2012).

FLEMING, JAMES (ed.), *Nomos 50: Getting to the Rule of Law* (New York: New York University Press, 2011).

FLETCHER, GEORGE, *Romantics at War—Glory and Guilt in the Age of Terrorism* (Princeton: Princeton University Press, 2003).

FLETCHER, GEORGE, "The Indefinable Concept of Terrorism," *Journal of International Criminal Justice*, 4 (2006), 894–911.

FRIED, CHARLES and GREGORY FRIED, *Because It Is Wrong: Torture, Privacy and Presidential Power in the Age of Terror* (New York: W.W. Norton, 2010).

FRIEDMAN, URI, "Targeted Killing: A Short History—How America Came to Embrace Assassination," *Foreign Policy*, August 13, 2012, available at https://foreignpolicy.com/2012/08/13/targeted-killings-a-short-history/.

FROWE, HELEN, *Defensive Killing* (Oxford: Oxford University Press, 2014).

FULLER, LON, "Positivism and Fidelity to Law: A Reply to Professor Hart," *Harvard Law Review*, 71 (1958), 630–672.

GILBERT, PAUL, *New Terror, New Wars* (Edinburgh: Edinburgh University Press, 2003).

GLOVER, JONATHAN, *Causing Death and Saving Lives* (Harmondsworth: Penguin Books, 1977).

GOVERN, KEVIN, "Operation Neptune Spear: Was Killing Bin Laden a Legitimate Military Objective?," in Finkelstein et al. (eds.), *Targeted Killings*, 347–373.

GROSS, MICHAEL, "Fighting by Other Means in the Mideast: A Critical Analysis of Israel's Assassination Policy," *Political Studies*, 51 (2003), 350–368.

GROSS, MICHAEL, "Assassination: Killing in the Shadow of Self-Defence," in Irwin (ed.), *War and Virtual War*, 99–116.

GROSS, MICHAEL, "Assassination and Targeted Killing: Law Enforcement, Execution, or Self-Defence," *Journal of Applied Philosophy*, 23 (2006), 323–335.

GROSS, MICHAEL, *Moral Dilemmas of Modern War—Torture, Assassination, and Blackmail in an Age of Asymmetric Conflict* (New York: Cambridge University Press, 2010).

GROSS, MICHAEL, and TAMAR MEISELS (eds.), *Soft War—The Ethics of Unarmed Conflict* (New York: Cambridge University Press, 2017).

GUIORA, AMOS, "Targeted Killing as Active Self-Defense," *Case Western Research Journal International Law*, 36 (2004), 319–334.

HAJJAR, LISA, "Anatomy of the US Targeted Killing Policy," *Middle East Report*, 264 (2012), 11–18.

HALBERTAL, MOSHE, "The Goldstone Illusion—What the UN Report Gets Wrong About Gaza—And War," *The New Republic* (November 2009).

HALBERTAL, MOSHE, "Moral Challenges in Asymmetric Warfare," available at http://www.law.nyu.edu/sites/default/files/upload_documents/a%20symetrical%20warfare%20publication%20(1).pdf.

HAMPSHIRE, STUART (ed.), *Public and Private Morality* (Cambridge: Cambridge University Press, 1978).

HARCOURT, BERNARD, *The Counterrevolution: How Our Government Went to War Against Its Own Citizens* (New York: Basic Books, 2018).

HELLER, KEVIN, "'One Hell of a Killing Machine': Signature Strikes and International Law," *Journal of International Criminal Justice*, 11 (2013), 89–119.

HENSON, R. G., "Utilitarianism and the Wrongness of Killing," *Philosophical Review*, 80 (1971), 320–337.

HOLDER, ERIC, "Remarks of Eric Holder at Northwestern University School of Law, March 5, 2012," in Jaffer (ed.), The Drone Memos, 191–199.

HONDERICH, TED, *After the Terror* (Edinburgh: Edinburgh University Press, 2002).

HONDERICH, TED, *Terrorism for Humanity—Inquiries in Political Philosophy* (London: Pluto Press, 2003).

HUMAN RIGHTS WATCH, "Targeted Killing under Donald Trump," available at https://www.hrw.org/news/2018/03/07/ngo-statement-reported-changes-us-policy-use-armed-drones-and-other-lethal-force.

HURKA, THOMAS, "Proportionality in the Morality of War," *Philosophy & Public Affairs*, 33 (1) (2005), 34–66.

ICRC, "Interpretive Guidance on the Notion of Direct Participation in Hostilities under International Humanitarian Law," *International Review of the Red Cross* 90 (no. 872): 991–1047, available at: http://www.icrc.org/eng/resources/documents/article/review/review-872-p991.htm.

IRWIN, JONES (ed.), *War and Virtual War: The Challenges to Communities* (Amsterdam: Rodopi, 2005).

ISSACHAROFF, SAM and RICHARD PILDES, "Targeted Warfare: Individuating Enemy Responsibility," *New York University Law Review*, 88 (2013), 1521–1599.

ISSACHAROFF, SAM and RICHARD PILDES, "Drones and the Dilemma of Modern Warfare," in Bergen and Rothenberg (eds.), *Drone Wars*, 388–420.

JACOBSEN, ANNIE, *Surprise, Kill, Vanish: The Secret History of CIA Paramilitary Armies, Operators, and Assassins* (New York: Little Brown, 2019).

JAFFER, JAMEEL (ed.), *The Drone Memos: Targeted Killing, Secrecy, and the Law* (New York: New Press, 2016).

KAMM, FRANCES, *The Trolley Problem Mysteries*, Eric Rakowski (ed.) (New York: Oxford University Press, 2015).

KANT, IMMANUEL, *The Metaphysics of Morals* (1797) trans. Mary Gregor (Cambridge: Cambridge University Press, 1991).

KANT, IMMANUEL, *Toward Perpetual Peace and Other Writings on Politics, Peace, and History*, Pauline Kleingeld (ed.), trans. David L. Colclasure (New Haven: Yale University Press, 2006).

KAPITAN, TOMIS, (ed.), *Philosophical Perspectives on the Israeli-Palestinian Conflict* (London: Routledge, 2017).

KETCHUM, RICHARD, *The Winter Soldiers: The Battles for Trenton and Princeton* (New York: Anchor, 1973).

KLAIDMAN, DANIEL, *Kill or Capture: The War on Terror and the Soul of the Obama Presidency* (Houghton, Mifflin, Harcourt, 2012).

KNUCKEY, SARAH (ed.), *Drones and Targeted Killings: Ethics, Law, and Politics* (New York: IDebate Press, 2015).

KOH, HAROLD HONJU, "The Obama Administration and International Law," Speech at the Annual Meeting of the American Society of International Law, Washington, DC, March 25, 2010, available at https://www.state.gov/documents/organization/179305.pdf.

KRETZMER, DAVID, "Targeted Killing of Suspected Terrorists: Extra-Judicial Executions or Legitimate Means of Defence?" *European Journal of International Law*, 16 (2005), 171–212.

KRIPKE, SAUL, *Naming and Necessity* (Oxford: Basil Blackwell, 1981).

LAZAR, SETH, "Necessity, Vulnerability, and Noncombatant Immunity," unpublished manuscript, cited by Meisels with the permission of the author (2010).

LAZAR, SETH, *Sparing Civilians* (Oxford: Oxford University Press, 2015).

LAZAR, SETH, "Evaluating the Revisionist Critique of Just War Theory," *Daedalus*, 146 (2017), 113–124.

LAZAR, SETH and HELEN FROWE (eds.), *Oxford Handbook of the Ethics of War* (New York: Oxford University Press, 2015).

LEVINSON, SANFORD (ed.), *Torture: A Collection* (New York: Oxford University Press, 2004).

LOCKE, JOHN, *Two Treatises of Government*, Peter Laslett (ed.) (Cambridge: Cambridge University Press, 1988).

MACHIAVELLI, NICCOLO, *Discourses on Livy*, trans. Harvey Mansfield and Nathan Tarcov (Chicago: University Of Chicago Press, 1996).

MACHIAVELLI, NICCOLO, *The Art of War*, trans. Christopher Lynch (University of Chicago Press, 2003).

MAXWELL, MARK, "Rebutting the Civilian Presumption: Playing Whack-A-Mole without a Mallet?" in Finkelstein et al. (eds.), *Targeted Killings*, 30–59.

MCDONALD, JACK, *Enemies Known and Unknown: Targeted Killings in America's Transnational War* (New York: Oxford University Press, 2017).

MCKELVEY, TARA, "Defending the Drones: Harold Koh and the Evolution of US Policy," in Bergen and Rothenberg (eds.), *Drone Wars*, 185–205.

MCMAHAN, JEFF, "The Ethics of Killing in War," *Ethics*, 114 (2004), 693–733.

MCMAHAN, JEFF, "Just Cause for War," *Ethics and International Affairs*, 19 (2005), 1–21.

MCMAHAN, JEFF, "Torture in Principle and in Practice," *Public Affairs Quarterly*, 22 (2008), 91–108.

MCMAHAN, JEFF, *Killing in War* (Oxford: Oxford University Press, 2009).

MCMAHAN, JEFF, "The Morality of War and the Law of War," in Rodin and Shue (eds.), *Just and Unjust Warriors*, 19–43.

MCMAHAN, JEFF, "Targeted Killing: Murder, Combat, or Law Enforcement?," in Finkelstein et al. (eds.), *Targeted Killings*, 135–155.

MEISELS, TAMAR, "Targeting Terror," *Social Theory and Practice*, 30 (2004), 297–326.

MEISELS, TAMAR, *The Trouble with Terror* (Cambridge: Cambridge University Press, 2008).

MEISELS, TAMAR, "In Defense of the Defenseless: The Deep Morality of the Laws of War," *Political Studies*, 60 (2012), 919–935.

MEISELS, TAMAR, "Preemptive Strikes—Israel and Iran," *Canadian Journal of Law and Jurisprudence*, 25 (2012), 447–463.

MEISELS, TAMAR, "Assassination: Targeting Nuclear Scientists," *Law and Philosophy*, 33 (2014), 204–234.

MEISELS, TAMAR, "Kidnapped—Kidnapping and Extortion as Tactics of Soft War," in Gross and Meisels (eds.), *Soft War*, 1–14.

MEISELS, TAMAR, *Contemporary Just War: Theory and Practice* (London: Routledge, 2017).

MELZER, NILS, *Targeted Killing in International Law* (Oxford: Oxford University Press, 2008).

MENUCHIN, ISHAI, "The Case of Israel: A Covert Policy of Political Capital Punishment," in Cohn (ed.), *Drones and Targeted Killing*, 205–217.

MEYER, RICHARD, "The Privilege of Belligerency and Formal Declarations of War," in Finkelstein, et al., *Targeted Killing*, 183–219.

MILL, JOHN STUART, *A System of Logic: Ratiocinative and Inductive, Being a Connected View of the Principles of Evidence and the Methods of Scientific Investigation* (London: John Parker, 1834).

MILLER, JOHN, *Cartwheel: The Reduction of Rabaul* (Washington, DC: Office of the Chief of Military History, 1959).

MILLER, SEUMAS, "The Ethics of Assassination and Targeted Killing," *Annual Review of Law and Ethics*, 19 (2011), 309–322.

MIRER, JEANNE, "US Policy of Targeted Killing with Drones: Illegal at Any Speed," in Cohn (ed.), *Drones and Targeted Killing*, 135–168.

MONTAGUE, PHILLIP, "Defending Defensive Targeted Killings," in Finkelstein et al. (eds.), *Targeted Killings*, 285–301.

MOORE, MICHAEL, "Targeted Killings and the Morality of Hard Choices," in Finkelstein et al. (eds.), *Targeted Killings*, 434–466.

MOREHOUSE, MATTHEW, "The Claws of the Bear: Russia's Targeted Killing Program," *Journal of Slavic Military Studies*, 28 (2015), 269–298.

MOTHANA, IBRAHIM, "How Drones Help Al Qaeda," in Knuckey (ed.), *Drones and Targeted Killings*, 82–85.

MURPHY, RICHARD and AFSHEEN JOHN RADSAN, "Due Process and Targeted Killing of Terrorists," *Cardozo Law Review*, 31 (2009), 405–450.

NABULSI, KARMA, *Traditions of War: Occupation, Resistance, and the Law* (Oxford: Oxford University Press, 1999).

NAGEL, THOMAS, "War and Massacre," *Philosophy and Public Affairs*, 1 (1972) 123–144.

NETANYAHU, BENJAMIN (ed.), *Terrorism—How the West Can Win* (New York: Farrar, Straus and Giroux, 1986).

NETANYAHU, BENJAMIN, *Fighting Terrorism*, 2nd edition (New York: Farrar, Straus and Giroux, 2001).

O'CONNELL, MARY ELLEN, "The Choice of Law against Terrorism," *Journal of National Security Law and Policy*, 4 (2010), 343–368.

O'DONOVAN, OLIVER, *The Just War Revisited* (Cambridge: Cambridge University Press, 2003).

OFFICE OF LEGAL COUNSEL, Memorandum for the Attorney General (July 16, 2010), re: Applicability of Federal Criminal Laws and the Constitution to Contemplated Lethal Operations against Shaykh Anwar al-Aulaqi, available at http://www.justsecurity.org/wp-content/uploads/2014/06/OLC-al-Aulaqi-memo.pdf.

POWER, MATTHEW, "Confessions of a Drone Warrior," in Knuckey (ed.), *Drones and Targeted Killings*, 163–182.

POWERS, ROBERT, "Insurgency and the Law of Nations," *JAG Journal*, 16 (1962), 55–65.

PRIMORATZ, IGOR (ed.), *Terrorism: The Philosophical Issues* (New York: Palgrave-Macmillan, 2004).

REIFER, TOM, "A Global Assassination Program," in Cohn (ed.), *Drones and Targeted Killing*, 79–90.

RODIN, DAVID, *War and Self-Defense* (Oxford: Oxford University Press, 2002).

RODIN, DAVID and HENRY SHUE (eds.), *Just and Unjust Warriors: The Moral and Legal Status of Soldiers* (Oxford: Oxford University Press, 2008).

ROSENBLUM, NANCY (ed.), *Liberalism and the Moral Life* (Cambridge: Harvard University Press, 1989).

ROTHENBERG, DANIEL, "Drones and the Emergence of Data-driven Warfare," in Bergen and Rothenberg (eds.), *Drone Wars*, 441–461.

ROUSSEAU, JEAN JACQUES, *The Social Contract and Discourses* (London: Everyman, 1762, 1993).

RUSSELL, BERTRAND, "On Denoting," *Mind*, 14 (1905), 479–493.

SCHAUER, FREDERICK, "Slippery Slopes," *Harvard Law Review*, 99 (1985), 361–383.

SCHEIPERS, SYBILLE (ed.), *Prisoners in War* (Oxford: Oxford University Press, 2010).

SEARLE, JOHN, "Proper Names," *Mind*, 67 (1958), 166–173.

SHAH, PAIR ZUBAH, "My Drone War," in Knuckey (ed.), *Drones and Targeted Killings*, 89–101.

SHKLAR, JUDITH, "The Liberalism of Fear," in Rosenblum (ed.), *Liberalism and the Moral Life*, 21–38.

SHUE, HENRY, "Do We Need a 'Morality of War'?" in his collection *Fighting Hurt*.

SHUE, HENRY, *Fighting Hurt: Rule and Exception in Torture and War* (Oxford: Oxford University Press, 2016).

SITARAMAN, GANESH, "Counterinsurgency, the War on Terror, and the Laws of War," *Virginia Law Review*, 95 (2009), 1745–1839.

SLUKA, JEFFREY, "Death from Above: UAVs and Losing Hearts and Minds," *Military Review*, 93 (2013), 70–76.

SOLIS, GARY, *The Law of Armed Conflict: International Humanitarian Law in War* (Cambridge: Cambridge University Press, 2010).

STANFORD LAW SCHOOL (International Human Rights and Conflict Resolution Clinic) and NYU SCHOOL OF LAW (Global Justice Clinic), *Living under Drones: Death, Injury, and Trauma to Civilians from US Drone Practices in Pakistan* (2012).

STATMAN, DANIEL, "The Morality of Assassination: A Response to Gross," *Political Studies,* 51 (2003), 775–779.

STATMAN, DANIEL, "Targeted Killing," *Theoretical Inquiries in Law,* 5 (2004), 179–198.

STATMAN, DANIEL, "Drones, Robots and the Ethics of War," *Zebis Ethics and Armed Force—Controversies in Military Ethics and Security Policies* (e-journal), 1 (2014), 41–45.

STATMAN, DANIEL, "Drones and Robots: On the Changing Practice of Warfare," in Lazar and Frowe (eds.), *Oxford Handbook of the Ethics of War,* 472–487.

STATMAN, DANIEL, "Jus in Bello and the Intifada," in Kapitan (ed.), *Philosophical Perspectives on the Israeli-Palestinian Conflict,* 133–156.

STATMAN, DANIEL, "Can Just War theory Justify Targeted Killing," in Finkelstein et al. (eds.), *Targeted Killings,* 90–111.

STIMSON CENTER, "Recommendations and Report of the Task Force on US Drone Policy," in Knuckey (ed.), *Drones and Targeted Killings,* 102–123.

STRAWSER, BRADLEY JAY, "Moral Predators: The Duty to Employ Uninhabited Aerial Vehicles," *Journal of Military Ethics,* 9 (2010), 342–368.

STRAWSER, BRADLEY JAY, (ed.), *Killing by Remote Control—The Ethics of an Unmanned Military* (Oxford: Oxford University Press, 2013).

STRAWSON, P. F., "On Referring," *Mind,* 59 (1950), 320–344.

TESÓN, FERNANDO, "Targeted Killing in War and Peace: A Philosophical Analysis," in Finkelstein et al. (eds.), *Targeted Killings,* 403–433.

THOMSON, JUDITH JARVIS, "A Defense of Abortion," *Philosophy and Public Affairs,* 1 (1971), 47–66.

TOBEY, WILLIAM, "Nuclear Scientists as Assassination Targets," *Bulletin of the Atomic Scientists,* 68 (2012), 61–69.

TURNER, ROBERT, "An Insider's Look at the War on Terrorism," *Cornell Law Review,* 93 (2008), 471–500.

TURNS, DAVID, "The United Kingdom, Unmanned Aerial Vehicles, and Targeted Killings," *American Society of International Law,* 21 (2017).

VALENTINE, DOUGLAS, *The Phoenix Program* (Lincoln: William Morrow, 1990).

WALDRON, JEREMY, *God, Locke, and Equality: Christian Foundations of Locke's Political Thought* (Cambridge: Cambridge University Press, 2002).

WALDRON, JEREMY, "Terrorism and the Uses of Terror," *Journal of Ethics*, 8 (2004), 5–35.

WALDRON, JEREMY, "Torture and Positive Law: Jurisprudence for the White House," *Columbia Law Review*, 105 (2005), 1681–1750, reprinted in Waldron, *Torture, Terror and Trade-offs*.

WALDRON, JEREMY, "Post Bellum Aspects of the Laws of Armed Conflict," *Loyola of Los Angeles International and Comparative Law Review*, 31 (2009), 31–55.

WALDRON, JEREMY, *Torture, Terror, and Trade-Offs: Philosophy for the White House* (Oxford: Oxford University Press, 2010).

WALDRON, JEREMY, *Dignity, Rank, and Rights*, Meir Dan Cohen (ed.) (New York: Oxford University Press, 2012).

WALDRON, JEREMY, "Justifying Targeted Killing with a Neutral Principle," in Finkelstein et al. (eds.), *Targeted Killings*, 112–133.

WALDRON, JEREMY, "Death Squads and Death Lists: Targeted Killing and the Character of the State," *Constellations*, 23 (2016), 292–307.

WALDRON, JEREMY, "Deep Morality and the Laws of War," in Lazar and Frowe (eds.), *Oxford Handbook of Ethics and War*, 80–95.

WALDRON, JEREMY, "The Rule of Law and the Importance of Procedure," in Fleming (ed.), *Nomos 50: Getting to the Rule of Law*, 3–31.

WALDRON, JEREMY, "The Image of God: Rights, Reason, and Order," in Witte and Alexander (eds.), *Christianity and Human Rights*, 216–235.

WALDRON, JEREMY, "Targeted Killing," *London Review of Books* (May 7, 2011).

WALZER, MICHAEL, "Political Action: The Problem of Dirty Hands," *Philosophy and Public Affairs*, 2 (2) (1973), 160–180, reprinted in Levinson (ed.), *Torture*, 61–76.

WALZER, MICHAEL, *Thinking Politically: Essays in Political Theory* (New Haven: Yale University Press, 2007).

WALZER, MICHAEL, "Targeted Killing and Drone Warfare," *Dissent* (January 2013).

WALZER, MICHAEL, *Just and Unjust Wars: A Moral Argument with Historical Illustrations*, 5th edition (New York: Basic Books, 2015).

WALZER, MICHAEL, "Just and Unjust Targeted Killing and Drone Warfare," *Daedalus*, 145 (2016), 12–24.

WEBER, MAX, "Politics as a Vocation," in Weber, *Political Writings*, 309–369.

WEBER, MAX, *Political Writings*, Peter Lassman and Ronald Speirs (eds.) (Cambridge: Cambridge University Press, 1994).

WECHSLER, HERBERT, "Toward Neutral Principles of Constitutional Law," *Harvard Law Review*, 7 (1959), 1–35.

WELLMAN, CHRISTOPHER, "The Rights Forfeiture Theory of Punishment," *Ethics*, 122 (2012), 371–393.

WICKS, ELIZABETH, *The Right to Life and Conflicting Interests* (Oxford: Oxford University Press, 2010).

WILLIAMS, BERNARD, "Politics and Moral Character," in Hampshire (ed.), *Public and Private Morality*, 55–74.

WILSON, GEORGE GRAFTON, and GEORGE FOX TUCKER, *International Law*, 9th edition (New York: Silver Burdett, 1935).

WITTE, JOHN and FRANK ALEXANDER (eds.), *Christianity and Human Rights: An Introduction* (Cambridge: Cambridge University Press, 2010).

YOO, JOHN, "Using Force," *University of Chicago Law Review*, 71 (2004), 729–797.

ZENKO, MICAH and SARAH KREPS, "Limiting Armed Drone Proliferation," in Knuckey (ed.), *Drones and Targeted Killings*, 124–136.

ZOHAR, NOAM, "Collective War and Individualistic Ethics: Against the Conscription of Self-Defence," *Political Theory*, 21 (1993), 606–622.

INDEX

For the benefit of digital users, indexed terms that span two pages (e.g., 52–53) may, on occasion, appear on only one of those pages.